Issue Evolution

ISSUE EVOLUTION

Race and the Transformation of American Politics

•

EDWARD G. CARMINES

JAMES A. STIMSON

PRINCETON UNIVERSITY PRESS

PRINCETON, NEW JERSEY

Library of Congress Cataloging-in-Publication Data

Carmines, Edward G.
Issue evolution : race and the transformation of American politics
Edward G. Carmines and James A. Stimson.
p. cm.
Bibliography: p.   Includes index.
ISBN 0–691–07802–5
1. United States—Race relations—Political aspects. 2. Afro-Americans—Politics
and government. 3. United States—Politics and government—1945–
4. Voting—United States—History—20th century.
I. Stimson, James A. II. Title.
E185.615.C35 1989   323.1′196073—dc19   88–25463

CONTENTS

LIST OF FIGURES

LIST OF TABLES

ix

LIST OF TABLES

PREFACE

Dwight Eisenhower was president. November 4, 1958, would be an early evening for those who awaited the outcome of the biennial exercise in American constitutional democracy. Beginning with the first scattered reports from the East, confirmed by everything later and to the West, the Democratic party was scoring a stunning victory in the congressional elections. The early picture was clear. Democrats were winning all the close contests, and they were winning some against heavy odds. The pattern was unbroken through the night. On the morning after, the *New York Times* observed the sweep of House and Senate contests by the Democrats:

> The greatest Democratic sweep since 1936 seemed to be in the making as the party scored spectacular gains in races for the House of Representatives. (p. 1)

> Mr. Nixon, who formulated the Republican campaign strategy, and President Eisenhower, who adopted it, sounded the cry that Democratic gains in the North and West would elevate "radical" Democrats and create troublesome opposition for the Southern Democratic conservatives and the Republican administration. . . . [W]hat was really at stake was . . . the fate of the old coalition of moderate Democrats and Eisenhower Republicans that had worked harmoniously with the White House since 1955. (p. 19)

The election had been fought in the context of two critical events, both unfavorable to the Republicans. Recession gripped the American economy for the second time in the Eisenhower presidency. With memories of Hoover still fresh and fears of worse to come, American voters were reasserting their now traditional distrust of Republican economic management. Less openly a matter for political discourse, if no less on the minds of voters, was Sputnik. The first of a series of early Soviet triumphs in space technology, Sputnik was a shock to American self-confidence, resting on the (thought to be) firm ground of the inherent superiority of American technological know-how. After years of advance publicity about the coming triumphs of American space exploration, the nation was unprepared to witness Russian success where the United States produced but delay and failure. National humiliation is a difficult matter for party politics in a democracy; it certainly does not lead to "issues"—in the normal sense of that word. But like the matter of hostages in Iran more than two decades later, it shook American confidence in the party of the White House.

We did not know it then but the 1958 election was a turning point, an irreversible event that was to help launch a decade of racial politics and thereby reshape American politics for the remainder of the twentieth century. If we hold to the conventional view of elections, as means to settle issues of public debate, then the events of 1958 are strange indeed. For the lasting significance of the 1958 contest would be to *unsettle* the coming issue of race in American life. It unsettled this issue—not yet significantly on the agenda of American party politics—by putting in place for the epic battles yet to come a large and cohesive body of Democratic liberals who would not defer to southern sensibilities and southern political power over the delicate matter of race. That by itself would be important, perhaps crucial. But at the same time, and this is much less appreciated, 1958 decimated the ranks of moderate and liberal Republicans. For the Democratic victories did not come at the hands of conservatives. Republican liberalism, theretofore an important, often even dominating, force, would never recover from the body blow of 1958, an event of signal importance for understanding the Goldwater conservative insurgence of 1964 and the absolute conservative control of the Republican party in the 1980s.

The black civil rights movement that was to erupt so dramatically in the early 1960s can be understood as an event rooted in the rural South, a product of racial oppression, black religion, and charismatic and innovative leadership. But to understand why civil rights became a decisive political movement, not limited to blacks, not limited to leaders, not limited to the South, we need to come to terms with why a party system was ready for the revolution when it came. We can understand the great words, "I have a dream . . ." from Martin Luther King, Jr., without reference to American electoral politics; the dream was not the stuff of party platforms or election outcomes. But if we are to understand why King's dream was spoken in the shadow of Abraham Lincoln's Memorial and why millions of ordinary Americans witnessed it, then we need to piece together how the centuries-old aspirations of black America captured the moment in a particular place and time. That will require us to understand American party politics.

On the morning of November 5, 1958, we knew none of this. Indeed, while the great events of the 1960s were underway we failed to appreciate their lasting significance. Now we know all this was part of a larger picture. Whether or not the participants knew it, the great battles of the 1960s were fought over not only the rights of black people in America but also the future direction of American politics itself. Events of profound importance, world wars, the American debacle in Vietnam, and so forth, have come and gone, leaving behind only ripples on the calm water of American party politics. The struggle over race, at its peak the dominant issue of American political life for only some three years in the mid-1960s (Smith 1985), permanently rearranged the American party system. That is the subject of this book.

This book is a half-century portrait of an issue evolution in progress. The issue is race. The issue, more specifically, is the yet unsettled matter of the role of the black man in a white society. Sometimes it is called "civil rights"—we do not often use the term because it commonly refers to only part of the larger question—sometimes more prosaically integration or desegregation. The questions it raises bite deep: How much is enough? And how hard should we, as a society, try to do better? That is why they are yet unresolved. In their easiest form they challenge the law and the Constitution; in their hardest form they question our morals. They cause discomfort, anxiety, unease. They do not go away.

"Race and the Transformation of American Politics," our subtitle, is an apt description of the book. We shall have much to say about race, but the issue itself is not our principal focus. We deal throughout with the fundamental question, what happened to American politics when race emerged as a political issue? That is not the only question that might be pursued, but it is the one that interests us. As students of American politics we are interested in institutions, their processes and behavior, and the public policies that result from them. We are interested in the mass electorate, in how and why it reacts as it does to the institutional environment. But more important than either of these, we are interested in the interaction between institutions and the electorate, how each influences the other. That interaction is necessarily studied as a dynamic process; it is seen in the adjustments and reactions of one to the other over time.

We, the authors, are not policy analysts, not specialists in the matter of race. No one of our generation could not have some personal interest in racial questions; for many it is the issue of our time. But we had no professional interest in race. We took up the research that led to this book without intending to study race per se. It was but one of many of the "issues" scholars of electoral processes might examine in the early 1970s. We first addressed the matter in what was intended to be a minor research note, a corrective to the emerging consensus of the 1970s that the politics of race had run its course, that it had become a matter for historians. That little note was intended to be the beginning and end of any special focus on race. For we were students of issue voting, and we shared in the procedural norm of that subdiscipline: issues, *in general*, were the proper focus of inquiry. But our data would not let us comfortably proceed to the general. Those data suggested that race was not merely one of many issues of the time. It was different. All issues are in some sense different, special each in its own way, but race was different because the evidence suggested that it was transforming the American political landscape. Then, more than now, when that landscape was taken to be almost wholly fixed, not to be moved or shaken by mere political issues, such evidence could not be ignored.

Despite having succumbed to the urge to pursue a single issue, we are political scientists of a theoretical and quantitative stripe. Not abandoning the urge to generalize, we have redirected it. Rather than study all issues in electoral behavior or all policy outcomes of Congress or all of anything produced by presidents, parties, conventions, and the like, we study one issue in all contexts. Because race is transforming American politics, we have chosen all of American politics as the basis for generalization. We attempt no less than an integration of our understanding of how the diverse aspects of American political life are connected: race is the connector. This is a common enough approach in the literature of policy case studies, but the cross institution focus of that genre is usually speculative. Our approach differs when we propose and test a theory of issue evolution that weaves together all of the partisan[1] actors of American politics.

[1] Because the theory of issue evolution is structured around political parties and partisanship, we shall have little to say of the (nonpartisan) judiciary. Obviously important in bringing racial issues to the forefront of American political life, the courts' lack of a partisan role in the American constitutional structure leads us largely to ignore their role in the evolution of racial desegregation. The

Issue evolution is a theory of political processes. Because processes are studied over time, so too will time be a fundamental structuring element of this book. Most of our analyses focus upon how the behaviors of one set of actors influence another set, over time. In the end we move beyond the racial case for a necessarily partial statement on the dynamics of American politics, our ultimate generalization.

Race makes interesting current history, but we are not historians; it is interesting public policy, but that is not our focus. Race raises the most perplexing issues of personal and social morality, important for understanding the staying power of the issue, but we are unequipped to be commentators on ethics. We are equipped to study race as leverage in the struggle for power, as justification for governance, as stimulant to an often lethargic mass electorate, as transforming element in political ideologies, as sustenance of a new issue alignment—as politics. That is what this book is about.

---

judicial role in racial matters is a central theme in a vast literature. We shall not attempt to improve upon it.

ACKNOWLEDGMENTS

Ten years is a long time. In that long time we have talked about our work to more audiences than we can remember, read dozens of anonymous manuscript and proposal reviews, interacted with hundreds of colleagues and graduate students. All these activities and interactions left their imprint. Most we could no longer trace. But they are all in this book in one way or another.

This book, which reports the results of a ten-year study of a fifty-year issue in transition, has benefited from the contributions, both financial and intellectual, of many organizations and individuals. Our greatest debt on the financial side is to the National Science Foundation, which supported our research under grant SOC-7907543.

Indiana University also contributed generously in the form of Research Grants-in-Aid, Summer Research Fellowship, and a sabbatical for Carmines. Both the Department of Political Science and the Workshop in Political Theory and Policy Analysis at Indiana University aided in the preparation of the manuscript. Nuffield College, Oxford, provided an hospitable and stimulating setting for the drafting of early portions of the manuscript.

The peripatetic Stimson has numerous institutional debts. The State University of New York extended a sabbatical leave that was critical to this project's origin. The Florida State University provided released time for the preparation of the National Science Foundation proposal. The University of Houston provided research leave that was a crucial bridge in the period after the NSF grant, when important work remained still to be done. At the final stage the Graduate College of the University of Iowa provided a small grant for manuscript preparation. The Southern Methodist University and Oregon State University have been homes away from home; their adjunct appointments made possible a reasonably continuous research schedule in the face of a discontinuous personal geography.

Our intellectual debts are more extensive. John McIver and Ann Shaw provided excellent research assistance; the former quickly moved from being student and assistant to colleague, critic, and collaborator. The ideas in this book were first tested on a generation of graduate students at four universities. Those ideas are different for that experience as, indeed, are the career orientations of the authors. Helpful commentary on various publications culminating in this volume came from Chris Achen, Paul Beck, Sam Bookheimer, Russell Dalton, Ray Duch, Lawrence Dodd, Richard Eichenberg, Robert Erikson, Scott Flanagan, James Gibson, Michael Giles, William T. Gormley, John Haraldson, Charles O. Jones, Kathleen Knight, Carolyn Lewis, Robert Luskin, James Kuklinski, Yvette Nowak, Elinor Ostrom, Vincent Ostrom, Bruce Oppenheimer, Glenn Parker, Samuel Patterson, John Pierce, Karen Rasler, Steven Renten, Leroy Rieselbach, Paul Sniderman, John Sprague, John Sullivan, William Thompson, Ronald Weber, Gregory Weiher, Herbert Weisberg, B. Dan Wood, Gerald Wright, and John Zaller. Lee Epstein, Robert Huckfeldt, and C. L. Kim read the manuscript and offered a number of useful comments. Richard Niemi and Gerald Pomper reviewed the manuscript for Princeton University Press and made suggestions for improving it, many of which have been incorporated into the final version. Finally, on a longer time scale, we would like to thank Roberta S. Sigel and Donald R. Matthews.

Some of the data used in this book were originally collected by the Center for Political Studies of the University of Michigan under a grant from the National Science Foundation and made available through the Inter-University Consortium for Political and Social Research, and by the Louis Harris Political Data Center of the University of North Carolina at Chapel Hill. Neither organization bears any responsibility for the analyses or interpretations presented here.

The *American Political Science Review*, the *Journal of Politics*, the *American Journal of Political Science* and Agathon Press published early reports on various aspects of the research. We thank them for permitting us to incorporate those analyses into this book.

It goes without saying that our wives—Ethel Carmines and Dianne Stimson—contributed greatly to the success of this collaboration. And we are especially grateful to Paige Alexandra Carmines, age two, who arrived at the end of this project and saw it through to fruition.

Issue Evolution

· 1 ·

THE DYNAMICS OF
ISSUE EVOLUTION

Evolution is one of the half-dozen shattering ideas that
science has developed to overturn past hopes and assumptions, and to enlighten our current thoughts.
—Stephen Jay Gould, *The Flamingo's Smile:*
Reflections in Natural History

The theory of the generation of [issue] alternatives de-
serves, and requires, a treatment that is just as definitive
and thorough as the treatment we give to the theory of
choice among prespecified alternatives.
—Herbert A. Simon, "Human Nature in Politics:
The Dialogue of Psychology with Political Science"

Where do issues come from? Why, when most do not matter, are
some the leading themes to the story of a polity? Some last when
most do not. Why that too? Some issues, like lines drawn in the
dust, define what it means to be a party to political conflict. Most
are easily stepped over.

To speak of politics is to speak of political issues, almost invariably. We speak of them as if we knew of them. But we truly do
not. We do not know why they arise, why one question rather
than another comes to seem important, why it happens at a particular time, rather than another, why some last, why most do
not.

These are familiar sorts of questions in the worlds of biology,
geology, paleontology. There we ask about species. But the questions are much the same. Why do they arise in one rather than
another form? Why do some persist, others not? Why do whole
groups of similar species thrive and then die out? These are all
questions about change, organic change.

The preeminent theoretical problem of this book is the explanation of change. We have turned to the biological theory of natural selection because it addresses that problem. It carries with
it a powerful system of reasoning. The analogy directs our thinking to certain kinds of questions and leads us to look for distinctive patterns. It is a useful organizing framework for considering

3

the question of organic change. We discuss the uses—and abuses—of grafting such a metaphor to our purposes below.

That large numbers of potential issues compete[1] with one another for the highly limited attention of the public in an ever changing political environment leads us to think of issue evolutions as biological evolutions. The life cycles of political issues are determined by the selective pressure of competition—in this case for public attention—in an environment that is itself always in flux.

Issues, like variations of species, arise in great abundance. A complex governmental environment produces policy questions, problems, and conflicts in far greater number than can ever be the subject of public discussion. Of these, most are not suited to the opportunities offered by the political environment at any given time and never gain a place on the public agenda. Some are the subject of unseen administrative decisions, some are non-salient acts of Congress, and some are the issue platforms of aspiring politicians that never quite strike a sensitive public response.

Some issues—a minute proportion of the potential—are well fitted into new niches provided by an evolving political environment. New environmental opportunities can emerge from unsatisfied constituencies, from political leaders in search of electoral leverage, or from exogenous shocks to the system. Darwinian "fitness," biologists agree, is not absolute but relative to the evolving ecological niche. "Most fit" then comes to mean "best adapted" to an available niche. And so it would seem with issues. Adaptation to the niche is readily understandable after the fact. But the evolution of the niche itself is but one of a nearly infinite number of possible outcomes dependent upon a long series of events in which chance plays a major role. Particular issues come to influence the life of a political system, not so much because they are fundamental to the system but because they fundamentally fit well to an opportunity provided by the evolving political environment.

[1] Issues, of course, do not compete. Nor in fact do animals in evolutionary theory. Individual organisms behave *as if* they intended to survive. What we observe then looks like "competition" for survival among species. But the "competition" comes from our outside human vantage point. So too issues, which more obviously lack intent, appear to compete for public attention. That appearance is created by the human actors on the stage who employ them—just as Dawkins (1976) argues that genes may be best understood as behaving as if they employed their host organisms to perpetuate themselves.

The political environment that evolves to create new issue opportunities just as surely dooms most issues to a temporary existence. Creation and extinction are two sides of the same coin of
system change. However, we shall see that issues, like species,
can evolve to fit new niches as old ones disappear. But, unless
they evolve to new forms, all issues are temporary. Most vanish
at their birth. Some have the same duration as the wars, reces-
sions, and scandals that created them. Some become highly associated with other similar issues or with the party system and
thereby lose their independent impact. And some last so long as
to reconstruct the political system that produced them; these are
the focus of our inquiry.

We wish to know where issues come from, why some thrive in
the competition for limited public attention and others do not,
and how the origin and development of new issues is capable of
transforming the organic system in which that development occurs. These are our next items of business: origins, developments,
and transformations.

Sources of Issue Competition

Accounting for "ultimate" issue origins is not a difficult explanatory problem. Like the origins of species, we can readily postulate the interaction of a complex environment and chance processes as the source of more numerous raw material in issue
innovations than can ever develop. Just as natural variation in
gene pools is filtered by chance processes to produce a plenitude
of variations in species, so a complex governmental environment
superimposed upon a disparate social order can be counted upon
to raise new issues in abundance. The regulation, distribution,
and redistribution of governing acts, multiplied by the number of
spheres of social and economic activity, in turn multiplied by
time and interaction at the boundary of government and governed is an engine for the production of new unresolved questions
of such power that we need never fear it will fail to produce
enough new material to supply our need for diverse possibilities.

The more important question is how issues are selected for development: Why do some thrive against the heavy odds of competition for too scarce attention? If far more issues are generated
than can ever gain space on the small stage of issue competition,
we must know what processes filter the possibilities from the
many potential issue conflicts to the few that can command sig-

5

nificant public attention, what mechanisms promote some and not others.

Four mechanisms will command our detailed attention: (1) the promotion of particular issues by strategic politicians as effective leverage in the struggle for power, (2) issues moved to the center of public discourse when highlighted by external disruptions to the established order, (3) new issue species that are old issues transformed by isolation and specialization in a new context to something quite different than their origins, and (4) cybernetic issues selected for importance because internal contradictions and imbalances in the political system generate corrective needs.

Strategic Politicians

Strategic politicians play the most obvious and perhaps most influential role in determining the relative competition among political issues. All successful politicians instinctively understand which issues benefit them and their party and which do not. The trick is to politicize the former, deemphasize the latter.

Every party alignment embodies a more or less explicit issue agenda—the set of policy conflicts around which the struggle for power has been fought. The winning party naturally seeks to maintain the salience and centrality of the current agenda, not only to preserve but also to perpetuate the distribution of power emanating from those salient political conflicts. After all, the exploitation of those issues has resulted precisely in success in the first place. Of course, one way of exploiting is to continue to emphasize the original aligning issues; another is to treat all new issues as logical outgrowths of the original agenda. In both cases the idea is to fight current political battles within the framework of the old. The existing majority, in short, has an obvious incentive to keep winning; the equally obvious strategy for victory is emphasizing the original aligning issues. Because these issues contributed to its current majority status, it sees no reason to deemphasize or discard them. Just as genes behave as if they seek to perpetuate themselves by becoming attached to viable species, so strategic politicians attempt to maintain their power by being associated with winning issues. For politicians of the existing majority, these are issues of the past.

Not so with the existing minority. Its ultimate goal is to upset the dominant party alignment, including the issue basis on which it has been constructed. Losing politicians naturally turn to new issues to improve their political situation. New issues—if they can split the majority coalition and sufficiently attract the electorate—offer the opportunity for converting old losers into new winners (and old winners into new losers); they are thus the stock-in-trade of successful politicians. This does not mean, of course, that all new issues will have this effect. On the contrary, the vast majority of new issue proposals are bound to fail, striking an unresponsive cord in the mass public and leaving the current majority party's coalition intact. Political losers may occupy an even more disadvantageous position than they did before introducing the proposal. Nor are new issues the only mechanism for undermining the majority coalition. The minority may also emphasize performance on old issues or attempt nonissue appeals, such as candidate personality. Be this as it may, sponsoring new issue proposals is one of the few strategies that losers have for permanently improving their political position. And on those rare occasions when losing politicians provide exactly what the public is seeking, the issues, as Riker (1982, 210) observes, "flourish, even to the point of completely reshaping the environment in which they arose."

Dissatisfied political losers, in sum, have an ever-present motive to unseat the governing status quo. Generating new issue conflicts is a natural vehicle for this purpose. The natural selection of issues thus reflects the dominant strategy of losing but rational politicians and their parties.

External Disruptions

Potential issues exist always on the periphery of awareness. Some are called to the center when the world outside a particular political system intrudes upon it. The external world causes disruptions and shocks, raises challenges and opportunities, and, in general, prevents any organic system from being driven entirely by internal imperatives. Most evident in the case of crises, wars, depressions, terrorism, and invasions of the economic sort, the external world is always a source of problems to be solved, opportunities to be exploited. Matters requiring public discussion generate issue conflicts over how best to deal with them. Thus, the relevant set of potential issue conflicts in the domain of intrusion is selected for greater attention, greater debate, and greater conflict.

7

Local Variations

The thesis of local variation is a leading account of the origin of
new species. When an interbreeding population and common
gene pool are physically divided by distance, geologic events, or
whatever, we reasonably expect that the local populations that
continue to interbreed will adapt more readily to the specialized
local environment than to the common environment of the original population. After a few generations of isolated adaptation
and sufficient variation in environmental conditions, the isolated
population may diverge quite substantially from the ancestral
population. Given enough time and variation, the divergence
may create a new species (no longer capable of interbreeding
with the old) and a closed gene pool.

We can readily imagine similar developments in political issues. A common issue (whether, for example, government ought
to intervene in the market economy) applied in diverse specialized settings over a long period of time may produce offspring
issues (e.g., the regulation of airline fare structures) so adapted
to the new specialized context that they take on an identity and
developmental path distinct from the ancestral issue.

Cavanagh and Sundquist (1985, 37) argue that this is precisely
what happened with repect to economic issues in the 1980s:

> The debate between the parties on the old role-of-govern-
> ment and economic policy issues has been placed in such a
> new ideological context in the 1980s by the radicalized Re-
> publican party of Ronald Reagan that the distinction be-
> tween the parties may have taken on quite new mean-
> ings. . . . To that extent the line of party cleavage can be seen
> as having shifted, with much the same impact on the party
> system that a new line born of wholly new issues might hy-
> pothetically have had.

Internal Contradictions

The world of systems in perfect balance and harmony is inspired
more by theology than empirical observation. In the real world of
politics harmony is partial, balance often nonexistent. Thus,
problems arise from the internal contradictions and imbalances.
Issues associated with those problems and their solutions may

then move to the fore from their tie to a growing consciousness of policy problems in need of solution.

Thus, by their very nature, all party alignments contain the seeds of their own destruction. The various groups that make up the party may be united on some issues, particularly on those that gave rise to the alignment in the first place. But lurking just below the surface a myriad of potential issues divides the party faithful and can lead to a dissolution of the existing equilibrium. In politics, as Riker (1982, 197–212) notes, because of the inevitability of internal contradictions, disequilibrium may only be one issue away.

A sense of predestination or inevitability is not to be found in any of these paths to issue development. That is a central theme of the literature on natural selection and equally in our approach to political issues. We see developmental paths as sensible and explainable after the fact. But given a world dependent upon context, variation, and chance, any possible outcome, including the one that did in fact occur, has a prior probability so low as to be all but unpredictable. That view of history and evolution, in marked contrast to much theorizing on party systems and realignment, will run through our treatment of the issue evolution of race. Many crucial events and decisions that mark the path of political response to race were marginal; they could easily have tipped differently than they did. Any could have altered the path of racial issue evolution.

Outcomes of Issue Competition

We have suggested that four sources determine the differential salience of issues in their competition with one another through time. But the ultimate object of our inquiry is not just to understand the pattern of competition among issues. We also want to understand the outcomes of this competition, to model the impact that evolving issues have on the larger party system of which they are the most dynamic part. We see three distinct outcomes— associated with three respective issue types—of this competition for public attention and influence.

Organic Extensions

The first is perhaps the most easily understood. Some new issues fit into the same niche that has previously existed. These are genuinely new issues; their content is novel. But because they continue already existing conflicts, or at least become interpreted in that way, their capacity for moving the political system in a novel direction is sharply curtailed. Federal aid to education, for example, an issue that occupied a prominent place on the political agenda of the early 1960s, posed the same kind of questions and invoked the same sort of reactions as did Roosevelt's New Deal. At most these "organic extensions" are likely to reinvigorate old issues and old conflicts, to redefine them in the direction of more current issue debates.

Unsuccessful Adaptations

Unsuccessful adaptations are of two subtypes, issues that never capture public attention at all, by far the largest in number, and those that do receive attention but cannot hold it very long. Even the former may have important objective consequences. They are, however, too complex, technical, and nonsalient to form an effective communication link between citizens and elites. For this reason, they tend ultimately to be resolved by the political elites themselves with little guidance from the public. Perhaps the best illustration of this issue type is the host of conflicts involved in national energy policy. Genuine policy disputes of unquestioned importance, these conflicts have so far failed to exert substantial influence on electoral politics for lack of shared referents between masses and elites.

Some issues have great impact in the short term but do not leave a permanent mark on the political system. These issues are linked typically to political events that cause disturbances in the existing political environment. The public may become aroused about them, even to the point of decisive electoral impact. These issues do not, moreover, reinforce the bases of the existing party system; instead, they may cut across the natural development in one or both political parties.

But their effects are short-term. They may influence system outcomes, but they do not change the system. These issues have the important limitation of being unable to sustain themselves beyond the events that brought them into being. Thus, as the events fade in public memory, the issues lose their salience and with it their ability to shape public opinion. The dramatic short-term electoral importance of these issues is thus more than counterbalanced by their inconsequential long-term effects on the political system. Vietnam and Watergate are two recent examples of this policy type.

Issue Evolutions

We define issue evolutions as those issues capable of altering the political environment within which they originated and evolved. These issues have a long life cycle; they develop, evolve, and sometimes are resolved over a number of years. The crucial importance of this issue type stems from the fact that its members can lead to fundamental and permanent change in the party system.

Issue evolutions, by which we always mean partisan issue evolutions, possess the key characteristics absent from each other issue types. Unlike organic extension issues, they do not merely continue the existing party system. They cut across the direct line of evolutionary development. They emerge from the old environment, but having once emerged they introduce fundamental tensions into the party system, inconsistent with the continued stability of old patterns. These issues capture the public's attention for more than a short span of time; they tend to be salient for a number of years. They are distinctive, finally, in their unique combination of short- and long-term effects.

Thus, they may result in voting defections among partisans, but more important, they also alter the fundamental link between citizen and party. They have the ability to alter the party system from which they emerged. Only issues of this type have the capacity to reshape the party system, replacing one dominant alignment with another and transforming the character of the parties themselves.

How much cognitive processing is required to deal meaningfully with an issue we have argued elsewhere (Carmines and Stimson 1980) is a critical dividing point between issues that may or may not lead to issue evolutions. "Easy" issues have the attribute that they may be responded to, indeed even understood in a fundamental sense, at the "gut" level. They require almost no supporting context of factual knowledge, no impressive reasoning ability, no attention to the nuances of political life. Thus, they produce mass response undifferentiated with respect to knowledge, awareness, attentiveness, or interest in politics; none of these is a requisite of response.

"Hard" issues, by far the more common type, require contex-

11

tual knowledge, appreciation of often subtle differences in policy options, a coherent structure of beliefs about politics, systematic reasoning to connect means to ends, and interest in and attentiveness to political life to justify the cost of expensive fact gathering and decisionmaking. Accordingly, hard issues are the special province of the most sophisticated and attentive portion of the electorate as well as of issue publics who have special reason to be concerned about particular sets of, but not all, public policies. Hard issues are not the stuff of issue evolutions, for they can generate neither large nor sustained public response.

Models of Issue Evolution

Thus far we have introduced two typologies: the first focuses on the sources of issue competition, the second on the outcomes of this competition. But to picture the full system we need a further typology of processes or models that link sources to outcomes. Without it the story has a beginning and end but no middle.

We postulate three basic models of issue evolution. The first, undoubtedly the most familiar to students of party realignment, is the critical election realignment or, stated in terms of its biological analogue, cataclysmic adaptation. The fundamental characteristics of change in this model are rapidity and discontinuity. Not only does the issue lead to a transformation of the system, but it does so dramatically and permanently. A long period of stability is followed by a sudden burst of dramatic change that shifts the party system to a new level of stability. The party system is stationary before the critical election—an intervention that leads to a radical and profound alteration of the system. The earthquake is an often used, appropriate metaphor of such change (see, for example, Burnham 1970).

To say that cataclysmic adaptation is rare in the biological world is an understatement. It is a category without any cases,[2] unless one treats biblical creationism as a serious theory. Indeed, Darwinian reasoning literally rules it out as a plausible model of biological change. Although it is clearly the dominant paradigm for thinking about political change, we doubt in fact if it is any more common in the political world, a topic we discuss in detail in Chapter 6.

[2] The one possible exception is the passing of the dinosaurs, which some controversial interpretations view as the result of cataclysmic adaptation (Raup 1986).

A second type of issue evolution is based upon Darwinian pure gradualism. The change effected through this transformation is permanent; it leaves an indelible imprint on the political land- scape. And the change can be quite substantial, fundamentally altering the complexion of the system over a long period of time. But the process is slow, gradual, incremental. This noncritical, wholly gradual model of partisan change is consistent with Key's (1959) notion of secular realignment.

"Punctuated equilibrium" notions in biology are the origin of our third, "dynamic growth," model of political change. It is dy- namic because it presumes that at some point the system moves from a fairly stationary steady state to a fairly dramatic rapid change; the change is manifested by a "critical moment" in the time series—a point where change is large enough to be visible and, perhaps, the origin of a dynamic process. Significantly, how- ever, the change—the dynamic growth—does not end with the critical moment; instead it continues over an extended period, al- beit at much slower pace. This continued growth after the initial shock defines the evolutionary character of the model.

Exciting discoveries in molecular biology and in the study of embryological development have reemphasized the integrity of organic form and hinted at modes of change different from the cumulative, gradual alteration emphasized by strict Dar- winians. Direct study of fossil sequences has challenged gradualistic biases (the "punctuated equilibrium" pattern of long-term stasis within species and geologically rapid origin of new species) and asserted the idea of explanatory hier- archy in identifying species as discrete and active evolution- ary agents. (Gould 1983, 14)

THE EVOLUTION OF RACIAL ISSUES

We intend our three sets of typologies to provide an analytic framework within which the evolution or life history of any issue can be analyzed. But it is obvious that not all issues are equally significant for the long-term development of the party system. Genuine issue evolutions are clearly the most important when viewed in these terms because they have the capacity to trans- form the system itself. But issue evolutions are rare, a tiny pro- portion of the total number of issue conflicts that can arise in any complex political system. Indeed, given the sharp limits of mass attention and the difficulty issues have in sustaining themselves through time, perhaps political systems can accommodate only a single-issue evolution during a given period. In any case we have chosen the single-issue dimension of race as the focus of our inquiry.

Although numerous issues since the formation of the New Deal have crowded onto the political agenda and competed for public attention, racial desegregation has clearly had the greatest long term impact on the party system. Race with its deep symbolic meaning in American political history has touched a raw nerve in the body politic. It has also been an issue on which the parties have taken relatively clear and distinct stands, at least since the 1964 presidential contest between Goldwater and Johnson. Moreover, the issue has a long political life cycle; it has been a recurring theme in American politics since the nation's founding. Most of that time it has been submerged, too contentious for the party system. But it reemerged as a partisan conflict in the early 1960s and has remained prominent since then. Thus, if a significant issue evolution is occurring in American politics, it is most likely to revolve around the issue of race.

The Actors in Issue Evolution

We have written thus far of an organic system of issue evolution, a contest between issues for dominance of scarce issue space. That takes little account of the human factor, for the species in question is issues, not human participants in politics. But politics at another, more familiar level of analysis is a uniquely human activity, driven by human emotion, motive, and calculation.

Human emotions and calculations are the stuff of normal accounts of politics. Some emphasize the emotional: the lust for power that drives politicians, the electorate's need for symbolic reassurance, and so forth. Others emphasize calculation: the intended pursuit of goals through political activities. But the human factor is always present.

One of Darwin's great insights is that the natural world can be explained as if driven by human emotion and calculation, even though it is not. Species that survive behave as if they intend to survive. We do not need to postulate consciousness or intent, but we merely note that the cold brutal workings of natural selection produce this result as a natural consequence of its logic. Behaviors and attributes that tend to promote survival are selected,

14

more likely to reappear in subsequent generations. Because we observe with extreme selection bias only those that did in fact survive, we observe patterns that appear calculated to promote survival.

Although we will choose not to do so, an account of politics could be similarly constructed. Calculating political leaders who push particular issue positions for leverage might be explained much like the Dawkins's (1976) "selfish genes." Genes behave as if they had an intent to spread their influence to subsequent generations, as if they consciously pursued their self-interest in survival, because those that make salutary contributions to the organism of which they are part do have a greater likelihood of survival. So, too, politicians attached to positions that are ultimate winners will tend to survive on the political stage as if the issue position were chosen to promote survival. This would occur if intent were present. But, like the selfish gene, it is also the prediction we would make as a result of unintended natural selection.

But we will deal with human behavior in the normal way, postulating consciousness, albeit sometimes at a low level, emotion, and calculation. The actors in our account—presidents, senators, congressmen, party leaders, those who aspire to those positions, party activists, and ordinary citizens—will be the normal ones, pursuing self-interest and, more in the case of some than of others, calculating the consequences of their acts. The guiding focuses for our study of every actor, each in itself much too large a topic, are the roles each plays in the evolution of issues, the role each played in the evolution of race.

Presidents and presidential contenders are figures of central importance in issue evolution generally, and no less in the specific case of race. Much of their centrality arises from their unique and hence idiosyncratic position at center stage. That makes them simultaneously highly visible and very difficult to study in any systematic manner. Our approach to the presidency—its occupants and its aspirants—is thus largely historical, largely idiosyncratic. Presidents, always conscious in our thoughts about issue evolution, appear in this book in our development of the history of racial desegregation policy in Chapter 2 and again, more secondarily, as central figures in congressional politics (Chapter 3).

Party leaders are central figures of Chapter 2, where we take up the issue of conscious calculation of party issue positions as expressed in party platforms. Parties themselves are diffuse in American politics; a very large proportion of all political behavior is partisan political behavior. Thus, parties loom large in our treatment of all other actors as well.

Senators and congressmen are the subject of Chapter 3. Sometimes key actors in issue evolution, as they undoubtedly were in the great legislative struggles over civil rights in the 1960s, the congressional actors and institutions are also invaluable even when not on center stage given the quality of the public record of their acts.

Citizen political activists, those largely ordinary people whose one distinctive attribute is relatively intense participation in partisan politics, have a special role in the theory of issue evolution. Highly sensitive to the context of politics and the issue stakes of elections, these actors, the subject of Chapter 4, appear to be leading indicators of issue change and, indeed, leading actors in its production.

The mass electorate is necessarily crucial in a representative democracy. We treat it as the environment of elite politics, where elites and institutions are the environment of mass politics. This leading agent of issue selection chooses to respond, or more often not to respond, to new issues and new issue definitions. That is its decisive importance. We deal with the mass electorate in two frameworks: first, we examine the question of how issues evolve in mass attitude structures, the subject of Chapter 5; second, in Chapter 6, we take on the issue of how mass electorates align and realign themselves with the contending parties to produce issue dominance of the mass party structures, the ultimate evidence of issue evolution.

We step back from dealing with individual actors, in Chapter 7, to a unified theory of issue evolution, which specifies the structure and sequence of the whole dynamic process for the racial case. It is our integrating treatment of how issues evolve. And in light of what we have learned from the racial case, we look, in Chapter 8, at the issue evolution process generally.

On the Use and Abuse of Evolutionary Reasoning

Metaphor, it is well known, is no stranger to scientific reasoning of all kinds. Quite explicit in Burnham's *Critical Elections and the Mainsprings of American Politics*, the explanation of change by physical analogy has a long history in American political science and a very long history in American political thought.[3] It has no need of a defense. But organic metaphors are considerably less common in social science. And because their abuse is associated with the political and ideological use of "science" to justify common prejudices, we feel some need to be explicit about our intent and usage.

The evolution of species by natural selection is a powerful theoretical system; its postulates are simple, its reasoning elegant. Its generality is much greater than the problem it was designed to explain, important though that is. Thus, we find merit in exploiting this system of reasoning to model a different phenomenon, the evolution of political issues.[4] This model and metaphor have been powerful stimulants to the work we report in this book. We have repeatedly found that they offered purchase on the organic world of politics unavailable in the prevailing, more mechanical modes of thinking about political systems and institutions. Thus, we choose to push the analogy to the limit, aware that at times it may lead us astray. We ask the reader's patience, for we think the payoff is worth an occasional bout of analogical strain.

Although we are enthusiastic about the heuristic value of natural selection as a means of coming to terms with issue evolution, we have a certain reticence about open exploitation of biological theory because the social use of biology has a disreputable history. More often exploited to justify politics and policy than to explain them, the social use of biology is littered with fraud, pseudoscience, and the abusive use of "science" to justify social and racial prejudices. Beginning with "social Darwinism," an absolutist misunderstanding of natural selection used in praise of the social status quo—the rich and well-born are obviously fittest, just look how well they survive and prosper, while poverty is "nature's" way of weeding out the unfit—the pseudoscience continues in the present day to assert genetic dominance of behavior, minus any empirical evidence for the case, and to claim

---

[3] But the earthquake, not the mainspring, is the physical analogy central to much reasoning about electoral realignment. Nowhere is it more central than in Burnham's work.

[4] The evolutionary perspective is beginning to gain attention and find application in areas far removed from its origins in biology. See Axelrod (1984), Boyd and Richerson (1985), Kingdon (1984), Nelson and Winter (1982), and Radnitzky and Bartley (1987).

17

genetic superiority for white male Northern Europeans (Gould 1981). Modern "biopolitics" lacks these abusive pseudoscientific elements, but as a field it is notably reluctant to test many of the theses that so readily spill out of fertile imaginations.

We differ fundamentally from all these schools; we do not assert a biological basis to behavior. Natural selection for us is a key to understanding the organic competition between issues, a powerful analogy used to draw insight from the great theoretical achievement of Darwin and his followers to explain what seems to us a fundamentally similar situation. We are simply not interested in "nature versus nurture" and similar sorts of controversies from the application of biology and genetics to society; they are quite irrelevant to issue evolution. Pursuit of a biological (or any other) metaphor sometimes leads one to ask certain kinds of questions and not others. Probably it shapes in part what answers are found to be satisfactory. In some cases the application is so limited that it has little effect at all. Some of it is conscious and intentional, some not. Certain principles are conscious and can be abstracted and advertised. Among these, three are worthy of particular note.

Although structured by human reason and calculation, sometimes self-consciously strategic, and constrained by social structure, chance is the fundamental driving force in producing change. That does not imply that change is either chaotic or unknowable but most explicitly that it is neither determined nor inevitable. We are intellectually at war here most particularly with any notion of inevitability, which unlike other Marxist notions, is not at all foreign to American social theory. We will encounter no situations in the political evolution of race where we will assert that it could only have happened as it did. Our scenarios will instead be more akin to Tolstoy battle scenes, where calculation, force, confusion, and chance commingle to produce an outcome, the appearance of which is orderly only after the fact.

We expect change to be dynamic—a process, not an event. That implies subtle movements over time. That does not commit us to gradualism; the punctuated equilibrium model we draw from Gould and others allows for bursts of rapid change, at least on the appropriate time scale. The notion of subtle dynamics is openly in conflict with the earthquake metaphor that so dominates much thinking on political change in the critical realignment tradition. The notion of a buildup of stress from unresolved tension over time, followed by a great shearing cataclysm, is appealing. But whether observed political changes resemble those suggested by such a model is an empirical issue, and for at least the case at hand we have found that they do not.

Finally, we borrow the notion that resultant change is neither unidirectional nor permanent. The species succeeds by being well adapted to a niche but not in any absolute sense superior to its ancestor. Change represents not a process of perfection but rather a randomly driven tryout of new survival possibilities, each successful or unsuccessful relative to the niche only. If the niches themselves are impermanent, from externally induced change, from competition from new species, even perhaps from competition with the same species, then the adaptations are not absolutely good or helpful; they are good only insofar as the conditions to which they were a lucky adaptation persist.

These assertions—that change is driven by randomness, that its form is dynamic, and that its result is impermanent—are not essentially biological. Highly consistent with Darwinian sorts of reasoning, they can be stated nonetheless as abstractions without organic content. We began this research without self-conscious theories of change. They developed from the impossibility of squaring the sorts of processes we observed with the available mechanical-deterministic modes of explanation. Much of that conflict and quandary is captured in the notion of electoral realignment, to which we now turn.

Issue Evolution: A Species of Realignment?

Realignment notions were a natural means of conceptualizing the transformations we will see to be associated with the infusion of racial issues into American political life. And in our earliest work on the question (Carmines and Stimson 1981), we attempted to use realignment concepts to express the racial transformations. We came to regard that attempt as unsatisfactory, a disillusioning experience that led us ultimately to develop our issue evolution alternative. A minimal interpretation of that experience is that realignment is not a satisfactory concept for the racial transformation; a maximal view, one we find increasingly persuasive, is that realignment is not a satisfactory concept for any political transformation. That requires some explanation.

Why Disillusionment?

Realignment is a dichotomous notion. Elections, or sequences of elections, are either realigning or they are not. There is no middle ground. Thus, to explain change in these terms, one must either assert realignment or deny the change. In fact, the natural critical response is the inevitable question of whether it is really a realignment.

We found the "is it or is it not" debate unhelpful in coming to terms with the racial transformation for two reasons. First, scholars can choose their favorite reputable set of definitions of realignment and come to either conclusion; this definitional confusion we address below. Second, and more important, neither conclusion satisfactorily fits the evidence. The issue evolution of race is not of a magnitude comparable to the better known realignments of American history—for example, the Civil War or the New Deal. It is a considerably more subtle phenomenon. Calling it a realignment seems to be stretching its impact beyond what the evidence will support. But denying the change is equally awry. No serious observer of American politics questions the evidence of the racial transformation, and few would deny its import. Thus, the conclusion that it is a "nothing," the only alternative to "realignment," is troublesome. Realignment notions, put another way, allow us to assert political change when the magnitude of that change is overwhelming, so obvious that it need not be documented, and deny that anything more subtle can matter. That is a formula for a simplistic science of politics. Documenting the obvious is the first task of a primitive science. It is time now to move on to matters of greater interest.

The prominent escape from this intellectual trap is amending the theory to make it speak to the evidence. Indeed, realignment theory has so often been amended when the evidence it purported to explain was not so much in conflict with its original terms but extraneous to them that the amendments are far more weighty than the original core of the theory. Because those amendments are also complex and confusing, further additions to the list are unlikely to produce scientific progress. Most scholars, we suspect, have stopped cataloging the too numerous amendments because to continue cataloging gives the matter more the feel of theology than of scientific theory. To move to a more explicitly scientific conceptualization is the wiser course.

WHAT IS REALIGNMENT THEORY,
AND WHY IS IT SO CONFUSED?

Electoral realignment can be an appealing notion. It imbues with drama the often too routine world of politics. The realignment produces an immediately visible change, promising permanency as well. Where the normal channel of communication between governed and governors is clogged with noise, the realignment provides a clean crisp signal of electoral intent. The stark drama of electoral realignment appeals to both the scholarly and the popular imaginations. This appeal is important, for it accounts for the resilience of the idea. It accounts in particular for the resilience of the idea of realignment in its simplest form. That resilience is indeed part of the problem.

To read the literature of realignment is to be impressed with how often scholars have searched for simple and dramatic realignments and how rarely they have found them. If simplicity is often the first casualty of scientific research, that is even more the case in realignment research: the simple and dramatic model of critical realignment, the one that so readily captures our attention, finds no supporting evidence.[5] Scholars search for evidence of realignment and find it, but the nature of the realignments found bears notably little likeness to the simple and resilient concept.

Starting with the simple concept of realignment, it seems reasonable to ask when realignments happen, who does the realigning, how it occurs, and with what result. On the "when" question it is natural to look for a date. Questions such as was 1984 a realignment? seem sensible from this point of view. But researchers find that dating can be accomplished only by ignoring much evidence. The closer we look, the more these "simple" realignments become movements over time, taking decades or multiples of decades to achieve their final form. When precursors and aftershocks are added, the multiple decade processes overlap, and the continuing effects of old movements are still manifested while new and different movements toward a still newer alignment are underway. There is no "normal" period left, no time when the reshaping of loyalties and behaviors is absent. From the fully de-

---

[5] The work of Burnham (1970) and others who rely heavily on aggregate election outcomes data comes closest to being an exception. The outcomes data are not rich enough for complex interpretations.

veloped time scale of realignment, such as in Sundquist (1983), to ask whether a particular election was a realignment is a senseless question. All elections are part of realigning progressions, and none are realigning in themselves. It is akin to asking whether a particular wave rearranged the sand on a beach; the answer is always, "Yes, and so did every other."

When we ask "who" shaped a new alignment and "how" that new shape was forged, the evidence is sparse, for the classic realignments occurred before serious survey research allowed us to track individual movements; but see Erikson and Tedin's (1981) attempt to do so with the primitive data available from the 1930s. The drama of the simple resilient notion implies conversion from one party to another on a notable scale. The evidence here is controversial, but a fair summary would be that enough conversion can be found to document that the process existed, but nowhere near enough to account for observed changes in party strength. When we relax the time scale, then other processes, principally the mobilization of newer voters (Andersen 1979), become more plausible accounts of "who" formed the new alignment. And even that more complex portrait would appear strikingly simple in contrast to the survey-based explorations of party movement (c.f., Norpoth and Rusk 1982) in the modern electorate.

If we ask "what resulted from" a realignment, we are tempted to search for coherent sets of programs dealing with the challenge of the events provoking the new electoral structure. As is so often the case in realignment research, one historical sequence—the Great Depression and New Deal—is the prototype for thinking about the policy consequences of realignment.[6] If we allow simplistic dating of realignment, that is, that the New Deal realignment "occurred" in 1932, then event, realignment, institutional change, and policy change (Brady 1978) can all be connected. Alas, we can also find realignments without notable policy change and notable policy changes without realignments.

Although we can treat realignment as a unified concept, two

[6] A skeptical view of the realignment literature would see that much of it is tailored to "explain" this single discrete historical event. Realignment scholars are not to be faulted for working with only five or so cases in the American context, for that is the universe of evidence. The fault lies in failing to demand that general concepts fit and empirical assertions hold true for all the cases. Many a list of requisites or defining characteristics of "realignment" fail such a test; they are instead historical particulars of the New Deal case.

major strands or emphases can be seen in the literature. Some authors—for example, Key (1955, 1959), Schattschneider (1960), and Sundquist (1983)—emphasize the "alignment" aspect of party realignment. For them a party realignment is an overlaid new issue cleavage along party lines. New issue cleavages may or may not have other consequences for party systems, policy outcomes, control of government, and so forth. The second strand—seen in Campbell, Converse, Miller, and Stokes (1960), Burnham (1970), and Pomper (1968)—emphasizes changing party fortunes at the polls as the essence of realignment. For this approach, and for popular use of the term, realignments are manifested when reversals of the majority and minority party status result from sharp and largely permanent movements of the electorate from one party to the other.

We may avoid conflict between the two uses by presuming them two sides of the same coin, in effect by assuming that movements of cleavages produce changes in majority party status or that changes in majority party status must presume underlying changes in the lines of party conflict.[7] But this common presumption is dangerous; it is theoretically possible that the two sorts of changes may occur independently. And, in our judgment of the historical evidence, they in fact do. This bifurcated connotation, the roots of which are as old as serious scholarly attention to realignment, causes confusion at the beginning. In addition to this conceptual discord, the realignment literature may be seen as a long string of amendments by typology, as successive scholars have applied the concepts to the raw materials of (usually American) political history and found the empirical materials too complex to be subsumed by the initial concept.

We have already seen some amendments in the conflicts over conversion versus mobilization as causal process and gradual versus cataclysmic (or secular versus critical) accounts of the pace of change. Some accounts emphasize social cleavages (Petrocik 1981), where others see issue cleavages (Flanagan and Dalton 1984) as the central phenomenons of party conflicts; sometimes the two are seen as the same, sometimes different. More recent accounts distinguish between realignments as overlays on old alignments and realignments as exclusive cleavages, between the sort of national realignment implied by the simple account

[7] See Clubb, Flanigan, and Zingale (1980) for an explicit treatment of this issue.

and realignments as sectional phenomenons, occurring at different times, in different manners, and even for different reasons in different sections of the nation (Bensel 1984). More recent still is the distinction between structural and performance-based realigning processes (MacDonald and Rabinowitz 1987).

If all these preceding distinctions (and this is by no means an exhaustive list of the possibilities or of the election outcome typologies) are to be taken seriously, then the number of possible types of realignment exceeds the number of cases by a considerable order of magnitude. That we have far more types and categories than cases to sort into them is not wholly indefensible, but it does suggest a considerable lack of theoretical power. And realignment theorists seem unnaturally eclectic about accepting this ever growing number of distinctions. One might imagine, for example, that those who defined realignment as if it implied cataclysmic change would reject assertions that realignments might be secular or regional or performance-based, all of which would appear inconsistent with the notion of change by an electoral uprising. There is instead a considerable tolerance for the introduction of new forms and types.

Tolerance is a good thing in politics, but it can be quite another in theory building. Its effect is to make genuine unresolved conflicts appear instead to be only minor disagreements about details. The refinement of the realignment notion to square it with empirical reality, most notably in Sundquist (1983), is a good thing. Troublesome is that this good thing is strikingly inconsistent with the simple resilient notion; event causes conversion causes new party system. And, if the simplistic notion is a straw man, it is straw man often and enthusiastically articulated; more than any contender it is the standard meaning of the term realignment.

That the concept of realignment has been refined is not troublesome. The difficulty is that the original unrefined idea is still current. If one were to ask for the best work on realignment, we think most would point to the refinements. But if one were to ask most political scientists for a definition, the answer almost invariably would be the simple original notion. How can a concept fundamentally modified by theoretical speculation and empirical investigation yet remain unaltered in much professional discourse and absolutely dominant in public discussions of politics? Part of the answer may be that realignment theory as refined lacks most of the drama and theoretical power that first stimulated interest in the concept. Another part, we will suggest, is that political scientists and other scholars do not "own" the concept and so cannot mold its usage.

We would suggest realignment belongs to that class of prescientific concepts (along with, for example, power and democracy) that predate the scientific study of politics and whose connotation is essentially in the public domain. All these concepts are difficult to deal with, not just because of the confusion of established usage but, more important, because of their resistance to scientific redefinition. Thus, just as nonspecialists speak of power in much the ordinary prescientific connotation (in textbooks, for example) so too does the original popular connotation of realignment remain relatively secure from scientific redefinition. It "belongs" to the popular political culture from which it derived. This is in considerable contrast to concepts of political science origin—of which "party identification" is a good example—which, though relevant to politics, remain scientific concepts. Although the authoritative source on the meaning of political science concepts is work in monographs and professional journals, prescientific concepts such as realignment are more likely to be redefined, if at all, by the *New York Times* or the *Washington Post*.

It is thus a safe prediction that the next decisive election in American politics—and decisive elections are not by any means rare events—will produce a debate, both public and scholarly, about whether it was or was not a realignment. And both the question itself and the terms of the debate will be the original simplistic idea of realignment. The matter is beyond scholarly control.

We are left with a scholarly morass. To take up the question of our section title, we cannot know whether issue evolution is a species of realignment because we cannot know what realignment means. Works on realignment invariably deal at length with definitional problems—in itself evidence of the morass—but none ever settles the matter; no connotation becomes consensually held. The research on realignment has both weaknesses and strengths. But if our analysis is correct, no additional work on the concept is called for because no additional work will extricate us from the morass.

Issue evolution, despite its other strengths or weaknesses as a concept, can be scientifically defined and controlled. It allows us to proceed to the business of theory, model, and empirical analysis without the burden of a contentious and uncontrollable concept. Our ensuing analysis will describe issue evolutions and demonstrate that the racial transformation belongs to that class of processes. We will not then have to bother with the unenlightening question of whether it is "real," but we can instead evaluate its contribution to the structure of American political life in empirical terms.[8]

[8] None of this is to say, of course, that our work does not draw on, often quite explicitly, previous research in the realignment tradition; our intellectual debt to this research is both obvious and substantial. But we have found the notion of issue evolution more adequate for a rich depiction of the racial transformation.

· 2 ·

THE POLITICS OF RACE:
FROM ROOSEVELT TO REAGAN

In Chapter 1, we presented a general theory of issue evolution. This theory specifies the sources, processes, and outcomes of issue competition. The theory is necessarily dynamic; issues do not appear fully developed on the political agenda. Instead, they evolve through time as they initially emerge, develop, mature, and are sometimes resolved. But not all issue conflicts have long-lasting, much less consequential life histories. Most are as fleeting as they are inconsequential. The vast majority of issues becomes extinct as quickly as the issues appear on the political scene, and, as a consequence, they lack capacity for transforming the political system.

Given this situation, it is not surprising that our attention as political analysts is directed to the few exceptions to the rule, to the tiny number of issue conflicts that truly matter to the long-term development of the political system. Race, as we pointed out in Chapter 1, clearly falls within this category. Over its long history it has had a profound impact on American politics.

Our purpose in this chapter is to trace the life history of this issue, especially its partisan evolution since the New Deal. Elite party actors, notably presidents and presidential contenders, play prominent roles in this history. We shall examine their roles in the evolution of race, focusing on the policy initiatives of presidents and the rhetoric of presidential candidates. We are especially interested in the changing racial positions of the parties as revealed in party platforms. How did party leaders respond to the growing salience of racial concerns? This is the theme we shall pursue in Chapter 2.

America's tragic struggle with the cause of racial equality did not, of course, begin with the New Deal. It has been a recurring theme in American history. After the painful resolution of the earlier slavery issue, it became a particularly salient national concern during Reconstruction, as white America first confronted the black man as a free, independent citizen. The early successes but ultimate failure of this first encounter set the stage for the later evolution of race. Thus, it is important to examine this earlier period, albeit briefly, so that the later reemergence of race as a national political issue can be seen in historical perspective.

RACIAL POLITICS DURING RECONSTRUCTION

In the immediate aftermath of the Civil War federal efforts to ensure racial equality took on a new reality in American politics. Three amendments to the Constitution explicitly removed racial barriers to the full enjoyment of citizenship by the newly freed slaves. The Thirteenth Amendment, adopted and ratified in 1865, outlawed slavery. The Fourteenth Amendment, passed by Congress in 1866 and ratified in 1868, guaranteed blacks federal and state citizenship, and provided for the "equal protection of the laws." Finally, the Fifteenth Amendment, passed in 1869 and ratified in 1870, provided that the right to vote could not be denied by the United States or any state "on account of race, color or previous condition of servitude." Between 1866 and 1875, Congress enacted five major civil rights and reconstruction acts to enforce these amendments.

For the first time, blacks gained and exercised political power in the South. Joining with the carpetbaggers and scalawags, they played an important role in the radical Republican state governments. Blacks served in all state legislatures, held significant executive positions in several states, including the lieutenant governorships in South Carolina, Mississippi, and Louisiana, and fourteen blacks were elected to the House of Representatives and two to the Senate. They were also prominent participants in the southern state conventions, organized by federal officials to write new state constitutions.

The Republican party embraced the freedman and his newly acquired vote. The black citizen responded in kind. The Republican platform of 1868 proclaimed: "We congratulate the country on the assured success of the reconstruction policy of Congress, as evinced by the adoption, in the majority of the States lately in rebellion, of constitutions securing equal civil and political rights to all, and regard it as the duty of the Government to sustain those constitutions . . ." (Johnson and Porter 1973, 39). The vast majority of black voters responded by becoming loyal Republicans, beginning a political tradition that was to last well into the twentieth century. Of course, blacks had little choice, for the alternatives offered them were "between a party that gave them civil and political rights and a party whose stock-in-trade was racist demagoguery" (Stampp 1965, 167).

During Reconstruction blacks, with the support of the Republican party, gained a measure of political power unprecedented in American history. What would have happened if this situation had been allowed to continue is matter only for speculation. For within a decade after the Civil War, Reconstruction had come to a tragic end, and the cause of racial equality had suffered a major defeat. With the Compromise of 1877[1] the last federal troops were removed from the South, the radical governments collapsed, and conservative Democrats gained eventual control of southern politics.

THE DECLINING SALIENCE OF RACIAL ISSUES

The ending of Reconstruction marked the end of race as a national political issue. For most of the next eighty years, race was predominantly a regional concern, fundamentally shaping the distinctive features of southern political life. Its life as a national political issue was only sporadic and inconsequential.

Left to the disposition of southern whites in the aftermath of the Reconstruction, blacks saw their civil and political rights almost completely eroded. Through a variety of mechanisms—including outright violence and intimidation, cumbersome and unreasonable registration procedures, literacy tests, and poll taxes—black voters were disenfranchised throughout the South. Without the vote, blacks lost what little political influence they had been able to acquire during Reconstruction. And without political influence, they were unable to effectively oppose the imposition of Jim Crow segregation laws. During the last two decades of the 1800s, racial separation, born and widely practiced in the North, became institutionalized throughout every corner of southern public life. From hospitals to prisons to funeral homes, the segregation of the races became a fact of everyday life in the South (Woodward 1974).

The Supreme Court was a powerful force in pushing race off the national agenda, leaving it as a matter for the states to decide. In the Slaughterhouse cases (1872) and the Civil Rights cases (1883) the Supreme Court took the position that the Four-

---

[1] The Compromise of 1877 allowed Republican Rutherford Hayes to win the presidential election of 1876 on the basis of contested southern electoral votes in exchange for a promise to remove the last federal troops from the South.

teenth Amendment did not place under federal protection "the entire domain of civil rights heretofore belonging exclusively to the states" and that the Fourteenth and Fifteenth amendments offered protection against state, but not private, action. Thus, in declaring the Civil Rights Act of 1875 to be unconstitutional, the Court maintained that:

> Until some State Law has been passed, or some State action through its officers or agents has been taken, adverse to the rights of citizens sought to be protected by the Fourteenth Amendment, no legislation of the United States under said amendment, nor any proceeding under such legislation, can be called into activity. (quoted in Pritchett 1984, 253)

What constituted "state action" thus became a crucial issue in deciding civil rights cases. The Court clarified the scope of appropriate state action in *Plessy v. Ferguson* (1896) by holding that a Louisiana statute requiring segregation on railroad facilities was constitutional so long as "separate but equal" accommodations were extended to blacks. That black facilities were invariably inferior to those provided for whites was a fact the Court persistently ignored.

In *Williams v. Mississippi* (1898) the Supreme Court upheld a state law that required citizens to pass a literacy test that included the ability to understand or interpret provisions of the state or federal constitutions in order to qualify to vote. Although it was clear that such tests were being widely used to disenfranchise blacks by requiring them to answer impossibly difficult questions not asked of whites, the Court held the law to be constitutional because on its face it did not discriminate against blacks.

While the Supreme Court led the retreat from the cause of racial equality, it was also joined by the other national political institutions. After Reconstruction Congress did not pass a single piece of civil rights legislation until the Civil Rights Act of 1957. No president until Harry Truman in 1948 had even sent a major civil rights program to the Congress. And both political parties, but especially Democrats, were also willing to see racial issues kept off the national agenda.

The reasons for the Democrats' lack of enthusiasm are easy to understand. Having freed themselves from the yoke of Reconstruction, the last thing they wanted was for race once again to become a focus of national attention. Thus, Democrats, dominated by their southern wing during this period, were perfectly willing for race to be treated solely as a state and local matter. Even a modest proposal condemning some activities of the Ku Klux Klan was removed from the 1924 Democratic platform at the insistence of southern delegates (Johnson and Porter 1973, 76).

The Republican party continued to express support for racial equality during this period, but issues of race were no longer a central motivating force for the party.[2] Thus, while the Democrats were silent, the Republican platform in 1896 and again in 1920 and 1928 expressed the party's opposition to lynching, the most important civil rights issue of the day. But Republicans were not able to make these platform promises the law of the land.

FRANKLIN ROOSEVELT
AND THE AVOIDANCE OF RACE

Racial issues could not, however, be kept off the national agenda for ever. For blacks and their white allies, racial equality was a dream deferred but not forgotten. The first concerted effort to bring racial issues before the Congress in this century occurred during the administration of Franklin D. Roosevelt. Between 1937 and 1946 more than 150 civil rights bills were introduced in Congress. These bills focused on three principal areas: lynching, the poll tax, and fair employment practices. But not a single piece of civil rights legislation prevailed in Congress during that period. One main reason for failure was Roosevelt's unwillingness to either take public positions in favor of the legislation or to do anything to encourage its passage. He resolutely refused to support federal antilynching legislation and backed away from his earlier support for a federal law abolishing poll taxes (Freidel 1965). The president simply refused to back any civil rights legislation before Congress, claiming his support would lead to southern opposition to his entire economic recovery program.

Roosevelt did issue two executive orders concerning fair em-

[2] One main reason that racial issues were no longer so crucial to the Republican party was that the South—and black voters in the South—were no longer critical to the Republican majority. Republicans had gained control of the Old Northwest after the Civil War, which, when combined with their already dominant position in the Northeast, gave them a majority coalition without the South. They could afford to be less attentive to the political situation of southern blacks.

31

ployment practices. In 1941, he issued Executive Order 8802, which made discrimination in government employment illegal, and established a Committee on Fair Employment Practices (FEPC) to enforce a nondiscrimination policy in all defense areas (Morgan 1970). This was the first executive order issued in the area of civil rights since Reconstruction. Soon Executive Order 9346 followed; it extended the scope of the FEPC to include all federal contract areas, not just defense. But these executive orders were actually quite limited in their effect on employment discrimination. They were concerned only with federal employment, their provisions were not always enforced, and the FEPC was abolished at the end of the war. Looked at in its entirety, the Roosevelt administration's record on civil rights was weak and halting; for varying assessments see Kirby 1980, Sitkoff 1978, and Weiss 1983.

The different party attitudes toward civil rights were clearly revealed in their 1944 platforms. The Democratic platform contained the simple assertion: "We believe that racial and religious minorities have the right to live, develop, and vote equally with all citizens and share the rights that are guaranteed by our Constitution" (Johnson and Porter 1973, 404). It is hard to imagine a more general and vague statement. In contrast, the 1944 Republican platform continued the party's long-expressed support for civil rights. The plank was clear, specific, and detailed, calling for: (1) a congressional inquiry concerning the mistreatment, segregation, and discrimination of blacks in the military, coupled with federal legislation to deal with any found abuses; (2) the establishment of a permanent Federal Employment Practice Commission; (3) a constitutional amendment abolishing the poll tax; and (4) legislation to make lynching a federal crime (Johnson and Porter 1973, 412).

But northern Democrats had grown uneasy with their party's steadfast reluctance to address racial issues. As long as northern blacks remained loyal Republicans, there was little incentive for northern Democrats to press for racial equality. However, with millions of blacks becoming "Roosevelt Democrats," many northern Democrats were ready to act on race.

The strategic situation, moreover, was becoming even more compelling because of the great migration of blacks out of the South into the major cities of the Northeast and upper Midwest after World War II. As Table 2.1 shows, a steady and very substantial increase in the proportion of blacks in these regions oc-

TABLE 2.1
Percentage of Blacks in Central Cities of
Twelve Largest SMSAs, 1930–1970

Twelve largest SMSAs	Central City				
	1930	1940	1950	1960	1970
All twelve SMSAs	7.6	9.0	13.7	21.4	30.8
New York	4.9	6.9	9.8	14.7	23.4
Los Angeles–Long Beach	5.0	6.0	9.8	15.3	21.2
Chicago	7.1	8.3	14.1	23.6	34.4
Philadelphia	11.4	13.1	18.3	26.7	34.4
Detroit	7.8	9.3	16.4	29.2	44.0
San Francisco–Oakland	4.9	4.9	11.8	21.1	32.7
Boston	2.9	3.3	12.3	9.8	18.2
Pittsburgh	8.3	9.3	18.0	16.8	27.0
St. Louis	11.5	13.4	5.3	28.8	41.3
Washington, D.C.	27.3	28.5	35.4	54.8	72.3
Cleveland	8.1	9.7	16.3	28.9	39.0
Baltimore	17.7	19.4	23.8	35.0	47.0

Source: Adapted from Leo F. Schnore, Carolyn D. Andre, and Harry Sharp, "Black Suburbanization, 1930–1970," *The Changing Face of the Suburbs*, ed. Barry Schwartz (Chicago: University of Chicago Press, 1976), p. 80; the figures here were transposed to yield data on black percentages.

curred during this period. With the Democratic party increasingly a national party with national aims and interests, it was crucial for it to compete well outside its natural base of support in the South. Indeed, its success in maintaining a majority coalition depended critically upon its electoral fortunes beyond Dixie. And winning the electoral vote of northern states depended upon winning central cities by large margins, which, in turn, depended upon appealing to increasing numbers of northern black voters. For a Democratic presidential nominee to win Illinois meant, in other words, that he had to win big in Chicago, which meant he had to do very well among black voters in the city. The logic of the New Deal coalition, in short, was forcing Democrats to begin to confront racial issues to an extent that they had not had to do since Reconstruction. And Democrats found in Harry S. Truman a man far more committed to civil rights than his predecessor.

TRUMAN AND THE ABORTED
CRITICAL MOMENT OF 1948

In 1946 President Truman had appointed a Committee on Civil Rights to examine America's racial situation. The committee's report, "To Secure These Rights" (1947), recommended the establishment of a permanent civil rights commission and FEPC, passage of antilynching and antipoll-tax legislation, increased protection of voting rights, and adoption of laws prohibiting discrimination in interstate transportation facilities. Speaking before the NAACP in June 1947 Truman endorsed these recommendations, concluding his address with the assertion:

> [T]here is much that state and local governments can do in providing positive safeguards for civil rights. But we cannot any longer await the growth of a will to action in the slowest state and the most backward community. Our national government must show the way. (Truman 1948, 311–13)

In February 1948 President Truman sent the first civil rights legislation to Congress since Reconstruction, calling for federal legislation in the areas identified in the civil rights report (Berman 1970; McCoy and Ruetten 1973). Many southern Democrats were appalled at Truman's actions, and the war for the racial soul of the party began.

The battle continued at the Democratic convention. Southerners first introduced several amendments to weaken the relatively mild compromise plank on civil rights adopted in the platform committee. When these amendments failed, the convention accepted a northern amendment commending Truman's civil rights program and explicitly calling for congressional action to guarantee equal rights in voting participation, employment opportunities, personal security, and military service. For the first time in its history, the Democratic party had taken clear and specific stands in support of racial equality.[3] The Mississippi and parts of

---

[3] One factor that made it possible for the Democrats to nominate someone as racially progressive as Truman in 1948 was the abolition of the two-thirds majority rule for the nomination of a Democratic candidate for president in 1936. Although little noticed at the time, this change in institutional structure markedly reduced the influence of the South on the nomination of Democratic presidential

the Alabama delegation bolted the convention, eventually leading to the formation of a third party, the States' Rights Democrats, to contest the presidential election. The Democrats won the election by a very slim margin, but lost the electoral votes of Alabama, Mississippi, Louisiana, and South Carolina to the States' Rights Democrats (Sitkoff 1971).

A RETURN TO NORMALCY

During the 1950s both parties took relatively moderate stands on racial issues, but Republicans reclaimed their traditional position of being more supportive of civil rights. The civil rights section of the 1952 Democratic platform was nearly identical to the plank that appeared in 1948. It called for federal legislation to guarantee equal rights in voting participation, employment opportunity, and personal security. The 1956 platform concerning civil rights was similar to that of 1952, with two major differences. For the first time since the beginning of the New Deal, the Democratic platform mentioned the importance of states' rights. The platform asserted that "the Party of Jefferson and Jackson pledges itself to continued support of those sound principles of local government which will best serve the welfare of our people and the safety of our Democratic rights" (Johnson and Porter 1973, 538).

The platform made only the vaguest and most general reference to the recent *Brown v. Board of Education of Topeka* decision (1954), which decisively overturned the "separate but equal doctrine" of *Plessy*. Without offering any support for school desegregation whatsoever, the platform simply noted that "recent decisions of the Supreme Court of the United States relating to segregation in publicly supported schools and elsewhere have brought consequences of vast importance to our Nation as a whole and especially to communities directly affected" (Johnson and Porter 1973, 542).

These changes in the party platform reflected the Democrats' attempt to steer a more conciliatory course on civil rights after the near disaster of 1948. The choice of a presidential nominee was also a reflection of this change in direction. Governor Adlai E. Stevenson of Illinois was a solid New Deal Democrat, but he was not deeply committed to civil rights (Martin 1979). He was

---

candidates. It also allowed the possibility for issues of race to gain a foothold on the national Democratic agenda (Rubin 1975).

much more concerned with the potential of this divisive issue—already amply demonstrated—to split the party. Speaking to northern Democrats during the 1952 presidential election campaign, he concluded a comparison of racial discrimination in the North and South by saying "just as it is chastening to realize our own failures and shortcomings in the North, so it is both just and hopeful to recognize and admit the great progress in the South." He went on to caution northern Democrats against moving too quickly on civil rights:

> I think—indeed, I know—that there are leaders in the South who are just as anxious as we are to move ahead. But we must frankly recognize their local difficulties. We must recognize, too, that further government interference with free men, free markets, free ideas, is distasteful to many people of good will who dislike racial discrimination as much as we do. (Stevenson 1953, 26–27)

In a later speech given in Richmond, Virginia, Stevenson commended southern political ideas to the rest of country, asserting:

> Among the most valuable heritages of the Old South is its political genius, which in many respects was far ahead of its time. Even today some of the finest products of Southern governmental thought are only beginning to win the general acceptance which they have so long deserved. A classic example, it seems to me, is the Constitution of the Confederacy. (Stevenson 1953, 153)

Stevenson, in short, was making a strenuous effort to be conciliatory toward the southern wing of the party. Apparently this effort succeeded, for the four Dixiecrat states all returned to the Democratic fold in the 1952 presidential election.

White southerners, on the other hand, did not find the Republican party of the 1940s and 1950s sympathetic to their racial views. The 1948 Republican platform on race was just as strong and outspoken as its Democratic counterpart.[4] But whereas the

---

[4] Not only did the 1948 Republican platform take a progressive stand on racial issues but the Republican presidential nominee Thomas E. Dewey was very much in the Republican tradition of racial progressivism. As governor of New York, Dewey "took credit for securing the first state fair employment practices act, for establishing a State Commission Against Discrimination, and for appointing influential Negroes to highly visible state posts" (Sitkoff 1971, 607). In short, 1948 could not be a critical moment in the partisan evolution of race because both parties were competing for the pro–civil rights pole of the dispute.

Democrats retreated from their strong position on civil rights during the 1950s, the Republicans continued in their progressive racial tradition. Their 1956 platform, for example, first pointed to their record of accomplishment in civil rights, claiming that "more progress has been made in this field under the present Republican Administration than in any similar period in the last 80 years" (Johnson and Porter 1973, 554). The platform offered explicit and strong support for the *Brown* decision:

> The Republican Party accepts the decision of the U.S. Supreme Court that racial discrimination in publicly supported schools must be progressively eliminated. We concur in the conclusion of the Supreme Court that its decision directing school desegregation should be accomplished with "all deliberate speed" locally through Federal District Courts. . . . The work of the courts [must be] supported in every legal manner by all branches of the Federal Government. (Johnson and Porter 1973, 554)

This stronger Republican commitment to civil rights could also be seen in the passage of the Civil Rights Acts of 1957 and 1960—the first civil rights laws passed since Reconstruction. The 1957 Act created the temporary Commission on Civil Rights, gave the Justice Department an assistant attorney general for civil rights matters, and specified those circumstances requiring jury trials in contempt cases (Anderson 1964). The 1960 Act provided for court-appointed referees to ensure that eligible blacks were allowed to register and vote. Both acts were criticized by civil rights advocates because they lacked strong enforcement provisions (Anderson 1964; Berman 1970; Sundquist 1968). But the very fact that they were enacted during a Republican administration reinforced the party's moderate image on racial issues (Duram 1981). Moreover, in 1957 Eisenhower sent federal troops to Little Rock, Arkansas, to enforce a school desegregation order. This was further evidence, if any were needed, that the Republican party was not yet a viable alternative for segregationist voters.

Kennedy, Johnson, and the Crisis of Civil Rights

The 1960s witnessed the full maturation of the struggle for racial equality. As both parties groped to find a way to deal with this highly divisive issue, the country itself was becoming increasingly polarized by antithetical racial forces. Civil rights leaders turned to protests and mass demonstrations to press their political claims. From the Montgomery bus boycott in 1955, to the lunch counter sit-ins in the late 1950s, to the Freedom Riders in 1961, to the Birmingham demonstration and the great March on Washington in 1963, to the Montgomery march in 1965, the country was faced with a mass civil rights movement that would no longer accept second-class status and treatment for black Americans. But the segregationist forces would not give in without a protracted struggle. Their protests were conducted in the halls of Congress and were reflected in the brutal manner of local police using fire hoses and attack dogs to quell nonviolent demonstrators.

The campaign of the 1960 presidential election was conducted in this atmosphere of heightened racial concerns. Both parties and their respective candidates took progressive positions on civil rights. Whereas the civil rights plank in the 1956 Democratic platform was written in compromise language so as to not offend southern Democrats, the 1960 plank contained strong and specific support for civil rights. Senator Sam Ervin of North Carolina introduced motions to the platform committee to delete portions of the proposed platform that called for establishing a permanent FEPC, continuing the Civil Rights Commission as a permanent agency, granting the attorney general the power to file civil injunction suits to prevent desegregation, and setting 1963 as the deadline for the initiation of school desegregation plans, but his motions were overwhelmingly defeated by the platform committee. A minority report by nine southern state delegations calling for the elimination of the platform's civil rights plank was similarly defeated on the convention floor (*Congressional Quarterly* 1983, 99–100). Democrats were determined to adopt a strong civil rights plank even if it meant overriding the strong objections of the southern wing of the party and possibly leading to a new split in the New Deal coalition.

But the Republicans would not be outdone on civil rights. Led by Senator John Tower of Texas, the platform committee initially adopted a fairly weak civil rights plank that did not express support for civil rights demonstrations or promise federal efforts to gain job equality for blacks. But Richard Nixon and Nelson Rockefeller met during the convention and reached consensus on several major policy issues. Their agreement, informally dubbed the "compact of Fifth Avenue," included a much stronger civil rights plank on which Nixon threatened to wage a floor fight if it were not accepted by the platform committee. The committee adopted the stronger plank by a margin of fifty-six to twenty-eight (*Congressional Quarterly* 1983, 101). The final plank included an extensive array of civil rights' commitments, including support for equal voting rights, establishment of a Commission on Equal Job Opportunity, and a prohibition against discrimination in federal housing and in the operation of federal facilities.

> We oppose the pretense of fixing a target date 3 years from now for the mere submission of plans for school desegregation. Slow-moving school districts would construe it as a three-year moratorium during which progress would cease, postponing until 1963 the legal process to enforce compliance. We believe that each of the pending court actions should proceed as the Supreme Court has directed and that in no district should there be any such delay. (Johnson 1978, 619)

"Although the Democratic-controlled Congress watered them down," the GOP platform also stated, "the Republican Administration's recommendations resulted in significant and effective civil rights legislation in both 1957 and 1960—the first civil rights statutes to be passed in more than 80 years" (Johnson 1978, 618). In short, the Republican platform statement on civil rights was at least as progressive as its Democratic counterpart.

During the campaign itself John Kennedy and Richard Nixon followed their parties' leads, adopting progressive and almost identical civil rights positions. The most dramatic event of the campaign—and the single symbolic event that gave Kennedy a closer identification with the cause of racial equality—was his well-publicized telephone call to Coretta Scott King inquiring about the status of her recently arrested husband (Brauer 1977; Oakes 1982).

While the 1960 Democratic platform called for strong action on civil rights, President Kennedy initially took a very cautious approach to racial issues. Like Roosevelt before him, civil rights was not a deep moral concern for the new president. Nor was he about to sacrifice his domestic and economic programs on the altar of civil rights. Kennedy initially decided that he would not sponsor a civil rights bill after all, and, although he made a number of symbolic gestures in support of civil rights, he was unwilling to bring racial concerns within the legislative scope of his

"New Frontier." His strategy, so reminiscent of Franklin Roosevelt's, may have worked if civil rights had been a normal political issue, its outcome determined largely by the interplay of political forces in Washington. But civil rights was not an ordinary political issue, and it could not be resolved within the confines of the Potomac. It was an all-consuming, passionate concern both for those who wanted to see segregation ended a generation earlier and for those who wanted it to last forever. And the nation was caught up in this unfolding political drama.

Kennedy's go-slow approach to civil rights continued into his third year in office. In February 1963 he submitted a modest civil rights bill to Congress asking mainly for legislation to broaden the existing laws to protect blacks' voting rights. Civil rights leaders were unimpressed and stepped-up action to put greater pressure on the federal government. The result was a national domestic crisis in which demonstrations and boycotts spread to the entire country, North and South. By the end of the year, demonstrations had taken place in 800 cities and towns. In the aftermath of one of the most dramatic of these confrontations—in which Birmingham's Commissioner of Public Safety, Bull Connor, employed dogs, clubs, and fire hoses to quell a nonviolent demonstration against the city's segregation policies—Kennedy finally acted. On June 11 he delivered the most memorable speech of his presidency, placing his administration squarely on the side of the civil rights forces. He concluded his televised address with an emotion-filled plea:

> We are confronted primarily with a moral issue. It is as old as the scriptures and is as clear as the American Constitution.... If an American, because his skin is dark, cannot eat lunch in a restaurant open to the public, if he cannot send his children to the best public school available, if he cannot vote for the public officials who represent him, if, in short, he cannot enjoy the full and free life which all of us want, then who among us would be content to have the color of his skin changed and stand in his place? Who among us would then be content with the counsels of patience and delay?...
>
> Are we to say to the world, and much more importantly, to each other that this is a land of the free except for Negroes; that we have no second-class citizens except Negroes; that we have no class or caste system, no ghettos, no master race except with respect to Negroes? (Kennedy 1964, 469–70)

On June 19, Kennedy sent a comprehensive civil rights bill to Congress, following through on his nationwide address. In it, he asked for legislation to guarantee blacks access to public accommodations, allow the national government to file suit to desegregate schools, allow federal programs to be cut off in any area that practiced discrimination, strengthen then existing machinery to prevent employment discrimination by government contractors, and establish a community relations service to help local communities resolve racial disputes. Here, at last, were the legislative proposals that civil rights advocates had demanded and expected since Kennedy's inauguration.

But it was one thing to propose such far-reaching legislation, and it was quite another for it to become the law of the land. For this to happen the proposals would have to work their way through that mine field known as the United States Congress. All the major civil rights groups believed that massive public pressure would be necessary in order to force Congress to enact the administration's civil rights bill. In this situation, the March on Washington planned by A. Phillip Randolph, president of the Negro American Labor Council, to protest the treatment of black citizens took on a larger meaning. Although Kennedy initially tried to persuade the civil rights leaders to call off the March, arguing that it might lead to violence and undermine public support for the bill, he reluctantly supported the action. The March on Washington was a resounding success in bringing together the diverse elements of the civil rights movement and demonstrating the extent to which racial issues had touched the moral soul of the nation. Whether it improved the bill's chances of getting through Congress was more difficult to determine. Administration strategists decided that the bill should first be passed in the House before coming to the full Senate and facing an expected filibuster. The House Judiciary Subcommittee initially agreed on a bill that went well beyond the scope of the administration's proposal, especially in the areas of public accommodations and the greatly expanded powers of the Justice Department to file suits in civil rights cases. The administration opposed the stronger bill, believing it would not command the necessary Republican votes to pass the full House. A compromise bill, stronger than the administration's original proposal but milder than the judiciary subcommittee's initial draft, was approved by the full House Judiciary Committee on October 29, 1963.

Within a month Kennedy was assassinated, and Vice-President Lyndon Johnson had assumed the presidency. Johnson's record on civil rights was mixed. When he ran for Senate in 1948, he made clear his opposition to civil rights in racially conservative Texas by declaring:

"The civil rights program is a farce and a sham—an effort to set up a police state in the guise of liberty. I am opposed to that program. I have voted against the so-called poll tax repeal bill; the poll taxes should be repealed by those states which enacted them. I have voted against the so-called anti-lynching bill; the state can, and does, enforce the law against murder. I have voted against the FEPC; if a man can tell you whom you must hire, he can tell you whom you can't hire." (Miller 1980, 118)

But Johnson's position on civil rights had moderated considerably by the time he became Senate majority leader. In fact, his moderate, compromising approach to civil rights together with his ability to deal with Republicans, liberal Democrats, and southern Democrats allowed him to play a pivotal role in the passage of the 1957 and 1960 civil rights acts. But his compromising stance raised questions in the minds of liberal Democrats concerning the extent of his personal commitment to civil rights. Would he now, as president, seek a compromise on the pending civil rights bill, trading its stronger features for possible southern Democratic support? As civil rights friends and foes were soon to learn, President Johnson would show no signs of hesitation; he quickly grasped the mantle of civil rights leadership.

"We have talked long enough in this country about equal rights," said Johnson in his first address to Congress on November 27. "We have talked for one hundred years or more. It is time now to write the next chapter, and to write it in the books of law" (Johnson 1965, 9). Johnson made it clear that enactment of the civil rights bill would be a top legislative priority, representing a living memorial to the slain president: "No memorial oration or eulogy could more eloquently honor President Kennedy's memory than the earliest possible passage of this bill for which we fought so long."

Having publicly committed himself to the pending civil rights legislation, Johnson was now determined to see it enacted into law. Using the full powers of the presidency and his own legendary political skills, he pressed Congress to action. On February 10, by a margin of 290 to 130 the House passed a bipartisan civil rights bill. Democrats supported the bill 152 to 96. Their vote revealed a sharp regional split; northern Democrats voted 141 to 4 in favor of the bill while southern Democrats voted 11 to 92 in opposition. Of the 177 Republicans, 138 voted for the bill and 34, including 12 southern Republicans, against.

Attention now shifted to the Senate where the key question was not whether there existed sufficient votes for passage of the actual bill, but whether the bill would ever come to a vote. To invoke cloture to end a filibuster, a two-thirds majority was then required. Such a majority had never before been produced on civil rights legislation. But on June 10, 1964, after months of legislative maneuvering, the Senate voted 71 to 29 to cut off debate on the civil rights bill; 44 Democrats and 27 Republicans voted in favor of cloture while 23 Democrats and 6 Republicans opposed the motion. The cloture paved the way for the bill's approval on June 19 by a 73-to-27 roll-call vote.

The Civil Rights Act of 1964 was comprehensive in coverage. Its eleven sections barred discrimination in public facilities and accommodations, granted the attorney general the power to initiate suits against public schools that practiced segregation, forbade job discrimination by employers or unions, extended efforts to assure the right to vote, allowed the Justice Department to sue to desegregate state and local facilities, and provided that federal funds would be withheld from any federally funded program or activity that practiced discrimination. Speaking before a nationally televised audience at the signing of the bill, President Johnson concluded his address with the ringing assertion: "Our Constitution, the foundation of our republic, forbids it [racial discrimination]. The principles of our freedom forbid it. Morality forbids it. And the law I will sign tonight forbids it" (Johnson 1965, 108).

Passage of the Civil Rights Act of 1964 signified two major and interrelated developments in American politics. First, it demonstrated that the national government could play a major role in bringing about equal rights. The mild and largely ineffective 1957 and 1960 civil rights laws had led many to believe that opponents of civil rights were too powerful to allow the national government to exert significant influence in this area. The 1964 civil rights act proved that this was no longer the case. Passage of this legislation also revealed just how far the Democratic party had come on civil rights. The party had finally taken up the challenge issued by President Truman in 1948. Democrats had altered their historic position on this issue and become the principal defenders of black civil rights. And they had done so not only with rhetoric and proposals but also with action.

THE GOLDWATER RESPONSE

But would the Democratic party continue to champion civil rights, and what would the political implications be if it did so? Obviously not all Democrats had embraced the cause of racial equality. Quite the contrary. The party was sharply and, it seemed at the time, irrevocably divided on this issue: northern Democrats against southern Democrats, integrationists against segregationists. The national Democratic party had now chosen to ally itself with the former groups, leaving the latter to either change their racial attitudes to accommodate this new reality or find more appropriate parties and candidates to reflect their racial views.

Into this political void marched Barry Goldwater and the modern conservative movement of the Republican party. Neither Goldwater nor the conservative movement he led had their origins in America's racial crisis. Indeed, both candidate and movement were largely unconcerned with the specific issue of racial segregation. Goldwater and his followers were motivated by their fundamental belief in conservative principles, one of which was that the national government should play only a minimalist role in domestic matters. Not only was this principle a key element of the conservative ideology, but it was also mandated by the conservative understanding of the Constitution.

Goldwater derived his position on desegregation directly from his conservative ideology. Goldwater was neither a racial bigot nor, in principle, a segregationist. "I believe," he said, "that it is both wise and just for negro children to attend the same schools as whites, and that to deny them this opportunity carries with it strong implications of inferiority" (Goldwater 1960, 38). But his conservative ideology would not allow him to support government ordered desegregation policies:

[T]he federal Constitution does not require the States to maintain racially mixed schools. Despite the recent holding of the Supreme Court, I am firmly convinced—not only that integrated schools are not required—but that the Constitution does not permit any interference whatsoever by the federal government in the field of education. . . .

. . . .

The problem of race relations . . . is best handled by the people directly concerned. (Goldwater 1960, 35, 38)

Although Goldwater was thus neither racist nor segregationist, his racial conservatism had a powerful appeal to anti–civil rights forces that had been deserted by the national Democratic party. In Goldwater, they found a presidential candidate who was willing to let states and localities continue their segregationist policies and practices, unaffected by the intrusion of the federal government. His vote against the Civil Rights Act of 1964, one of only eight from outside the South, was fully consistent with his ideology, and it reinforced his appeal to southern whites.

Goldwater was no Republican aberration. The conservative movement he led controlled the 1964 Republican convention and dominated the platform committee. Republican Senator Hugh Scott from Pennsylvania introduced an amendment on the convention floor to strengthen the weak civil rights section of platform: increasing the enforcement authority of the Justice Department, setting specific compliance dates for desegregating school districts, guaranteeing voting rights in federal and state elections, and requiring federal commitment to ending employment discrimination. The amendment was resoundingly rejected (*Congressional Quarterly* 1983, 103–4). The platform's brief civil rights plank did call for "full implementation and faithful execution" of the 1964 Civil Rights Act but went on to state that "the elimination of any such discrimination is a matter of heart, conscience and education, as well as of equal rights under the law" (Johnson 1978, 683). Clearly, the Republican platform did not endorse racism. Nor did it call for segregation. But it embodied a racial conservatism that had great appeal to southern whites. The Republican party was to go "hunting where the ducks are"— a strategy that sent them right to the heart of Dixie.

In the ensuing election Goldwater suffered an overwhelming defeat, winning the electoral votes of only six states. But five of those states were in the Deep South, and Goldwater won each of them by large margins: 87 percent of the vote in Mississippi, 70 percent in Alabama, 59 percent in South Carolina, 57 percent in Louisiana, and 54 percent in Georgia. Republican presidential candidates had not carried these states since Reconstruction,

45

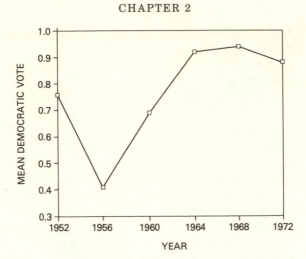

Figure 2.1 Vote for Democratic Presidential Candidates in the Black Precincts of Twenty-four Southern Cities, 1952–1972. *Source*: Bartley and Graham (1978).

again demonstrating the potency of Goldwater's appeal to southern white constituencies.

Although Goldwater's attraction to southern whites was impressive, his candidacy proved disastrous for the party's long-term relationship with black voters. Historically, as we have seen, blacks had had a close tie to the Republican party—a tie that had not been broken until the presidency of Franklin Roosevelt when millions of northern blacks became "Roosevelt Democrats." But the Republican party continued to be a viable alternative for black voters, often capturing a sizable if minority proportion of their votes. Approximately 40 percent of blacks had voted for Eisenhower in 1956, and about one in three voted for Richard Nixon in 1960. But Barry Goldwater in 1964 won the support of less than 10 percent of black voters. Blacks had gone from being solidly to overwhelming Democratic in casting their presidential ballots.

Figure 2.1 indicates the dramatic nature of this change. It shows the mean proportion of the vote for Democratic presidential candidates in the black precincts of the twenty-four largest southern cities from 1952 to 1972. Stevenson in 1952 and Kennedy in 1960 did well in these precincts, capturing roughly 76 and 70 percent of their votes, respectively. But Eisenhower cut deeply into the metropolitan black southern vote in 1956, win-

46

ning a clear majority in these precincts. The Johnson candidacy in 1964, however, represents the fundamental break in the series. Johnson won more than 90 percent of the votes in these black precincts; that figure was slightly exceeded by Humphrey in 1968 and almost matched by McGovern in 1972.

The 1964 presidential election thus marked the decisive turning point in the political evolution of racial issues. With the nomination of Goldwater the Republican party—the party of Lincoln and emancipation—turned its back on one hundred years of racial progressivism and instead undertook a strategy designed to attract the support of racially disaffected Democrats. At least this aspect of Goldwater's electoral strategy was clearly successful, marking the end of the "solid Democratic South" in presidential elections. But this strategy also led to severing the historic ties between the Republican party and the black electorate.

Conversely, the Democratic party, historically the party of slavery and segregation, had now become the home of racial liberalism, representing the views of the desegregationist forces in the struggle over civil rights. In so doing, it had strengthened its ties to blacks and white liberals but severely strained them with southern whites. The Roosevelt Democratic coalition, which counted upon southern electoral votes, was shattered beyond recognition. Not for many years would the full effects of this election work their way through the American party system. But it was already clear, in retrospect, that the 1964 presidential election had set into motion political forces that would transform the nature of American politics.

The Post-1964 Period

Several things could have happened in the post-1964 period that would have reversed or at least halted the political transformation marked by this election. The 1964 presidential election may have been a critical moment in the partisan evolution of racial desegregation. But if the moment had not been reinforced by future developments, its effects may have been temporary and thus ultimately inconsequential. Three developments in particular seem crucial in understanding the long-term significance of the 1964 election: Johnson's actions after the election, the racial orientation of the Democratic party in the post-Johnson era, and the response of Republicans to the Goldwater candidacy.

47

Johnson's Racial Policy Agenda

One possible course of action for Johnson after his overwhelming victory in 1964 was to be conciliatory toward the white South— to moderate the strong stand he had taken on civil rights. Johnson, of course, did nothing of the kind. Instead he pressed for congressional action in a new area of civil rights—black voting rights. The 1964 civil rights act had touched on voting rights, but it had not challenged a system in which millions of southern black citizens were being denied this fundamental political right. The immediate impulse for the Voting Rights Act of 1965 was the march from Selma to Montgomery led by Martin Luther King, Jr., to protest racial voting discrimination. As the nation watched in horror, state troopers, acting on orders from Governor George Wallace, used tear gas, night sticks, and whips to halt the peaceful marchers. As a result of this action Johnson not only put 700 federal troops on alert to protect the marchers from further violence, but he also called on Congress to pass a far-reaching voting rights act. Speaking before the Congress in a nationally televised address on March 15, the president bluntly told his fellow southerners: "To those who seek to avoid action by their National Government in their own communities, who want to and who seek to maintain purely local control over elections, the answer is simple: open your polling places to all your people" (Johnson 1966, 287).

Within a week of this address Johnson submitted a comprehensive voting rights bill to Congress, and on August 4 Congress approved the final bill. The main provision of the Voting Rights Act of 1965 gave the attorney general the power to appoint federal examiners to supervise voter registration in states and localities where a literacy test was in force and where fewer than 50 percent of voting-age residents were registered or cast ballots in the 1964 presidential election. Seven states would be subject to this federally funded and directed registration process: Alabama, Alaska, Georgia, Louisiana, Mississippi, South Carolina, and Virginia.

The 1965 Voting Rights Act dramatically increased registration among blacks in southern states, as shown in Table 2.2. In Mississippi, for example, the proportion of blacks registered to vote increased from 0.067 in 1964 to 0.675 in 1970. There were similar, if less spectacular, increases in the other southern states as well. The increases were especially impressive in precisely

TABLE 2.2
Proportion of Blacks Registered to Vote in Southern States, 1960–1970

	1960	1964	1970
ALABAMA	0.137	0.230	0.640
Arkansas	0.377	0.544	0.716
Florida	0.390	0.637	0.670
GEORGIA	NA	0.44	0.636
LOUISIANA	0.309	0.320	0.618
MISSISSIPPI	0.061	0.067	0.675
North Carolina	0.382	0.468	0.548
SOUTH CAROLINA	NA	0.388	0.573
Tennessee[a]	0.641	0.694	0.765
Texas[b]	0.337	0.577	0.847
Virginia	0.230	0.457	0.607

Source: Congressional Quarterly (1967; 1970).

Note: States in small capital letters cast their electoral votes for Barry Goldwater in 1964.

[a] The 1960 proportion for Tennessee is based upon data from 63 counties.

[b] The 1960 proportion for Texas is based upon data from 213 counties.

those five deep southern states that had voted for Goldwater in 1964. There was a certain logic to this pattern, of course. These states were most angered by the racial policies of Kennedy and Johnson and found a sympathetic voice in Goldwater. These were also the states in which racial discrimination was most deeply entrenched; consequently they had the lowest levels of black voting participation prior to 1965. Given the opportunity, large numbers of blacks in these states registered to vote for probably the first time in their lives.

The Voting Rights Act also made sense from the perspective of Democratic party strategy. It was clear from the voting results in 1964 that Democratic presidential candidates could no longer count on winning the electoral votes of the Deep South. Indeed, given the scale of the defeat, the opposite seemed more likely; the party would not be able to win electoral votes in this region for the foreseeable future. One possible way to alter this outcome was to add large numbers of likely Democratic voters to the voting population, trying to offset defections among white voters—

precisely the effect of the voting rights act. That this strategy ultimately did not succeed says less about the wisdom of the strategy itself than about the disdain with which white southerners now held the national Democratic party.

The Civil Rights Act of 1964 and the Voting Rights Act of 1965 had dealt with most important areas of civil rights except one: housing discrimination. In 1966 Johnson asked for legislation to ban discrimination in housing. The legislation passed the House but with a much more narrow margin than the earlier civil rights bills: 259 favored the legislation, and 157 opposed. The winning margin was provided by 183 Democrats and 76 Republicans, who were opposed by 95 Democrats and 62 Republicans. The voting pattern revealed a substantial decline in support for civil rights among Republican congressmen. Whereas the 1964 and 1965 legislation had received overwhelming support among House Republicans, the party membership was sharply split on the 1966 bill.

This bill was never enacted into law because it was subject to an intense and successful Senate filibuster. The Senate was unable to cut off debate because southern Democratic senators were joined by a large group of Republicans in opposing cloture. In 1964, forty-four Democrats and twenty-seven Republicans had voted for cloture; in 1965, forty-seven Democrats and twenty-three Republicans supported the cloture motion. But in 1966, the forty-two Democrats were joined by only twelve Republicans in voting to cut off debate while twenty-one Republicans and twenty-one Democrats opposed cloture. An almost two-to-one majority of Republican Senators opposed cloture, a sharp departure from previous years. The lack of Republican support for the Civil Rights Act of 1966 was due partly to the specific content of this legislation. Northern Republican senators and representatives, who had been willing to end segregation and voting discrimination in the South, were much less willing to end housing discrimination prevalent in the North as well as the South. But the lack of Republican support probably also reflected the growing racial conservatism of the GOP.

Johnson, however, would not be dissuaded. In 1967, he again asked for housing legislation, and again the legislation was approved by the House. On the fourth cloture vote minority leader Dirksen was able to produce just enough Republican votes to end the Senate filibuster, and the bill was subsequently passed by the Senate. On April 11, 1968, Johnson signed the bill into law. In sum, Johnson could have tread softly on racial issues after 1964 in an effort to bring white southerners back into the Democratic fold. That he chose to do just the opposite further solidified the Democratic party's relationship with blacks but strained even more the party's now extremely tenuous ties to the white South.

The post-1964 Democratic Party

If Johnson would not be conciliatory toward the racial views of white southerners, perhaps his successors would be. As we have seen, Stevenson, in a similar situation, had made a supreme effort to rebuild relations with the white South in the post-Truman era. Perhaps Johnson's successors would do the same. But the Democratic party, having moved toward the racial left under Kennedy and Johnson, stayed there. Three of the party's post-1964 presidential candidates—Humphrey, McGovern, and Mondale—came from the programmatic liberal wing of the party. Their racial liberalism was outspoken and uncompromising. None showed the slightest inclination to retreat from Johnson's stand in support of civil rights.

Nor did the party itself retreat from racial liberalism. Instead of downplaying the racial policies of the Johnson administration, the 1968 Democratic platform spoke in glowing terms about those policies:

"The Civil Rights Act of 1964 . . . and the Voting Rights Act of 1965, all adopted under the vigorous leadership of President Johnson, are basic to America's long march toward full equality under the law. We will not permit these great gains to be chipped away by opponents or eroded by administrative neglect." (Johnson and Porter 1973, 734)

The 1972 Democratic platform, the most consistently liberal statement ever made by a major American party, contained a section on civil rights that spoke of a renewed effort to bring about greater racial equality:

"The Democratic Party in 1972 is committed to resuming the march toward equality; to enforcing the laws supporting court decisions and enacting new legal rights as necessary, to assuring every American true opportunity, to bringing about a more equal distribution of power, income and wealth and equal and uniform enforcement in all states and territories of civil rights statues and acts." (Johnson and Porter 1973, 790)

51

Moreover, in one of its most controversial statements the 1972 platform offered support for busing as a means to eliminate school desegregation: " 'Transportation of students is another tool to accomplish desegregation. It must continue to be available . . . to eliminate legally imposed segregation' " (Johnson and Porter 1973, 804).

Jimmy Carter's candidacy in 1976 is especially revealing, for it confirmed the new reality of Democratic politics in the post-1964 period. Carter was a politician of the deep South. His speech, religion, and character were firmly rooted in rural southern political culture. Southerners were justly proud of him not only because he was one of their own but because he had won the Democratic presidential nomination against great odds.

But Carter was part of the new breed of southern Democratic politicians. He was a racial liberal whose political success depended upon putting together a coalition of blacks with a segment of mainly working-class white voters. He won the 1970 general election for the Georgia governorship with this coalition and there his chances for the presidency in 1976 rested. In the ensuing election, Carter carried the South but won only 46 percent of southern white votes compared to 53 percent who voted for Gerald Ford. Carter's victory margins in the South were due to the overwhelming support he received among black voters. Thus, in spite of Carter's close identification with the white South, he was unable to win a majority of the southern white vote. Carter's candidacy both confirmed the new direction of the Democratic party on issues of race and demonstrated the continuing estrangement between the Democratic party and the white South.

Our point is simple and straightforward: the post-1964 Democratic party showed not the slightest remorse concerning its past support for civil rights and indicated no hesitation about present and future support. The Democratic party had gradually but unmistakably become the home of racial liberalism.

The post-1964 Republican Party

But if the Democratic party had turned permanently leftward on race, what about the Republican? Would it now disavow Goldwater's racial conservatism and return to its tradition of racial progressivism? Or was the move to the racial right to be lasting?

There is no simple answer to this question. Clearly, Richard Nixon and Gerald Ford were not Goldwaters; neither embraced racial conservatism to that extent. But one can say with a fair degree of certainty that Republican presidential nominees in the post-1964 period were always more conservative on racial issues than their Democratic counterparts, and often strikingly so.

It is particularly instructive to compare the Richard Nixon of 1960 with the Richard Nixon of 1968 and, especially, of 1972. As we saw, Nixon in 1960 not only ran on a racially progressive platform, but he made a major personal effort to win black votes. Nixon's candidacy in 1960, in short, was still part of the racially progressive tradition of the Republican party. But in 1968 Nixon was far more interested in appealing to southern whites than to blacks. The day before the balloting for the Republican presidential nomination Nixon met with southern delegations to assure them that he was sympathetic to their racial situation. He told them that "he would not run an administration which would 'ram anything down your throats,' that he opposed school busing, that he would appoint 'strict constitutionalists' to the Supreme Court and that he was critical of federal intervention in local school affairs" (*Congressional Quarterly* 1983, 107).

In contrast to the Democratic platform of 1968, the Republican platform made no mention of the recently-enacted civil rights statutes. Indeed, the Republican platform did not include a full section on civil rights, offering but a single phrase on the topic: " 'We pledge . . . energetic, positive leadership to enforce statutory and constitutional protections to eliminate discrimination' " (Johnson and Porter 1973, 749).

In 1968 Nixon won the presidency with only a small proportion of black votes but with a number of states from the once-solid Democratic South in his electoral column. He proceeded to pursue a course of action on racial issues that had great appeal to white southerners. During his first term, he nominated three southern conservatives to the Supreme Court, forced the liberal chairman of the Civil Rights Commission to resign, opposed the extension of the Voting Rights Act of 1965 in its original form, and directed the departments of Justice and Health, Education, and Welfare to request a federal court to postpone the desegregation of Mississippi's public schools.

In 1972, Nixon followed these steps by requesting that Congress place a moratorium on school busing orders by federal courts. The Republican platform of that year echoed Nixon's position, stating that " 'we are irrevocably opposed to busing . . . we regard it as unnecessary, counter productive and wrong' " (Johnson and Porter 1973, 862). Nixon, in sum, made a special effort to court the white South in his comeback bid in 1968 and especially in his reelection in 1972, when he pursued a visible "southern strategy." His actions as president, moreover, more than fulfilled his promise to white southerners that " 'If I'm president of the United States, I'll find a way to ease up on the federal pressures forcing school desegregation—or any other kind of desegregation' " (Murphy and Gulliver 1971, 2).

Although Nixon and later Ford were not Goldwaters in the extent of their racial conservatism, Ronald Reagan's racial views closely match those of the Arizona senator. On the one hand, Reagan, like Goldwater, is clearly no racial bigot or segregationist, declaring: "I am opposed with every fiber of my being to discrimination" (Reagan 1982–1983, 38). On the other hand, Reagan's racial views parallel Goldwater's in his assertion that the federal government should do little or nothing to bring about desegregation. He opposed the Civil Rights Act of 1964, the Voting Rights Act of 1965, and the Fair Housing Act of 1968 (Dugger 1983, 197–98).

During the Reagan administration, the federal government has put hundreds of school desegregation cases on hold, tried to weaken the Voting Rights Act, supported tax breaks for segregated schools, and molded the Civil Rights Commission, always before a bastion of racial liberalism, into an open opponent of it. In short, Reagan has been a chief apostle of contemporary racial conservatism, breathing new life into the Republican's southern strategy. After winning the electoral votes of the southern states by very narrow margins over Carter in 1980, Reagan scored a landslide in the region against Mondale in 1984. At the same time, he received the lowest percentage of black votes of any Republican presidential candidate for which we have voting statistics and, quite likely, the lowest of any Republican candidate in American history.

Thus, political developments in the post-1964 period tended to reaffirm the historic partisan transition that had taken place in the 1964 presidential election itself. President Johnson continued to be a strong advocate for civil rights, further aligning the Democratic party with the cause of racial equality. The Democratic nominees who succeeded Johnson, moreover, kept the party on the racial left by adopting tough pro–civil rights stands on a variety of racial issues. The Republican party, by contrast, having moved to the racial right in 1964, more or less stayed

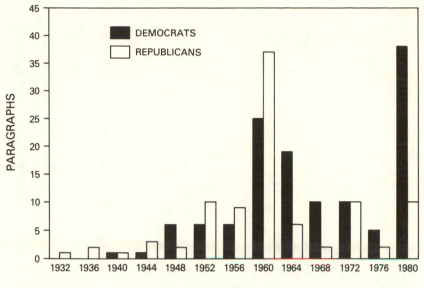

Figure 2.2 Number of Paragraphs on Race in Party Platforms, 1932–1980. *Source*: Computed by the authors from Johnson (1978, 1982) and Johnson and Porter (1973).

there after 1964. Republican party elites learned at least one crucial lesson from Goldwater's 1964 candidacy: there are millions of southern white votes to be won by positioning the party to the right of the opposition.

A More Systematic Look at the Party Platforms

We have traced to this point the changing responses of the Democratic and Republican parties to racial concerns by examining the rhetoric and actions of presidents and presidential candidates since FDR. In this effort, we have quoted liberally from the racial statements found in party platforms. We turn now to content analyses of these same platform materials. Quantitative indices from content analysis speak crudely to be sure, but they limit subjectivity, the analyst's ability to find what fulfills preconception and then quote it selectively. Figures 2.2 and 2.3, differing from one another in measurement strategy, report the results of this more systematic analysis of the racial content of the platforms.

55

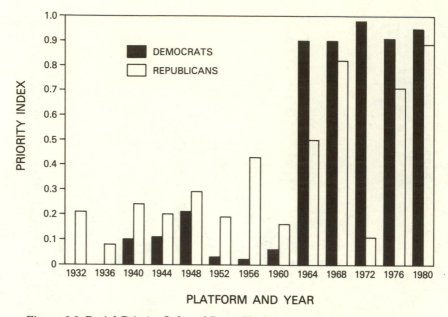

Figure 2.3 Racial Priority Index of Party Platforms, 1932–1980. *Source*: Computed by the authors from Johnson (1978, 1982) and Johnson and Porter (1973).

One simple measure of the importance of a topic is the space devoted to it. In Figure 2.2 we examine in the Democratic and Republican platforms from 1932 to 1980 the number of paragraphs that focus on racial concerns. The figure indicates the emphasis given to race by the two parties during this period, which, in general, is very little for both parties before 1960 and a great deal after that. That comes as no surprise, although it is worth noting that the surge in party attention to race, indeed its high point, comes in 1960, before the civil rights revolution of the early 1960s. Of more interest are the interparty differences. Before 1960, with the notable exception of 1948, Republican platforms always gave at least as much, and usually considerably more, attention to racial concerns than Democratic platforms. This pattern changed abruptly and permanently in 1964; after that Democratic platforms uniformly accorded more importance to racial issues than their Republican counterparts.

A second measure of the subtle concept "importance" is where, in the list of competitors for attention, an item gets mentioned. We assume that position in the program is an indicator, albeit a crude one, of relative priority among issue domains. We define a "priority index" as 1.0 minus the number of the paragraph containing the first discussion of racial policy (i.e., the number of paragraphs in the platform preceeding the first race paragraph) divided by the total number of paragraphs in the platform. Thus, the index is at its maximum value when race is at the very beginning of the program and declines to smaller values as it moves toward the end. If the issue is not mentioned at all, we give the index a zero.

Looking at the priority index of race in the Democratic platforms in Figure 2.3, one sees a clear and obvious pattern. Before 1964 racial concerns were positioned at the end of the party platforms. Beginning in 1964 and continuing through 1980 issues of race moved to the forefront. Racial issues, in other words, were given a great deal more emphasis in Democratic platforms beginning in 1964.

Comparing the relative position of race in the Democratic and Republican platforms, one can see that prior to 1964 Republicans gave relatively more emphasis to racial concerns. In each of the eight platforms 1932 to 1960, race is placed consistently more toward the end of Democratic platforms than Republican. Again this pattern changes dramatically and permanently beginning in 1964. Although the post-1960 Republican party gives relatively more emphasis to race than the pre-1960 Republican party, it always places race in a secondary position to the post-1960 Democratic party. That is, in 1964 and in each succeeding year, Democrats accord race a more prominent position in their platforms than Republicans do in theirs.

THIS QUANTITATIVE ANALYSIS of the racial content of party platforms confirms the picture that emerged from our earlier, mainly qualitative assessment of these documents—namely, that 1964 was a critical moment in the partisan evolution of racial issues. It was critical not merely because it marked a fundamental change in the parties' response to issues of race but, more important, because the transition was permanent.

It is difficult to overestimate the significance of Barry Goldwater in this partisan transformation. Before Goldwater, the Republican party was dominated by candidates and party leaders committed to racial progressivism. The party's history and lack of support in the South made this a natural stance. But a party committed to progressive racial ideas and policies was not going to be able to take advantage of the growing split between the national Democrats and white southerners. In this case, racial conflict would lie outside the two-party system, leading the white South to support third-party efforts as in 1948. Goldwater's candidacy fundamentally altered the likelihood of this possibility, not because he was a racist or a segregationist but because his racial conservatism struck a responsive cord among racially disaffected southern Democrats. Goldwater showed how Republicans could develop a powerful appeal in the white South without becoming outright segregationists.

No one individual represents the transformation in the Democratic party in the way Goldwater does for the Republican party. Truman, Kennedy, Johnson—all were key figures who moved the party toward racial liberalism, as was Carter, who sustained it at a moment of possible reversal. But if the change were more protracted in the Democratic party, it was no less significant. The party altered its historic position on race, becoming the home of racial liberalism.

The American party system, in sum, was fundamentally transformed during the mid-1960s. The progressive racial tradition in the Republican party gave way to racial conservatism, and the Democratic party firmly embraced racial liberalism. These changes unleashed political forces that permanently reshaped the contours of American politics. This fifty-year portrait of race and American politics, told of the materials of presidents, speeches, and platforms, is familiar in its general contours, and it provides a useful starting point. But issue evolution is much more routine business, involving the daily behaviors of a host of political leaders, most more or less unknown, and the multitudes that constitute the mass electorate. This history is perhaps the shell of a story of issue evolution. To get inside the shell we look now to the behaviors of others. We begin with Congress.

· 3 ·

THE POLITICS AND POLICY OF
RACE IN CONGRESS

The U.S. Congress is sometimes a policy initiator, sometimes a forum for response to presidential initiatives. Sometimes it is in the vanguard of policy articulation, sometimes the collective voice of resistance to innovation. Sometimes it debates and does nothing; sometimes it sanctions policies with the stamp of law. In each of these roles, Congress claims a central position in issue evolution.

If Congress acts or fails to act, it produces a public record of response to issue challenge. Its collective foot dragging through the late 1950s had a clear interpretation to racial activists, presidents, courts, and the public. The unmistakable message was that racial equality in all its forms was not the business of the United States government. But by 1964 Congress had written racial equality into law.

No presidential order or Supreme Court ruling can hope to achieve anything like the official sanction of legislation, particularly when the issue debate and the roll call are in the public eye. And more than any other policy in the postwar era, that has often been the case with race. Taken together, the string of congressional actions on racial issues comprise the most memorable acts of policy making in the post–World War II period. When civil rights legislation was offered repeatedly in the 1950s, it fell repeatedly to highly publicized filibusters in the U.S. Senate. The modern Senate is a drab contrast to the confrontations of the 1950s, where a small group of aging Southerners used its right to debate continuously to beat back a less determined civil rights majority.

Failure, repeated painful public failure, moved racial issues to the top of the liberal agenda in the 1960s. The early—and, in retrospect, small—victories for the civil rights coalition were all the more dramatic because they were so long in coming. Following the shifting tide of the 1958 Senate elections the old struggles were reenacted, but this time fragile bipartisan majorities managed at last to threaten the Southern filibusters. The drama built to a peak in the Civil Rights Act of 1964, probably the single

59

most publicized act of the twentieth-century Congress. The exclusive business of the Senate from February to June 1964, final passage of the act came only after 124 consecutive roll-call votes. The decisive role in this public drama was left to Minority Leader Everett Dirksen who, after satisfying his concern about the hypothetical "Mrs. Murphy's Boarding House," lined up his Republican troops to finish the job.

Only slightly less dramatic was the subsequent Voting Rights Act of 1965. Amidst national turmoil over violence directed toward civil rights activists in the South, Lyndon Johnson stood in the well of the House and, before a national television audience, with great emotion proclaimed the voting rights bill the solution to a national dishonor. When he concluded with "we shall overcome," he effectively incorporated the motto of the civil rights movement into national policy. A large bipartisan majority settled the issue.

Congress has addressed racial issues many times since 1965, but none of its action has achieved comparable public notice. Racial issues still arouse intense emotions, but congressional actions on them are no longer in the spotlight of sustained public attention.

We will examine the congressional role in racial politics in this chapter. Although it would be foolish to assert that congressmen are unresponsive to constituent desires on this issue—of all policy domains it is usually the single best case of policy representation—the primary role for all institutional actors in our issue evolution scheme is to lead public opinion. Policy making institutions, unlike the public, are confronted with specific questions that demand resolution. The public could be for or against "equal access to public accommodations," for example; Congress had to decide the question of principle and also apply it to "Mrs. Murphy's Boarding House." Policy-making institutions must lead the public in the important sense of having to confront issues earlier in time. And when they act, they add both policy and political definition to the issue.

Our approach in this chapter is two-pronged. We will raise and answer two questions: What happened? And how did it happen? The first requires a close look at the racial vote time series. That entails, among other things, measurement of the racial positions over time (to be found in Appendix 3), description of the observed evolutionary pattern, examination of the coalitions for and against desegregation over time, a chronology of key events and issues, and, finally, a first attempt at explanation (through intervention models) of the impact of two particularly important elections.

We will then turn to the "how did it happen" question. Our answers there will have more the flavor of systematic political science. Our concern will be to understand the mechanism of change, to apportion the observed evolution of party positions into their component pieces, among them conversion, replacement (intergenerational and interparty), shifts in the party base in the mass electorate, and the like. We will use the racial issue for leverage, ultimately, to examine the quality of representative democracy, the continuing question that haunts students of politics.

What Happened: The Partisan Evolution

A natural way to begin our narrative is to trace "the" origin of racial issues in American politics. And we have indeed pursued that question, always unsuccessfully. The problem with this strategy is that any postulated origin of the modern form of racial issues is invariably predated by an even earlier plausible origin. We have, for example, always considered the Johnson versus Goldwater election of 1964 a critical event in the partisan evolution of racial issues. But it was preceded by almost three years of dramatic sit-ins, freedom rides, and other attention-getting nonviolent protest. But the peak years of the civil rights movement were preceded by court-enforced school desegregation leading to violent response (e.g., Little Rock, 1957), in turn preceded by the *Brown v. Board* cases in 1954 and 1955. And there were the famous bus boycotts, most notably in Montgomery, Alabama, in 1955–1956.

These seeming origins in the mid-1950s were preceded in turn by desegregation of the armed forces (1948) and by extremely violent race riots during the war years. The riots were replicas of similar events twenty years before. And all this time there was quieter agitation against "Jim Crow" laws in the South and counteragitation by the Ku Klux Klan. Jim Crow and the Klan were products of Reconstruction, in turn a reaction to the Civil War. Historians have filled many volumes tracing the precursors of the war, abolitionism, Dred Scott, the Missouri Compromise, and so forth. Before that was the constitutional compromise that recognized a black slave as three-fifths of a person. Before that slavery and slave trade created controversies in the colonies. The only time that seems a reasonably certain origin for racial controversy in America would be the date the first black slave was brought ashore. And if that is a historically safe judgment, it is also certainly trivial. It does, however, suggest the folly of the enterprise; we ought not look for the origin of racial issues in American politics because racial issues predate American politics.

If we cannot find the origin of race in American politics, we can more reasonably assess the origins of partisan evolution on race in the modern period. And, unlike tracing the origins of the issue, that task is tractable. Although obviously not the beginning of our story, 1945 does mark a good point to begin systematic analysis of congressional response to race. The politics of race differed at the end of World War II from that at the end of Reconstruction, but not by much. The Republican party still marched under the banner of Lincoln. Enlightenment came naturally to its urbane Northeast heartland. And it was a cheap commodity to rural Republicans across the land who saw racial segregation as a southern issue.

Congressional Democrats at the end of the war were first and foremost southern Democrats. Representatives of the decaying urban political machines of the North and Midwest were also prominent. Like the designer of the New Deal himself, the urban Democrats managed to avoid conflict between social welfare and race by ignoring race. With extremely violent race riots of the 1930s and 1940s still fresh in memory, they had no grounds for illusion about how their constituents would respond if the issue were squarely confronted.

Notably absent in this picture are the northern Democratic liberals who later became so important to racial politics. The congresses before Humphrey, Douglas, and Lehman produced no well-known civil rights advocates. When Harry Truman began to advocate racial policies closer to Eleanor Roosevelt's than to Franklin's, he had to turn mainly to the opposition party for support.

All of this has, of course, changed. Figures 3.1 and 3.2 present the basic evidence of partisan issue evolution in the Senate and House time series, respectively. Although they differ in detail, both Senate and House figures demonstrate evolution of partisan voting patterns on race. Republicans, significantly more liberal than Democrats in both houses early in the period, become decid-

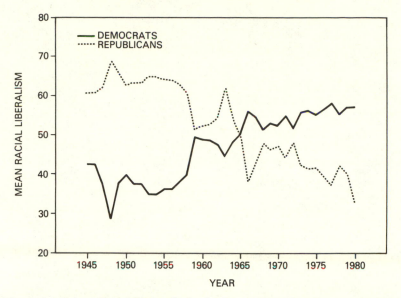

Figure 3.1 Senate Racial Voting Scales by Party, 1945–1980. *Source*: Compiled by the authors from analyses of annual roll-call votes of the U.S. Congress, 1945–1980.

edly more conservative after the mid-1960s. Our ensuing task is to describe this evolution.

The alignment of party and voting on racial issues is notably stable for the first fourteen years of the Senate series (Figure 3.1). Every year before 1959 Republicans are in the aggregate substantially more liberal than Democrats (and, not seen in Figure 3.1, about comparable to northern Democrats). The first evidence of change, the tentative origin of partisan issue evolution, is seen in the Senate series following the 1958 elections. By 1965, the greater racial liberalism characteristic of the Republican party since its origin before the Civil War vanishes, never to reappear. Similar but much weaker tendencies appear in the House series in Figure 3.2, where large scale movements would await the stimulus of the 1964 election.

We postulate membership replacement as the principal agent of interparty change over time. Thus, replacement mechanisms assume a central role in explanations. That leads immediately to two conclusions. First, elections are the probable causal forces that drive the system. And second, where replacement mechanisms differ, as they do between House and Senate by constitu-

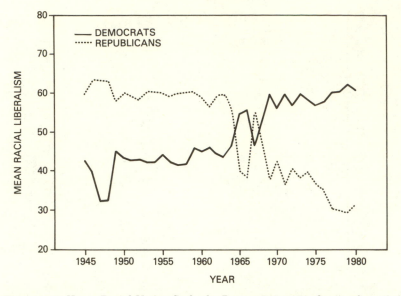

Figures 3.2 House Racial Voting Scales by Party, 1945–1980. *Source*: Compiled by the authors from analyses of annual roll-call votes of the U.S. Congress, 1945–1980.

tional design, change processes should also differ. The first conclusion leads us to look at elections as external causes of change in Congress; the second leads us to look at the two houses separately. We begin with the U.S. Senate.

Racial Policy Change in the Senate: *An Intervention Analysis*

Eighteen elections exerted potential influence on our thirty-six-year desegregation series. But we do not expect to see actual change associated with many of them. Two conditions influence the likelihood of election-induced interparty change for any policy: the magnitude of turnover and the potential systematic influence on the election outcome. Combining these two conditions, as shown in Table 3.1, provides a crude intervention scenario that is nonetheless good enough to allow us to sort out interesting possibilities.

Two of the four contingencies can be ruled out at the beginning. Category A includes most postwar Senate elections; turnover is small and unsystematic with regard to race. These elec-

TABLE 3.1
Election Outcomes and Partisan Change:
Some Hypothetical Effects

| Election Turnover | Desegregation Policy Role | |
	Spurious	Causal
Small	A. No Change	B. Systematic change possible
Large	C. Accidental change possible	D. Critical change possible

tions cannot explain change. Category D (large, causal turnover) would have been of great interest if it contained any cases, but it does not. The peak years of racial policy salience—roughly, the 1960s—produced no large turnovers in Senate membership. The racial salience of the Goldwater presidential candidacy makes 1964 a prospect for Category B, small but systematic turnover.[1] We know that contest is associated with issue evolution at the mass level;[2] it is reasonable to postulate similar effects in the Senate.

Very large turnovers in a very small body may produce substantial policy change between parties, even in the absence of policy influence on the election (Category C). The 1958 Senate election appears to be a case of this kind. Propelled by Khrushchev's first Sputnik and Eisenhower's second recession, Democrats scored nearly a clean sweep, effecting large-scale and long-lasting turnover of Senate personnel.

We are now ready to examine the impact of these two elections on the Senate series. We will explain the difference between Senate Republicans and Democrats on desegregation. The proposed

[1] See Converse, Clausen, and Miller (1965) for evidence of the racial salience of the Goldwater candidacy. They argue (327–30) that Goldwater attempted to portray himself as a racial conservative and that he met with striking success in conveying that message to voters. An electorate that had failed to perceive much racial policy difference between Richard Nixon and John Kennedy four years earlier, consensually separated Goldwater and Johnson and also the parties they represented.

[2] We develop the mass level evidence in Chapter 6; see also Pomper (1972).

explanations are the replacement effects of two elections, 1958 and 1964, using Box-Tiao intervention analysis.

Our goal is to test the intervention impacts of the two elections. Both are hypothesized to have sharp immediate impacts (except, of course, that senators take office in the year after they are elected) that decay over time back toward the original equilibrium level of the series. Because their apparent effects are almost identical, we impose the same Model 3.1 on both interventions, rather than fitting them separately. The model is a first order transfer function:

$$Y_t = [\omega_0/(1 - \delta_1 B)]I_{t-1} + \theta_0 \qquad [3.1]$$

where:

Y_t is the net difference series (Republican − Democratic)
I_t is 1 for 1958 and 1964, 0 for other years
δ_1 is the rate of decay of the intervention impact
ω_0 is the initial impact, and
θ_0 is the estimated mean of the series.

Model 3.1 describes a series in equilibrium around its mean that encounters shocks (two in the case at hand) that drive it away from equilibrium. Because the shocks are temporary, their impacts decay, and, given enough time, the model projects a return to the original equilibrium.

This decay model proves unsatisfactory in several regards. The dynamic parameter takes on an unacceptable (greater than one) value. The 1970s portion of the series is badly and systematically misestimated, and that in turn leads to a distortion in the estimated intervention effects. The fit of the model is not good (residual mean square = 32.6). None of these problems would have arisen if the model were fit to the pre-1970 series alone.

The problem with the 1970s portion of the series is that the earlier intervention effects do not decay after 1970. We see instead a steady growth in differentiation (see Figure 3.1) between the parties over that period. Because this secular differentiation cannot be accounted for by the earlier interventions, we must modify the model to account for it.

The form of the 1970s secular differentiation model differs from earlier interventions. Rather than an impulse with decaying impact, we model here a slow steady growth pattern. The choice of a starting point is neither as obvious nor as important

TABLE 3.2
Senate Party Differences on Desegregation:
An Intervention Model

	Parameter	Value	t	Description
Intervention 1:	δ_1	0.95	56.3	decay rate parameter
1958 and 1964 Pulse	ω_0	23.1	10.2	initial impact
Intervention 2:	δ_1	0.89	11.3	growth rate parameter
1970 Step Function	ω_0	4.4	2.6	initial impact
Noise Model	θ_0	-27.5	-27.5	mean (preintervention)
	θ_1	0.30	1.6	moving average (1)

Note: Residual mean square = 23.9.

for these sorts of models as in the impulse decay case. For that role we have chosen 1970, the first Senate election of the Nixon presidency. Model 3.2 leaves the 1958–1964 intervention model unchanged and adds an additional intervention for the 1970s:

$$Y_t = [\omega_{01}/(1 - \delta_{11}B)]I_{1t} + [\omega_{02}/(1 - \delta_{21}B)]I_{2t-1} + \theta_0 - \theta_1 a_t \quad [3.2]$$

where:

the first intervention is as before (except for the double subscript notation)

δ_{21} is the rate of growth of intervention 2
ω_{02} is the initial impact of intervention 2
I_{2t} is zero until 1970, one thereafter, and
θ_1 models a modest first order moving average noise process.

The estimated parameters for Model 3.2 are displayed in Table 3.2. The party difference series (Democratic mean minus Republican mean), actual and modeled, are displayed in Figure 3.3. Fitting a model of the modest complexity of Model 3.2 is a challenge to our statistical methodology when the series in question consists of only thirty-six time points. That the challenge is easily met tells us something of importance about the desegregation series; its variation is highly patterned. The net difference series of Figure 3.3 very clearly shows sharp impacts following the Senate elections of 1958 and 1964, each of which decays slowly back to-

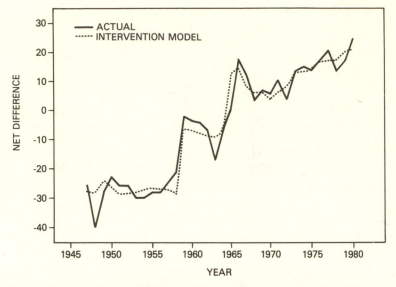

Figure 3.3 Senate Interparty Desegregation Differences, Actual and Intervention Model. *Source*: Interparty differences recomputed from Figure 3.1.

ward the preintervention mean of the series. This is as hypothesized. Almost equally clear, but not hypothesized (see Carmines and Stimson 1981, where the same effect was hypothesized for citizen attitude alignments) is the dynamic evolution of the 1970s.

Figure 3.3 leaves little doubt that Model 3.2 is an adequate description of the evolving party alignments on racial issues. It does not, however, tell us why the intervention effects occurred. We turn now to that question.

THE WHY OF ISSUE EVOLUTION IN THE SENATE

Before we can explain why a series of Senate elections could provoke a new race/party alignment, we need a picture of the world of racial politics as it existed before November 1958. Quite probably one side effect of issue evolution is the development of perceptual screens that leads modern observers to see a past more like the present than it truly was. Thus, a picture of the past in its own terms is a useful starting point.

Table 3.3 begins our picture of the racial policy status quo of the late 1950s. There we map the composition of the liberal and

TABLE 3.3
Racial Liberalism and Conservatism in
the Eighty-fifth Senate, 1957–1958

Desegregation Voting Pattern	Republican		Democrat	
	Nonsouth	South and Border	Nonsouth	South and Border
Liberal	37	5	20	1
Conservative	4	0	5	22
	41	5	25	23
Mean[a]	61.8	67.0	58.8	19.2

[a] Unrecoded Eighty-fifth Senate scale.

conservative racial coalitions by party and region.[3] The coalitions in Table 3.2 are quite different from those expected in later senates. Most important, there are twice as many Republicans as Democrats—forty-two to twenty-one—in the "liberal" category. Two pre-1958 factors go far in explaining this anomalous, by modern standards, situation. The more important of the two is that there were always far more northern Republicans than northern Democrats. Even if the northern Democrats had been uniformly liberal—and they were not—the Democratic party in the Senate was half southern during this period. The Democratic party could not become liberal in the aggregate without a massive reorientation of its electoral base from South to North.

The smaller, perhaps more interesting, phenomenon to be seen in Table 3.3 is that southern Republicanism—virtually all of it in the border states—was then a liberal alternative to the more traditional and conservative southern Democracy. The five border Republicans of the Eighty-fifth Senate—Cooper and Morton (Ky.), Beall and Butler (Md.), and Revercomb (W.Va.)—were actually more consistently liberal than the northern segments of either party.

The mean desegregation scales of Table 3.3 allow us to rule out

[3] Members are categorized by averaging votes from 1957 and 1958 and recoding. The mean for all members (50) is the division point between "liberal" and "conservative."

69

composition effects as an explanation of greater Republican liberalism. The Republican senators were more liberal overall, which we already knew, and they were also more liberal than the Democrats within each region. Although the northern Republican/northern Democrat difference of means is not statistically significant, its direction clearly rules out region as a spurious explanation for interparty difference.

With this context established, it is now easy to understand the impact of the Democratic landslide victory in 1958: eleven Republicans were replaced by Democrats; ten were racial liberals, each in turn replaced by a liberal Democrat. The forty-two Republicans to twenty-one Democrats found in the liberal ranks of the Eighty-fifth Senate became thirty-two to thirty-one in the Eighty-sixth Senate purely by virtue of interparty electoral change. In addition to the ten seats that stayed liberal but changed parties, the Democrats picked up another three seats as Alaska and Hawaii were admitted to the Union, tilting the balance even further. And while about one-fourth of all liberal Republicans ended their careers in only one election, the list of their Democratic replacements reads like a "who's who" of the Democratic coalition that would dominate the Senate for two decades.[4]

The summary of the 1958 Senate elections is simple: it was a bad year for Republicans. Although it would be very difficult to rule out any causal influence of racial issues on the outcome, neither do we have reason to postulate it. Racial issues were salient in 1958,[5] but the patterns of change do not suggest a systematic sorting process along racial lines, and we know from the later Kennedy/Nixon contest that voters perceived no interparty differences on racial desegregation. It is ironic that this first event in an unfolding issue evolution appears unrelated to the issue in question.

Whether the cause of the 1958 phenomenon was random or systematic with regard to race, the effect was certainly systematic. That single election ended the pattern of greater Republican liberalism on race, then called civil rights. Liberal Republicans were never again the dominant force in the civil rights coalition. At the same time, the Democratic party in the Senate developed

[4] Among them: Steven Young, Thomas Dodd, Clair Engle, Philip Hart, Vance Hartke, Frank Moss, Edmund Muskie, Eugene McCarthy, Harrison Williams, and William Proxmire (off-year).

[5] Even in 1958, well before the civil rights movement, racial issues provided the single strong case of policy representation in Congress. See Miller and Stokes (1963).

its more modern image: the hard core of northern liberalism was sufficiently large and sufficiently liberal that it counterbalanced the traditional southern contingent. This event must have been an important precondition in the struggle for control of the Democratic party that soon followed in the early 1960s.

Accounting for realignment on race following the 1964 Senate elections is an easier task. After the tumult of the civil rights movement, both on the streets and in Congress, there was clear evidence that racial issues were highly salient.[6] In that year American voters clearly perceived the Democratic party as more liberal on race issues than the Republicans.

The 1964 Senate elections contributed to further issue realignment on race in two ways. First, the liberals of the class of 1958, who would have been expected to suffer considerable attrition because they owed their initial success to a Democratic landslide, experienced no attrition at all because they had the good fortune to seek reelection during the Goldwater debacle—another bad year for Republicans.

Second, two more of the dwindling band of racially liberal Republicans, Beall of Maryland and Keating of New York, were replaced by highly visible liberal Democrats, Joseph Tydings of Maryland and Robert Kennedy of New York. Republican gains were small and uniformly conservative, including J. Strom Thurmond of South Carolina, who switched parties. Few seats changed hands in 1964, but "trading" Beall and Keating for Murphy of California and Thurmond pushed the Republicans ever more to the right. This shift occurred while Tydings, Mondale of Minnesota (replacing Hubert Humphrey), and Robert Kennedy gave increasing visibility to the Democratic left.

Small but systematic evolution through replacement is difficult to document precisely because it is small. But this much is clear: of the seats that changed hands, some (e.g., Keating/Kennedy) reinforced tendencies toward partisan issue evolution, some (e.g., Humphrey/Mondale) had no net effect, but none followed the pre-1958 pattern of greater Republican liberalism. Even Barry Goldwater, who evidently played a central role in realigning race and party, was replaced by a Republican (Fannin) whose racial conservatism was more consistent than his own.[7]

[6] See Converse, Clausen, and Miller (1965) for elaboration of this point.

[7] There is irony in the fact that 1964 marks a turning point in mass perceptions because, except for the purely regional voting rights issue the following year,

Racial Liberalism and Conservatism in
the Eighty-ninth Senate, 1965–1966

Desegregation Voting Pattern	Republican		Democrat	
	Nonsouth	South and Border	Nonsouth	South and Border
Liberal	10	0	37	8
Conservative	18	4	4	17
	28	4	41	25
Mean[a]	45.5	29.1	67.7	30.9

[a] Unrecoded Eighty-ninth Senate scale.

Table 3.3 is a snapshot of racial voting alignments before the first shock of the 1958 election; Table 3.4 is a similar portrait taken after 1964. In the Eighty-fifth Senate, two-thirds (forty-two of sixty-three) of all racial liberals were Republicans; in the Eighty-ninth, the comparable figure is 18 percent (ten of fifty-five). Before 1958 the GOP was significantly more liberal overall, and it was also more liberal in both the North and South separately; after 1964, it was more conservative within each region. All these changes appear on both sides of the ledger. The GOP not only lost seats in the Senate, it lost most of its 1957 liberal seats (roughly thirty-two of forty-two) and gained conservative seats during an era when the party was faring badly at the polls. The Democratic party meanwhile suffered minor loses to its conservative wing and made massive gains (from twenty-one to forty-five) among liberals. All these changes proceeded more or less equally in both North and South. Two elections produced an issue realignment in Senate voting.

Secular Realignment in the 1970s

Barry Goldwater made it respectable for Republicans to oppose federal intervention to enhance desegregation. We will see in

1964 was the last high point of Republican racial liberalism in the Senate. Only a handful of Republican senators voted "no" on the Civil Rights Act of 1964, but the handful included the party's presidential candidate.

Chapter 6 that the 1964 campaign appears to have set in motion an issue realignment among citizens.[8] Both the new respectability of conservative racial positions and the assurance of mass support, particularly support in Republican primary elections, would be likely to produce a systematically more conservative crop of Republican senatorial candidates. In contrast to the big jolts of 1958 and 1964 the process is slow and circular. Racially conservative candidates give the party a more conservative image, which filters the recruitment of party identifiers toward a more conservative norm, which in turn makes the nomination of more conservative candidates yet more likely, which in turn. . . . A process of this sort is evident in the secular realignment of the 1970s.

Secular issue realignment, the slow steady growth of inter-party issue differentiation, might be manifested either singly in any number of potent casual scenarios or multiply in weak versions of all of them. The latter appears to be the case. We give only brief illustrations here; we have already seen the systematic evidence.

The clearest manifestation of issue realignment occurs within parties. When Buckley ousted Goodell for the New York seat in 1970, for example, the Republican party not only lost one of its dwindling band of liberals but also gained a conservative. With much less drama, because the departures were usually voluntary and at advanced age, the old hard core of "segregation forever" southern Democrats has given way to racial moderates. The 1970s witnessed the departure of segregationist stalwarts such as Ellender, Ervin, Fulbright, Holland, Jordan, McClelland, and Russell. Their replacements were and are moderate in the aggregate; most have moderate voting records individually as well. Chiles, Stone, Gambrell, Edwards, Johnston, Nunn, Bumpers, Hodges, and Morgan are all southern Democrats, but they are cut from a mold closer to Jimmy Carter than to the old breed. Newly elected southern and border Democrats are not merely different than their predecessors in style. In every year after 1972 they are more liberal in racial voting than southern Republicans; this comes as no surprise. But those elected in the last two elections of our series are even slightly more liberal than northern Republicans. Distinctive primarily for its total opposition to desegregation, the "Dixiecrat" wing of the Senate Democratic party

[8] Also see Carmines and Stimson (1981) for an elaboration of this evidence.

was dead by the end of the 1970s.[9] That the old Dixiecrats could not hold on forever was to be expected. That they would be replaced only by moderates from their own party or conservatives from the opposition connotes issue evolution.

Interparty replacements have less direct effects on issue evolution. But two of the kind that matter can be seen in the 1970s. One is a long-term decline in Republican control of New England. Predictably liberal on racial matters and predictably Republican in Senate voting, New England was until recently a major force for (Republican) racial liberalism in the Senate. New England's six states produced nine Republican senators prior to 1958, all racial liberals. Twenty years later the Republican delegation was still liberal, but only four in number. Obviously much smaller than Republican heartland areas in the West and Midwest, New England now contributes even fewer Republican senators than the South.

The South itself is the final piece of the puzzle. Growing Republicanism has been expected since the early 1950s. That expectation has not been translated fully into Senate seats with any regularity, even through the 1970s. But the type of Republicanism now dominant in the South has changed. Once a racially liberal alternative with electoral success primarily in the border states, Republicanism has moved into the heart of the South, and it is now uniformly the conservative choice on racial issues.[10] The hard line on race is led increasingly by southern Republicans, such as Helms and Thurmond.

The Voting Rights Act of 1965 must surely have played some role in moderating at least the style, and probably the substance, of the racial positions of old southern Democrats. The asymmetry of impact of the new participation of large numbers of black voters is simple. Blacks now constitute large proportions of eligible voters in Democratic, but not Republican, primary elections. Racism was once a free shot in southern politics; an appeal to bigotry was certain to gain votes at almost no cost. The bigots are still out there—probably in somewhat lesser numbers—but now the southern Democrat who openly appeals to them does so with the certain knowledge that the appeal will cost a great deal.

We have examined Senate voting at length because the U.S.

[9] Of the warriors from the big segregation battles of the 1960s, only John Stennis and Russell Long remained at the beginning of the 1980s.

[10] It has also remained successful in the border states, but, except for Maryland, it is uniformly the conservative alternative.

Senate is a small body in which trends over time can be accounted for by the comings and goings of relatively few "household" names. A briefer, more systematic look at the House of Representatives is now in order.

MODELING ISSUE EVOLUTION IN THE HOUSE

Issue evolution in the U.S. House of Representatives occurs in the same political environment as that of the U.S. Senate. The House moves to the same external forces, the tides of electoral fortune, the bias of incumbency, the alignment of issues and parties in the mass public. But the House response is different.

In an era characterized by "vanishing marginals"[11]—the phenomenon of increasing electoral security for members of both parties—the House better resists electoral boom-and-bust cycles. Contrary to constitutional design, the lower house is better insulated from shifting public moods (Carmines and Dodd 1985). It responds just as surely to long-run change as the Senate, but its response is slower, more inertial, more deliberate.

The difference between the two bodies is partly a matter of numbers. With only 33 Senate seats at stake every two years, the size and policy predisposition of each party's contingent can vary considerably from the idiosyncratic events of a few states. Or, as in 1958, an electoral clock that accidentally exposes a distinctive wing of the party, racially liberal Republicans that year, to a heavy electoral current in the wrong direction can spark even more dramatic change. The House, in contrast, follows baseball's mystical concept, "the odds." With all 435 seats at stake in each election, there is little room for accidental replacement patterns. Because all members are equally exposed, there is a large theoretical possibility for systematic replacement, as undoubtedly occurred in 1964, but very little prospect of issue evolution by the accident of local or idiosyncratic factors.

Regional composition "accidents" do occur in the House; we shall see evidence of one in 1958. Before the confusion of later issue evolution there was a simple logic to regional composition. Seats in the South were Democratic through thick and thin; consequently, the South was the Democratic party base. Seats in the North, except the urban machine districts, were much more marginal. During bad times for the Democratic party, as in the early

[11] The phrase is from Mayhew (1974).

75

years of the Eisenhower administration, the southern base became a very large proportion of the party in the House. Good years, on the other hand, could only be good in the North because there were no seats to gain in the already "solid" South. Because race and region were closely associated, high tides for the Democratic party produced a party more northern and liberal in composition, and bad electoral fortunes produced a more southern and conservative party. And all of this was inevitable. It would have happened if no member changed position and no voter had racial issues in mind at the polls.

Because the House faces the same external environment as the Senate, we postulate the same interventions, the 1958 and 1964 elections, as causal forces. House electoral mechanisms are different; therefore, we expect a difference in response. Reflecting larger numbers, the House should be more orderly.

Racial Policy Change in the House: An Intervention Analysis

Figure 3.2 leaves no question about the fact of racial issue evolution in the House. Republicans were always more liberal than Democrats before the mid-1960s, always more conservative after. The evolutionary pattern is simpler than we saw with the Senate. A single election—and its dynamic aftermath—accounts for most of the observed shift. The 1964 election produced a large group of northern liberal Democrats elected largely at the expense of racially liberal Republicans; this is unlike the Senate, where turnover was small at that critical moment.

That Lyndon Johnson's landslide victory produced a large crop of liberal congressional Democrats is well known. One must also appreciate that liberal Democratic victories came largely at the expense of liberal Republicanism. Of the House Republicans who did not return for the "fabulous Eighty-ninth" Congress, roughly two of every three had voted in support of the strong House version of the Civil Rights Act of 1964. House Republicanism of the early 1960s was conservative on fiscal issues and proud of the heritage of Lincoln on race. The 1964 elections began the process, now nearly completed, of purging Lincolnism from the GOP.

For the earlier 1958 House elections we postulate a regional composition effect. Democratic success that year meant Democratic success in the North. Whether or not the emerging issue of race was on voters' minds, the northward move of the party's cen-

TABLE 3.5
House Party Differences on Desegregation:
A Dual Intervention

	Parameter	Value	t	Description
Intervention 1:				
1958 Step Function	ω_0	8.86	4.7	permanent impact
Intervention 2:	δ_1	0.77	14.3	growth rate parameter
1964 Step Function	ω_0	7.97	5.2	initial impact
Noise Model	θ_0	-19.1	-24.2	preintervention mean
	θ_2	0.78	4.5	moving average (2)

Note: Residual mean square = 31.0.

ter of gravity would have produced a more liberal Democratic party. But the shift could not be large, for the Democratic victory in the House was much smaller than its Senate counterpart.

Our intervention model of racial issue evolution in the House (see Table 3.5) is technically quite different from our earlier Senate model. The 1958 intervention produces a small permanent shift, not the impulse-decay pattern of the Senate. The 1964 intervention is a dynamic evolution toward a new equilibrium. That in turn obviates the need for an additional explanation of continuing evolution; the 1964 shift is still moving toward equilibrium through the 1970s. The differences do indeed provide evidence that constitution makers can influence the way in which institutions respond to a changing environment, but that point needs little support.

We see much more similarity than difference in the responses of the two houses. A comparison of racial voting in the two houses (in Figures 3.1 and 3.2) suggests that both evolutionary patterns were about the same, except that big changes came earlier in the Senate. In Figure 3.4, both actual and predicted House interparty differences also look much like the earlier Senate series. Two errors of prediction stand out. Both early in the series, 1947–1948, and two decades later differences are mispredicted by a parsimonious model. The former we regard a fluke. The 1967–1968 effects are probably real; they show the compositional change of losing in 1966 all those seats so easily won in 1964. Because the

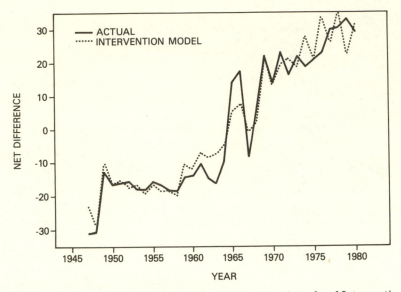

Figure 3.4 House Interparty Desegregation Differences, Actual and Intervention Model. *Source*: Interparty differences recomputed from Figure 3.2.

shift is evidently temporary, we prefer not to model it as an additional intervention.

Getting beneath the surface of the House racial polarization series is a task of a different order than our more informal approach to explaining change in the Senate. With few familiar names and some 1,600 members serving during the period, systematic analysis requires a different, somewhat more complex treatment. Those 1,600 members allow us some leverage in estimating systematic influences on issue evolution. Our chosen focus is region.

House Issue Evolution in Space and Time

Evolution and issue evolution[12] are inherently dynamic concepts, but racial desegregation is an issue framed in a regional context. Levels of popular support for desegregation have varied across regions as long as the issue has existed. And there is every rea-

[12] This section draws on Stimson (1985) where both the substantive example of House issue evolution and the statistical procedure are developed in considerably greater detail.

78

son to believe that similar variation is to be found in the voting patterns of regionally defined subgroups of the House of Representatives. We ascribe that variation to regional political culture, a term we shall use as an empty vessel to capture the multitude of factors—social, historical, economic, and so forth—that impinge upon the typical outlooks, beliefs, and behaviors of geographically defined populations.

American political parties are not and have never been national parties. They are organized at various levels, from precinct to national committee, but their character seems but modestly associated with any level of formal organization. They are diverse, but that point may easily be overstated. Each party is composed of fifty state units; however, each subunit does not have a wholly distinctive character, a political world of its own. The parties are more cohesive than that. The lines of division are fewer, largely regional; they are drawn by the distinctions between shared and not shared interests, shared and not shared experiences, shared and not shared values, shared and not shared speech.

Race has a longitudinal dimension; we have seen it evolve over time. It also has a regional basis. We might frame an analysis in terms of which it is, spatial or temporal, or which dimension accounts for more of its variance. But accepting that it is in fact both suggests a more useful strategy, modeling the issue evolution in space and time simultaneously. To do so we develop not one time series on the interparty differences on race, as earlier in this chapter, but eight independent time series, one for each of the eight standard regions[13] of the United States. Our analysis, a pooled cross-sections of time series regression, allows us to model the evolution and at the same time to specify how that common national evolution proceeded differently in the different regions.

Our dependent variable for this analysis is as before interparty differences or polarization on racial desegregation. Although race is clearly a regional concern, it is not obvious where we should expect to see greater or lesser polarization over it. For polarization reflects not whether the region is generally liberal or conservative on race but whether the parties typically differ

[13] We employ the Inter-university Consortium for Political and Social Research (ICPSR) standard region scheme. The eight regions are: New England, Middle Atlantic, East North Central, West North Central, South, Border, Mountain, and Pacific.

much or little on the matter. The degree of polarization depends on whether parties in the region typically differ on issue positions in general or whether views are so homogeneous that both parties are likely to converge on the same popular position.

We have some a priori expectations of what we are likely to see in the separate regions. Because the South and Border South have somewhat more salient and uniform views on racial issues, we would expect to see less party polarization there than is generally the case. Rational parties and candidates do not offer policy choice where views on one or the other side clearly predominate. New England should display a similar pattern at the opposite end of the scale, relatively little polarization because both parties hew to the predominant liberal position. It is less clear that we should expect to see greater than normal polarization in any particular region, but we shall indeed see that pattern.

We begin with the Ordinary Least Squares (OLS) analysis of the first column of Table 3.6. Essentially a replication of Table 3.5, but for the time period 1957–1980 only, the OLS estimates of the 1964 election intervention are quite similar to those we have already seen. Eight separate regional issue evolutions look like one national phenomenon. The model describes a polarization that begins after the 1964 critical moment and grows ultimately some six times greater than its initial level.

But OLS is not the estimator of choice in this situation; effects associated with the regional components may introduce specification bias of potentially serious magnitude. And the high level of residual autocorrelation (0.55) makes OLS an inefficient estimator, with potentially overstated significance and model fit.

The model is respecified after a series of analyses not reported here in the second column of Table 3.6 as a (pseudo) Generalized Least Squares (GLS) model with correction for autocorrelation and unit effect dummies for regions with lower or higher levels of polarization than the national norm. The region dummy variables, except for the special New England case, may be understood as adjustments to the regression intercept. The − 10.50 adjustment for the South means that the region is always ten and one-half points below the national level of issue polarization over the entire twenty-four-year series. This reflects the relatively slight issue contrast between parties typical of the region and, to a lesser extent, the neighboring border region.

No dummy variables are introduced for the Middle Atlantic,

TABLE 3.6
**Two Intervention Models of Racial Issue Polarization
in the U.S. House of Representatives**

Region	Ordinary Least Squares	Generalized Least Squares with Dummy Variables
1964 Election (ω_0)	4.82	4.97
	(0.36)[a]	(0.36)
Dynamic growth (δ_1)	0.83	0.83
	(0.08)	(0.08)
Preintervention mean	3.42	4.17
	(1.28)	(1.46)
New England (interaction)		−14.31
		(3.30)
South		−10.50
		(2.51)
Border		−5.64
		(2.85)
Mountain		6.13
		(2.94)
Pacific		9.16
		(2.84)
R^2 (adjusted)	0.485	0.549
ρ_1[b]	0.55	0.27
Estimated equilibrium level	28.35	29.23
($\omega_0/(1-\delta_1)$)		

[a] Standard errors are indicated in parentheses.
[b] The autocorrelation estimate ρ_1 is a weighted composite of within region residual autocorrelation.

East North Central, or West North Central regions. Each of these industrial heartland areas is close to the national norm of issue polarization and thus requires no special attention. Two regions, the Mountain and Pacific states, are significantly more polarized on racial matters than the national norm. Republican racial conservatism—as opposed to old fashioned racism—has significant roots in the American West, as do its most stalwart proponents

81

of the period, Barry Goldwater and Ronald Reagan. In this area with no long-standing tradition of racist politics, the new racial conservatism, associated from the very beginning with the Republican party, seems most completely to have permeated party divisions. The West utterly lacks the old segregationist sentiment of Democrats east of the Mississippi or any of the moderation often displayed by eastern Republicans.

New England is a special case. The evidence there suggests that alone among regions New England has resisted the tide of Republican movement to the racial right. Distinctive about the region is that while the rest of the country displayed a new party polarization over race New England did not change. Both Democrats and Republicans were predominantly liberal before the issue evolution, and both remained so. New England therefore is modeled with a dummy variable that is off (0) through 1964 and then on (1) for the rest of the series. The -14.31 estimate for New England then implies that the region *became* less polarized by that amount after the issue evolution began; in effect, it remained constant when all other regions changed.

The issue evolution itself, the dynamic component of the model, is virtually unchanged from earlier analyses, actually slightly strengthened by the regional controls. This evidence has an important implication: the issue evolution cannot be understood as an artifact of regional politics, an apparent national pattern that truly results from the aberrant behavior of one region, as is sometimes claimed by devotees of southern politics. It is a national pattern, the evidence for which is uniform across seven of the eight regions.

POLICY POLARIZATION IN CONGRESS: A SUMMING UP

We have now seen systematic evidence of an issue evolution on race in Congress.[14] Although we shall deal more fully with each, two aspects of the evidence are worthy of note here: first, the phenomenon is mainly dynamic; second, although associated with election outcomes, issue evolution is not associated with anything resembling "critical" elections.

Whether one looks at statistical parameter estimates or merely

[14] But the organization of this book does not reflect the chronology of our research. We were aware of issue evolution as a mass phenomenon before we ever thought to look at Congress. See Carmines and Stimson (1981).

stares at a graph of party movements over time, the same point emerges: most change over time is accounted for by what happens not at election times, which may be thought of as ultimate causes, but *after* them. The dynamic adjustment subsequent to signal changes accounts for most movement in the congressional party polarization series. Movements immediately following the signal events are more noticeable, but they account for little of the ultimate evolution. The institutions of American political life mediate response to electoral forces, producing dynamic response—effects that are neither immediate nor one-shot but cumulative from gradual adjustment processes over time. That response, if no less certain than immediate reaction, is more interesting. Moreover, it tells us what we have always known about institutions: they affect outcomes in general, and more specifically the effect is not entirely immediate but takes place over time. The theory of issue evolution is very much at peace with institutional approaches to political life.

The racial issue evolution is an instance of major policy and political change proceeding apace in national institutions and, as we shall soon show, in the mass electorate. Not only is most change dynamic rather than than critical, but none is associated with "critical" elections as commonly understood. We have singled out 1958 and especially 1964 as crucial electoral events that respectively started and greatly accelerated the racial issue evolution. But 1958 belongs in every analyst's "normal" category, and 1964, sometimes considered "critical," is most often considered and then rejected. Whether critical election realignments are sufficient to produce dramatic policy change we shall not consider. But our evidence does speak to the question of whether they are necessary; they are not.

In closing we note that issue evolution may have interesting consequences for issue representation. The dynamic trace etched by the parties in Congress will be seen as highly congruent with similar alignments of policy attitudes and party support in the mass electorate, producing policy representation at its full bloom that was not at all present at inception of the process. But the irony, which we will explore in some detail in Chapter 7, is that the representation runs in a direction counter to normal democratic expectation. For we shall see policy "response" from national institutions preceding the mass awareness alleged to cause it.

All this evidence speaks to connections between elite behavior and its mass response. It raises a series of questions about how the two are connected. For the beginnings of some answers to those queries we turn to an intriguing group of actors, neither political professionals nor ordinary citizens but something in between.

APPENDIX

*Measuring Racial Policy Change
through Roll-Call Votes*

The basic data for Chapter 3 are the roll-call votes cast by all members of both houses of Congress from 1945 through 1980. From that massive array, we selected in each year those with racial content. Sometimes manifest, as in the long series of "Civil Rights" acts, sometimes latent, as, for example, antilynching or poll-tax bills, the judgments were tedious but not difficult. Where we were in doubt about the true content of a vote, we included it.

In a second stage, all roll-call votes selected were subjected to a principal components analysis[15] to see for each whether extraneous issue or strategic dimensions were operative. When decisions were difficult, validating information (e.g., who sponsored? how did known proponents or opponents of civil rights vote?) was brought to bear. Votes that survived both stages of scrutiny were then recoded ("1" pro, "0" con) and summed into annual scales with implicitly equal weights for each member. Transformed into ratios:

$$\frac{\text{number of pro votes}}{\text{number of votes}}$$

the scales become indicators of racial policy liberalism.[16]

As a final check, "between Congress" correlations of the scale scores for individual members were computed for returning

[15] See MacRae (1970) for a treatment of the perils of choosing appropriate correlation coefficients for principal components with roll calls. After lengthy experimentation with all options, each of which is unsatisfactory in one regard or another, we settled for phi, the simplest, which is reasonably well behaved in the absence of extreme marginals.

[16] For this analysis we have standardized the annual scales to produce constant means (fifty) and standard deviations (twenty-five) in the aggregate for all years. Although the scales in their natural (percentage) metric do not vary greatly from these norms, variation could quite clearly occur because some congresses face easier or tougher versions of the same legislation.

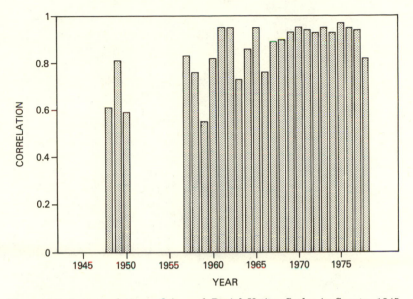

Figure 3.5 Autocorrelations of Annual Racial Voting Scales in Senate, 1945–1978. *Source*: Compiled by the authors from analyses of annual roll-call votes of the U.S. Congress, 1945–1978.

members. It is vivid testimony to the clarity and intensity of race that these correlations are large not only for adjacent congresses but also for congresses decades apart in time. The specific content of legislative actions on racial issues has changed quite substantially over time, but these data suggest no change at all in the basic segregation/desegregation dimension.

Figure 3.5 displays year-to-year autocorrelations for the Senate desegregation scales.[17] The autocorrelations are a first indication of the continuity of the racial dimension. The pattern of Figure 3.5 is high year-to-year autocorrelation with relatively little fluctuation. All exceptions to the pattern are produced by years where measurement reliability is constrained by a small number (minimum: two) of roll calls.

The evidence of Figure 3.5 does not close the case. If the meaning of an issue dimension were evolving, it would be possible to observe high year-to-year autocorrelations and yet witness strik-

[17] Years for which no autocorrelations are presented involve pairs of adjacent years, at least one of which had no identifiably racial votes. In later analyses we estimate individual scale scores for those years from earlier, if available, or later behavior.

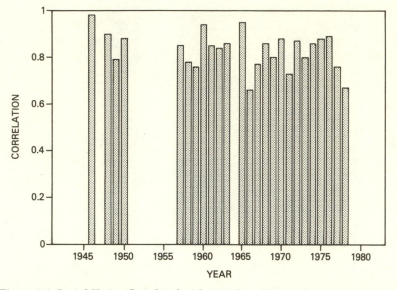

Figure 3.6 Racial Voting Correlated with 1964 Base Year in Senate, 1946–1978. *Source*: Compiled by the authors from analyses of annaul roll-call votes of the U.S. Congress, 1946–1978.

ing change from the beginning to the end of the series. For that reason we examine the correlations of each year with a base year to fix the content of the dimension. The base year chosen is 1964. In that year our measurement is reliable because a very large number of roll calls contributed to the scales. And because every one of those roll calls involved the omnibus Civil Rights Act of 1964, we have no question that it is a valid measure of the deseg-regation concept.

If the meaning of the desegregation dimension were changing over time, we would expect an inverted "V" pattern around the base year; moving away from the base in either direction in time would be expected to lower correlations, but that does not occur. Only two of the Carter years show some tailing off in the corre-lations of Figure 3.6. But the lowest correlation in the series is the almost adjacent 1966.[18] Very high associations occur in the

[18] The relatively low association of the 1966 votes with the earlier pattern in the Senate is reflective of real change. That session was an important turning point in the nationalization of civil rights issues and the decay of the bipartisan desegregation coalition.

86

Truman years, and they are matched through the Ford presidency.

It is commonly believed that the nature of racial issues changed after the landmark civil rights legislation of the mid-1960s; after securing legal rights, the agenda of racial politics was redefined toward far less tractable social and economic issues. Certainly the rhetoric shifted; "segregation forever" disappeared from public speech, and "black power" was born. But insofar as racial politics is reflected in roll-call votes, there is no evidence of the postulated change. Figure 3.6 shows that the continuing senators from 1964 behaved as if nothing had changed. Desegregation was the black/white issue of the Truman presidency; Figure 3.6 suggests that it was much the same under Eisenhower, Kennedy, Johnson, Nixon, Ford, and Carter. Anyone who lived through this era knows that important redefinitions of the grounds of racial politics have occurred. But our evidence, stated in its most limited sense, says that the core dimension of congressional response to questions of the federal government's racial policy is constant.

This same longitudinal stability of racial issues is evident in the House of Representatives. Figure 3.7 plots bivariate correlations between the racial issues of the Eighty-ninth House[19] and all other years. As in the Senate series, there is no indication of change. Votes of members who served in 1946 and were still present in 1965–1966 are correlated at 0.92 for the two independent issue scales. The comparable correlation between the Eighty-ninth and 1977, almost the end of the series, is 0.88. The early 1950s, the one period that seems a bit distinct, is also a time when almost nothing was happening on race. We are quite comfortable with the assumption that the House series taps a single common dimension over time.

The continuity is not as anomalous as it might at first seem. Part of the explanation for congressional constancy amid environmental change is that the newer issues were fought out in different arenas. Because the issues were nonlegal, they were also nonlegislative. "Black Pride," for example, might have been quite important in the shifting racial politics of the late 1960s, but it is not the subject of any of our roll calls.

---

[19] The two sessions of the Eighty-ninth House are chosen over the 1964 baseline used in the Senate for superior measurement reliability. The Civil Rights Act of 1964 was settled by a single vote in the House.

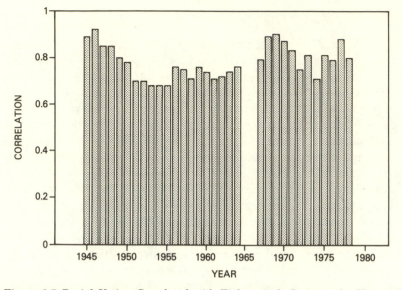

Figure 3.7 Racial Voting Correlated with Eighty-ninth Congress for House of Representatives, 1946–1978. *Source*: Compiled by the authors from analyses of annual roll-call votes of the U.S. Congress, 1946–1978.

A second explanation for constancy is our own decision to exclude matters that, though relevant to racial policies, are not themselves specifically racial. Black Americans were important actors in Lyndon Johnson's "poverty" legislation, for example, as well the Nixonian counterattack in the name of "law and order." Perhaps in the popular perception only blacks were poor and only blacks were muggers, but neither of these perceptions was true and neither written into law. In part then, the desegregation dimension is constant over time because it is the only specifically racial policy almost by definition.

· 4 ·

POLITICAL ACTIVISM AND
THE PARTY SYSTEM

Americans in the norm are passive observers of politics. A peripheral concern in their lives, politics commands attention infrequently. For most, a few hours devoted to the every four-year horse race of the presidential election sweepstakes is the full extent of involvement. They join no clubs or caucuses, attend no meetings, display no bumper stickers. Generous contributors to community good works, most Americans give no money to political parties or candidates.

Political activists—those Norman Rockwell good citizens who give money, ring doorbells, and wear buttons with candidate, not designer, names—are abnormal. Their interest is atypical. Their conspicuously political behavior, in a culture of mass noninvolvement, is deviant. But we entertain the reasonable suspicion that their weight in the political process is considerably greater than their number; that in a society where few care about politics, those few are unusually important actors.

Coming to terms with the attributes, behaviors, and institutional roles of the activists is our task in this chapter. It is challenging, for the literature offers hints but little guidance on the topic. The activists fall between the well-studied mass electorate on the one hand and the professional politician on the other. The activists' atypicality suggests that established theory and research on mass behavior will be of little help. And those Nexon (1971) labeled "occasional activists" are also unlikely to much resemble full-time professional politicians. To play the "game" of politics for sport and good citizenship cannot be similar to the grim business of protecting a livelihood.

Issue innovations, we have argued, arise from the strategic calculations of politicians, particularly those expected to be losers, from external shocks, internal contradiction, and local variation. Only the first of these posits actors or motive. The others, logical processes, also must work their force through human behavior. To give them life we need to understand who are the carriers of the germ, and that problem is more difficult than might at first seem the case. Abundant evidence indicates that ordinary citizens are unlikely sources of change; their response to political life is often restrained by lifelong commitment and filtered and dampened by inattention. As agent of change the mass public will not do. Elected public officials strain toward consistency rather than change, but for different reasons. They are rooted in place by thoughtful approach to issues, the weight of which produces over-time stability, by the constraint of party affiliation, and by the political danger of appearing unsteady of approach. None of these forces prevents change, but all forces act to dampen the prospect.

Who then can be an agent of change? To move quickly to new ideas demands more thought and involvement than we expect of mass electorates, more freedom and flexibility than we expect of politicians. Citizen activists, fired by zeal and standing to lose no more than an investment of time committed to the cause, are well situated to respond quickly to new ideas, to be the carriers of new themes. Although we expected only limited change from people deeply committed to any set of ideas, the structural position of activists, the fact that they move in and out of activity, frees them to be the dynamic element in issue evolution. Because activity itself is occasional, we expect change between occasions. Because new ideas may themselves motivate activity, the activists are well situated to be the vanguard of issue evolution.

Occasional Activism

Activism is occasional in American politics. Button wearing and doorbell ringing are intermittent activities, dated by the electoral calendar. The death of political machines that once dominated organizational politics by default has moved amateurs to the fore. Campaign and party activities lack routine and stable division of labor, but most important they lack personnel. Our early prejudice against standing armies has been abandoned to necessity for war making, but we have transferred it to political organization. There, each new campaign begins with the recruitment of an officer corps of campaign managers, pollsters, media consultants, and the like. But with rare exception, there are no continuing foot soldiers, no political garrison troops.

Each campaign faces anew the problem of recruiting its foot soldiers. Political campaigns need citizens with the personal attributes of good salesmen, for selling is what the campaign is all about. From the citizen activist the campaign needs his or her costly time, energy, and emotional involvement. In compensation it offers a sense of good citizenship and, sometimes, the opportunity to advance a personal ideology. Because the campaign needs are costly and the inducements to political activity are limited at best, failure to recruit adequate numbers of workers is a normal attribute of political campaigns. Such failure is nearly universal in campaigns for state and congressional offices. It is frequent even in presidential contests, where campaign induced press hype about "armies of volunteers" usually describes mere patrols, led, often as not, by mercenaries.

Sometimes a presidential campaign succeeds in producing widespread political activity. And this, unlike Nexon's usage, is a second sense in which activism is "occasional." The pool of potential activists is evidently much larger than the number of activists in any given year. All activists are "occasional activists" in Nexon's sense; they are active only "in season." But quite a number participate in some seasons and skip others; they are "occasional" on a larger time scale. Generalizations about activists and activism are accordingly hazardous. Activists are always present, but they are not necessarily the same people from one election to the next. This chameleon coloring is unkind to hypotheses derived from either single elections or even a short series of them. Among the more prominent casualties are, as we shall soon show,[1] the staple hypothesis of political commentators: "Activists in both parties are more extreme than the mass parties, Republican activists more conservative, Democratic activists more liberal." Democratic activists are sometimes more liberal than their party; Republican activists are sometimes more conservative. But neither is always the case, and it is rare that the activists of both parties deviate from their party norm in the same year.

Nexon's asymmetry variation of the hypothesis—Republican activists, not their Democratic counterparts, are more extreme than their party—was a nice adaptation of the staple hypothesis to the 1956–1964 period he studied, and particularly to 1964. But it was no sooner written than the asymmetrical extremism disappeared from the Republican party only to reappear on the Democratic side (Beck and Jennings 1979, 1984).

[1] See Beck and Jennings (1979) for a more general, multiple-issue treatment of the issue/participation link based upon the Jennings-Niemi student/parent 1965–1973 panel study and the National Election Study series from 1956 through 1976. The work is extended to 1980 in Beck and Jennings (1984).

91

The Verba and Nie (1972) thesis that middle age produces peak participation rates was disconfirmed by an influx of young adult activists in the very year *Participation in America* went to press. And as soon as commentators became accustomed to associating "activist" with "youthful," the pattern quickly reverted to its pre-1972 norm.

The moral to this failure to describe the attributes of campaign participation is that the phenomenon is variable over time and changing electoral context. To accommodate contextual variability in the attributes of political foot soldiers and the motivations to political activity we must examine the phenomenon over time. Before we take up that task, we digress to a brief discourse on data and method. Then we will proceed to a portrait of activism and a theory of the activist role in issue evolution.

DATA AND METHOD

The National Election Series is our basic data resource for all presidential elections, 1952 through 1984, and for some but not all the intervening congressional elections (1962, 1970, 1974, and 1978). The criterion for inclusion in our examination is simple; all studies that measure political activity are included.

The twelve studies provide a pool of over twenty thousand citizens who were interviewed during the period. From this very large—and largely inert—pool it is possible to isolate that tiny fraction of citizens who report active involvement in politics. Depending upon the rigor of our criteria for determining who is an activist, it is possible to extract a thirty-year activist subsample of about one thousand citizens, about one out of every twenty respondents interviewed. Thus, although the samples of activists in any particular election (averaging around one hundred) are too small for any but the most perfunctory analyses, the thirty-year pool allows considerable leverage, particularly for over-time analyses.

Measuring Activism

The literature on activism shows more diversity than consensus on the question of who are the political activists. The activist concept has partly been fit to what or who is available in a particular research design. In contrast to professional politicians on the one hand and the mass electorate on the other, both of whom are readily identifiable, the identity of activists is quite variable. The citizen activists we study are quite different from such alternatives as convention delegates or large contributors. Citizen activists are far less committed to party activity than the convention delegates and no doubt considerably less well-heeled than the large contributors.

The citizen activists we study share many characteristics of the national mass samples of which they are a selection. They differ principally in taking the opportunities to become involved in politics that others shun. They are in many regards the "opinion leaders" identified in the early voting studies (Berelson, Lazarsfeld, and McPhee 1954): citizens situated in their diverse settings who become disproportionately influential in their particular social contexts because they care more about political affairs than their friends, family, and coworkers. We shall take up below a fairly direct test of the opinion leader thesis.

We have isolated three overlapping sets of activists from the election study samples. The first, and most important for subsequent analyses, are campaign activists, identified by self-reports of engaging in multiple common political activities such as attending political rallies, wearing buttons, donating money, and the like. Our measurement technique is a simple summary count of the number of acts performed.[2] The behavioral activites are: 1) voting, which discriminates only at the passive end of the continuum; (2) attending political rallies or meetings; (3) wearing a campaign button or displaying a bumper sticker (not available for 1952); (4) working for a party or candidate; (5) attempting to influence others, and (6) donating money (not including the one dollar federal income tax check-off). Where we classify into an activist/nonactivist dichotomy, the criterion for activist classification is four or more acts, which isolates the most active 5 or 6 percent of the electorate.[3]

Working in the campaign, one of the six acts of the activity scale, is our second measure of activism. This second approach is a close conceptual fit to the ordinary connotation of "activist." We make limited use of this single criterion because it is a blunt

[2] See Verba and Nie (1972) and Beck and Jennings (1979) for validation of similar scales.

[3] Necessarily excluded by the design of the election studies are the sizable numbers of young people who become campaign activists before attaining the right to vote. This exclusion is no doubt more serious in the years before 1972, the year when the national eligibility age was lowered to eighteen.

93

measurement instrument. For many election studies it is a dichotomy—reported working or did not—that fails to capture any notion of an activity continuum. And it suffers from the inherent reliability limitation of any single-item measure.

"Informational activism," our third measurement approach, is based upon respondent reports of paying attention to the campaign in various media—newspapers, magazines, radio, and television. Not activism at all in a behavioral sense, informational activism measures passive involvement in the world of politics. Informational activism is a less rigorous standard of involvement than behavioral activism; the merely well-informed can become so in their living rooms. Because the overlap between informational and behavioral involvement is modest, we shall make limited use of the informational measure. Indeed, its greatest contribution is to make the point that actually doing something in a campaign is very different from psychological or intellectual involvement.

The Personal Attributes of
Political Activists

Inertia characterizes the behavior of the major actors in American politics. Three decades of scholarship on Congress, for example, paint a picture of members who generally come and stay. And while they stay in position, they are pretty much locked into policy positions on continuing issues. Both factors, continuity and stability, produce inertial response; new patterns of behavior are initially resisted, but they diffuse over time as the proportion of "old guard" members declines year by year.

The mass electorate, too, is inertial. Its membership change is gradual. Habit and inattention tie voters to particular combinations of party identification and policy positions. Where ties to party are frequently unaltered over a lifetime and attitudes are notoriously resistant to change, inertia is perhaps the most prominent characteristic of the American electorate.

It is arguable that neither form of inertia was expected when political scientists first began to examine the behavior of either politicians or citizens. The prevailing "rational activist" view of American politics had citizens transmitting strong policy views to representatives, who responded from fear of electoral retribution. But the behavior we observed forced an accommodation to the idea of inertia, now quite widely held. In this regard political activists resemble neither their fellow citizens nor political professionals. Variability is perhaps their most striking characteristic. Not capricious, that variability is responsive to the context of politics. Activists we presume are stable voters, but they come and go as activists in response to the times.

Two similar sorts of explanation can account for activist variability. If we presume that activists are perennial—from ideology, a sense of party membership, or whatever—then we must account for why they are sometimes inactive. Alienation from their party's candidate or platform is one natural line of explanation. Its drama makes good copy in political columns, where it is frequently seen.

If inactivity is the normal state of affairs—at least inactivity beyond the modest expectations of good citizenship—then we must account for why the potential for activism is sometimes realized. Activity is costly, and we must explain why citizens sometimes bear that cost. Here a natural line of explanation would focus upon the inducements that overcome inactivity in a particular election, the sense that activity might make a difference, that the policy stakes of a particular contest are great, or whatever.

The two explanations are opposite sides of the same coin: one accounts for why those expected to be active are on some occasions not; the other accounts for unexpected activity. Our data cannot settle the question of which is closer to the truth. But we are impressed with the barriers to activism, especially continuing activism, and so prefer the latter account.

The essential explanation for activist variability, for either line of argument, lies then in the fact that decisions to participate in election-year politics are made anew every two or four years. Unlike standing decisions of party identification or lifelong dispositions such as ideology, the decision to participate actively (beyond voting, which may indeed be habitual) is discrete. We posit the decision to result from more or less self-conscious weighing of costs and benefits. It would then be responsive to year-to-year changes in those costs and benefits. The costs of participation may be relatively fixed, but there is reason to suspect considerable variation in perceived benefits.

Whatever explains it, the variability of citizen activist involvement in electoral politics may prove to be of striking theoretical importance. Issue evolution or, for that matter, any theory of electoral change is hard pressed to account for change in the electoral system when most of the main actors in the process behave inertially. As we will argue below, the activists then may be crucial to our understanding of change precisely because they are highly susceptible to short-term behavioral alteration when all other elements in the system are not.

What then describes the activist? We can say much more than "variability," but we must always keep in mind that the picture of activism is dynamic. It changes over the three-decade scope of our examination. And we must be wary that it will change again, perhaps in unanticipated directions, in the future.

A Thirty-Year Portrait

The citizen activists of our thirty-year sampling are fairly constant on some dimensions, always predominantly middle-aged and disproportionately Republican, and highly variable on others, in both general ideology and more specific commitment to one or the other side in the contest over racial desegregation. The composition of the activist segment will be seen to be highly responsive to the electoral context.

Age: If the Activists are Middle-Aged in Numbers, Why is "Youth" so Visible?

Much popular commentary about political activists is of one particularly observable demographic characteristic, age. It is a peculiar characteristic of observers of American presidential election politics that almost no four-year interval passes without the discovery of a "new politics," directed toward and manned and womanned by the young. And if all these "new" politics cease to look in any sense new after the first blush of campaign season, it is equally the case that the average age of political activists seldom strays from the early forties. Why the young are so crucial in journalistic accounts and, by their own accounts, such a minute proportion of politically active Americans involves where campaigns occur, how they are reported, what is reported, and how activism is studied. The first three issues bias reporting in the direction of overstating the role of the young; the last biases studies, our own included, in the direction of understating it. We consider them in order.

The overwhelming proportion of citizen political activity occurs in both the neighborhood and the workplace, where the middle-aged dominate political activity. Reporting of campaigns, on the other hand, occurs "on the road," where the candidates go. The visible activists are thus those seen in numbers on the road. They are disproportionately young, below the age where career and family compete for priority, for the simple reason that they alone are available for on-the-road campaign activities in large numbers. Whereas others have personal and professional responsibilities that cannot be abandoned, those of high school and college age have free summers and no career or family responsibilities to keep them at home. The young thus seem to be everywhere during political season; in fact, they are only at every place where active campaigning and political reporting are occurring.

Youthful political activity is good press. The candidate with an army of youthful political volunteers is seen in favorable terms. To the extent that candidates can control what is reported about the campaign, for example by making volunteer work visible and public while keeping professional and traditional efforts such as "boiler-room" set-ups away from the visible campaign, they are likely to do so. That again tends to overstate the reporting the youthful activity.

Finally, youthful activity is overreported because it is inherently newsworthy. A stable two-party system that deemphasizes sharp issue cleavages produces relatively little hard news. Politics is continuous from year to year, the campaign continuous from day to day. Genuinely new stories are much in demand and short of supply. Thus, the sympathies and activities of the young are always reported because they are always new. The young activists on the campaign nearly always are engaging in significant political activities for the first time; their intense commitment to one or the other side is nearly always new. In an inertial political system dramatic change of any kind is unlikely, but, if it occurs at all, it is mostly to be seen among the young who lack the previous commitments that tend to produce inertial response. "Young people support Joe Blow" is news. "Again, as in the past, [group] supports [party]" is not. Therefore, youthful activity is overreported.

The countervailing bias occurs because the people we study when we study activism—convention delegates, campaign contributors, or as here, ordinary eligible voters who choose to be active—are all of minimum voting age. Particularly before the reduction in the minimum voting eligibility age in most states

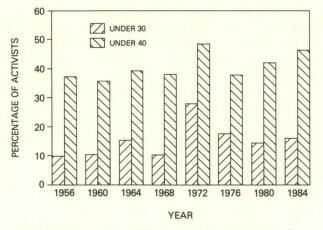

Figure 4.1 The Age Composition of Party Activists, 1956–1984. *Source*: SRC/CPS National Election Study Series, 1956–1984.

from twenty-one to eighteen, many visible young activists, and also the less visible and more numerous young people who volunteer at local party headquarters, were not eligible voters. They were not, therefore, represented in the populations we study. Even after the reduction of the voting age, enough such activity of the ineligible remains as to make quantitative assertions about the age of active citizens subject to understating the roles of the very young.

We take a brief glimpse of the age of activists in Figure 4.1. Although subject to bias as it is, variations over time in the typical ages of the party workforce tell us something of the dynamics of the political system. Figure 4.1 shows the proportions of all activists in two age groups—under thirty years of age and under forty, which includes the under thirty—over time. The notable pattern in the figure is a surge in the number of young activists in the early 1970s. That coincides in part with the peak of Vietnam and campus protest movements of that era, which produced unprecedented levels of unconventional activity, and in part with the reduced voting age. The context of the times, and in particular the issue context of symbolic and highly charged controversy of that era, would seem to be the larger part of the explanation. The change in the voting age was permanent; the surge of youthful activism was not.[4] Whatever the explanation of this phenom-

---

[4] A bit of the growth in proportion of the young activists is probably an artifact

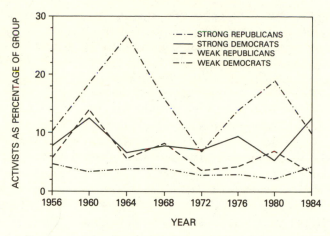

Figure 4.2 Percentage of Activists Among Strong and Weak Party Identifiers, 1956–1984. *Source*: SRC/CPS National Election Study Series, 1956–1984.

enon, it illustrates the repeatedly visible composition of activists as strikingly variable over time.

Party: Disproportionate Republicanism

Citizens who choose to become active in electoral politics—at least in the biennial elections, the focus of the National Election Study series—do not merely become active in community affairs, they choose sides. Or stated more accurately, having chosen sides, at any given time they choose whether or not to become active. One of the more important things we can know about them is which side they choose.

Our data suggest an unambiguous answer to the "which side" question. Republicans are far more likely to engage in electoral activism than are Democrats (Verba and Nie 1972). Because during this period there were far more Democrats to begin with, the higher proportions of Republican activists produce a relatively even split between the parties in total numbers of activists. Figure 4.2 portrays much of this variability over time, but it shows on balance that self-identified "strong" partisans in both parties are always more active than those who qualify their commitment

---

of the mere size of the "baby boom" cohorts. But the duration of the large cohorts is nearly twice as long as the surge of Figure 4.1 and so cannot account for much of the phenomenon.

to party, as would be expected. But among both "strong" and "weak" identifiers, Republicans are nearly always the more active and sometimes by as much as two or three to one.

The two parties differ not only in the level of campaign participation but also in its variability. Strong Democrats and the weak identifiers of both parties report activity levels that move but modestly from year to year around apparently stable equilibriums. The strong Republicans, in contrast, report strikingly variable behavior. The pattern of Republican activism over time is highly consistent with an explanation of activism as a response to ideological presidential candidacy. The Republican party twice in the three-decade period nominated as its standard bearer a candidate clearly identified with the party's ideological right— Barry Goldwater in 1964 and Ronald Reagan in 1980. It seems an unlikely coincidence that these two elections produce peak activism among the strong Republicans that more than doubles the normal level.

No such variability exists on the Democratic side. The weak Democrats report virtually constant and very low levels of activism over the period, while the activity level of the strong Democrats does not coincide with that party's one experiment in ideological presidential candidacy, George McGovern in 1972. Aggregation by party here obscures some individual variability that we shall show below; unlike the Republicans, large numbers of Democrats are drawn from both ideological wings of American politics, and the Democratic party would not be expected to respond uniformly to an ideological candidacy. This is particularly true in the first half of the period, when it formed the basis for the Nexon asymmetry thesis.

One component of activism is actual campaign work for a party or candidate. Because campaign work is probably the costliest of the activities open to citizen involvement—it consumes substantial personal time for a segment of the population that highly values its time—we might expect it also to be most variable. Campaign work is nether habitual nor an expected behavior of the "good citizen." Thus, those who choose to do it in a particular election are likely to respond to something about the election that makes it seem worth its cost. When we look at this indicator of activism in Figure 4.3, we see a pattern similar to the more general indicator. The strong Republicans emerge again as the group most likely to participate, most variable over time, and most likely to respond to ideological appeals. However, the pat-

100

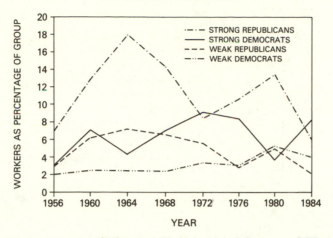

Figure 4.3 Percentage of Campaign Workers Among Strong and Weak Party Identifiers, 1956–1984. *Source*: SRC/CPS National Election Study Series, 1956–1984.

tern of Figure 4.3 diverges from the earlier figure: when it comes to campaign work, strong Democrats also display an over-time pattern of activity that seems responsive to ideological cues, with a notable surge in response to the 1972 McGovern candidacy.

Liberals and Conservatives:
Responsiveness to Ideological Cues

For partial confirmation of our ideological account of activism we turn to a direct measure of left versus right position, the Center for Political Studies "liberal-conservative" scale. Available only for the last of our three decades, it nonetheless allows a different and more direct observation of the ideological coloration of active citizens. Classified by party and the activist/nonactivist dichotomy, Figure 4.4 shows that the great mass of both parties remains virtually constant in aggregate ideological position from 1972 through 1984. That is what we expect, but it serves to anchor the scale and highlight the more variable composition of the activists. Activist behavior is again both more variable and more consistent with an ideological interpretation; those from each party who choose to be active in a given election mirror the ideological stances of their party's presidential candidate. Thus, peak liberalism occurs among Democratic activists in 1972, and,

101

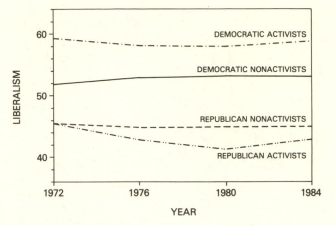

Figure 4.4 Liberalism Among Active and Nonactive Party Identifiers, 1972–1984. *Source*: SRC/CPS National Election Study Series, 1972–1984.

more dramatically, peak conservatism among Republicans is witnessed in the 1980 Reagan election.

Racial Attitudes: Dynamic Variability

Citizen activists may be expected to differ sharply from the mass electorate in the degree to which their specific policy attitudes are constrained by more general ideological positions; they are among the most sophisticated of a generally unsophisticated electorate. Having seen that the ideological composition of the activists is responsive to the candidate choices put forward in a given electoral contest, it comes as no surprise to see that the composition of racial attitudes is also responsive. But racial attitudes are not merely similarly variable and responsive; they are more variable and more responsive than general ideology.

With regard to liberal-conservative ideology (Figure 4.4) we saw that the parties in the electorate have always been differentiated, that the activist segment sometimes highlights that distinctiveness, and that the movement of the activists is highly responsive to context. We see in the racial policy case (Figure 4.5) that the parties have not been distinctive all along; there is general confusion in the attitudinal composition of both activists and mass electorate before 1964. After 1964 the activists are often more distinctive than the mass parties, although usually not in both parties at the same time. But what may be most crucial in

102

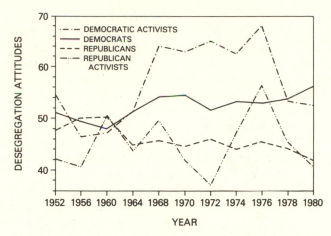

Figure 4.5 Desegregation Attitudes of Party Activists and Identifiers, 1952–1980. *Source*: SRC/CPS National Election Study Series, 1952–1980.

the racial case is that the activists are strikingly variable from year to year. That variability, most notable on the Republican side, is very closely tied to electoral context.

Movement in racial policy position is fairly simple on the Democratic side. Beginning in 1964 the Democratic mass party begins a movement to the racial left that continues, more or less unabated, through the end of the period. Excepting 1978 and 1980[5] the Democratic activists are starkly more liberal throughout the post-1964 period. That is as it should be, for the Democratic commitment to racial desegregation was unwavering in word and deed throughout the period. The Republican party, however, offered varied racial cues from year to year, to which the Republican activists were highly responsive. Barry Goldwater in 1964 first established the conservative racial agenda as a Republican position, and the composition of the Republican activists shifted to the racial right.[6] The "new" Nixon of 1968, like the old Nixon

[5] We choose not to make much of the 1978 and 1980 deviation because these studies present measurement comparability problems. Beginning with these studies the Center for Political Studies dropped most of the mainline items on attitudes toward segregation and desegregation from the NES series. The dominant remaining item, a seven-point scale on government aid to minorities, although associated with desegregation attitudes, also raises new and different questions of compensatory aid that go considerably beyond the realm of desegregation.

[6] The measured shift almost certainly understates the case in 1964, for the

of 1960, had little to say of racial issues and was generally perceived to be moderate, particularly in contrast to the flamboyant
Goldwater of 1964. Nixon had moved to the right by the time he
sought reelection in 1972, with a visible southern strategy in
both electoral politics and, more visibly, in the attempted nomination of two Supreme Court justices with strikingly segregationist past public records. Gerald Ford in 1976 was somewhat a
throwback to the old Republican moderation on race, in marked
contrast to his leading Republican opponent, Ronald Reagan;
both his past moderation as a congressional leader and his southern opponent Jimmy Carter mitigated against conservative racial appeals. In consequence, Republican activists were racially
moderate and relatively liberal in that year. When Ronald Reagan claimed the Republican nomination in 1980, racial conservatives moved into Republican activism.[7]

One way to inquire what a party stands for, a theme we will
develop in detail below, is to aggregate the positions of its members, those who express a sense of identification with the party,
and presumably also with its goals. But however correct this
strategy may be as accounting, it overlooks the fact that policy
views for most citizens are private. Looking at the policy views
of the mass electorate permits the survey research measurement
of views whose only public expression is in the survey interview.
If we ask instead what a party visibly stands for, then we need to
focus on those viewpoints that might reasonably be expected to
be expressed, to be seen and heard in the neighborhood, workplace, or wherever government and politics are discussed.

For this analysis we assume that one thing that distinguishes
activists from typical citizens is the public expression of political
views; indeed, "talking about politics" is one item we employ to

---

Goldwater appeal was across party lines to the Democrats and Independents of
the South. Because we do not know in which party a respondent was active, we
classify by party identification. That means that conservative Democrats who actively supported Goldwater are counted as activist Democrats and conservative
Independents are not counted at all. Goldwater could not mobilize large numbers
of racially conservative Republicans because there were not large numbers to be
mobilized. That ceased to be true after 1964.

[7] The Reagan 1980 effect is again probably understated because the ranks of
Republican activists in that year include an unknown number of moderate-to-
liberal types who worked against Reagan in support of the independent candidacy
of John Anderson. Liberal Democrats who moved into independence to support
Anderson would also detract from the normal liberal coloration of Democratic
activists.

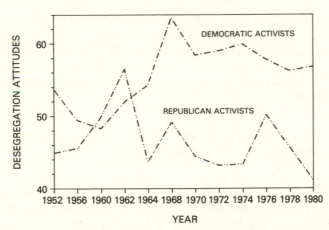

Figure 4.6 Desegregation Attitudes of Party Activists Weighted by Degree of Activity, 1952–1980. *Source*: SRC/CPS National Election Study Series, 1952–1980.

define activism. If we assume, furthermore, that the visibility of a citizen's views is in rough proportion to his or her activity, a matter of degree, not kind, then a method of examining visible party positions suggests itself. The logical extension of a simple accounting of identifier positions, equally weighted for all, is to weight views by the degree to which they are publicly expressed, operationalized in this case by activism. Thus, the citizen who reports no activity beyond voting is altogether removed from this "public" opinion analysis, while the more active are weighted by degree of activism.[8]

Looking at the positions of the two parties through the views of their active supporters, which we show in Figure 4.6, displays a cleaner glimpse of an issue evolution in progress. The same basic patterns are in evidence as in Figure 4.5, but they are stronger than the more inertial mass electorate sample and a bit less variable than the activists, treated as a discrete category rather than a continuum of activity. When weighted by activity levels, the identifiers of the two parties display a polarization over race that begins in 1964 and continues unabated through the end of the period, reaching its largest dimension in 1980, the final year of the period. If we take the next step and assume that

[8] This purposive weighting scheme is derivative of Converse, Clausen, and Miller (1965) who employed a similar scheme for a similar purpose; they observed not a cross-section of American public opinion but a cross-section of opinion likely to have been publicly expressed.

105

a similar process may be the mechanism by which ordinary citizens come to "know" what the parties stand for, on any number of issues, then a number of puzzling problems, seeming contradictions, and unanswered questions may all have a straightforward solution. We turn now to a detailed analysis of the logic of that solution.

THE DYNAMIC ELEMENT IN ISSUE EVOLUTION: HOW CITIZENS COME TO KNOW PARTY POSITIONS

Voters repeatedly tell us that they do not follow public affairs, have little interest in politics or policy, view government as relatively remote from their lives, and have little concern over which particular set of public officials ought to be in charge. But, in the aggregate, these same voters seem surprisingly well-informed about the choices they make. This contradictory set of facts—one of the longest running conflicts in the study of mass electorates—presents no easy way out.[9] We can deny one or the other set of facts, but after two decades of argument between the "voters don't pay attention" and "voters are not fools" schools of thought, the evidence marshaled on both sides is impressive. It seems that most citizens do not pay enough attention to public affairs to have a decent understanding of the issues with which they must come to grips to make informed choices. And yet it also seems that choices are informed by a decent understanding.

Public officials, such as U.S. congressmen, repeatedly tell us, in a similar vein, that the public is almost wholly unaware of their official behavior, often despite their own best efforts to inform. But these same officials worry, and not just a little, about the electoral consequences of their acts. Are they irrationally fearful, ignorant of the true level of public information? Or is there some way in which a public that does not know about a single individual act, such as a roll-call vote, somehow comes to understand a pattern of behavior?

Electoral history provides many examples of a singularly interesting variety of voter perceptions of facts at variance with the truth, as best as it can be objectively observed; yet, from the viewpoint of the relative choice between parties or candidates,

[9] For an intriguing attempt to resolve this conflicting set of findings and resulting contradictory view of the American electorate see Neuman (1986), who also accords a strategic role to those small numbers of citizens displaying unusual levels of political sophistication and activity.

these perceptions provide the basis for a sound expression of the voter's preferences. For example, how may we come to terms with the probably common perception that George McGovern in 1972 stood for "acid, amnesty, and abortion," when McGovern in fact had a mixed and largely private view of the abortion issue and certainly did not favor illegal drug use or the legalization of any substance as harmful as acid. But in the two-candidate choice of that year, inaccurate as those assertions are, they do capture the notion that McGovern was the one likely to sympathize with the left counterculture to which these themes were tied.

Even more contrary to fact was the widespread belief, of no small consequence to the election outcome, that Jimmy Carter was weak on defense, meaning specifically defense spending, in 1980. The fact of the matter was that Carter presided over the first defense spending increase in real terms since the Vietnam buildup and perhaps the most impressive peacetime buildup since the onset of the cold war era. But applied to the choice between Carter and Ronald Reagan, the public's misperception of Carter formed the basis of an accurate relative assessment of which candidate would likely spend more.

If we inquire closely into public policy as debated in the policy conscious environment of Washington, we must be impressed with how truly difficult most policy disputes can be. For when interesting policy debates arise they are only rarely of the for or against variety readily communicated for mass consumption. More often they are complicated and specific, involving disputes over facts and assumptions, not basic values. Values and ideologies do have a role, almost invariably, but that role is often so subtle that only the day-to-day experts in a particular policy area correctly know which side is which. When, for example, we debate nuclear deterrence strategy, the debate is framed by calculations of strategic behavior in regard to an event that has never before occurred, by knowledge of the differing technical capabilities of each contending side, and so forth. When we contrast this with the knowledge base of the electorate, we must be amazed that anyone ever figures out who are the hawks and who are the doves. But question after question presents issues of similar complexities; voters do at least sometimes seem to be making choices on issues they cannot reasonably understand, but these relative choices accurately reflect their underlying preferences (Carmines and Kuklinski 1989).

These contradictions and many more can be resolved if we but abandon the notion of individual citizens as atomistic fact collectors and decision makers. If instead we view the collection of factual information as a social process in the same way that Berelson and his colleagues (1954) long ago characterized the formation of voting intentions, as a two-step flow of communication, then we can come to terms with how millions of inattentive citizens somehow acquire reasonably accurate information about policy positions and policy choices. All we need do is assume that the normal economics of specialization and division of labor apply also to the collection of political information, and then both an account of information flow and a resolution of otherwise contradictory facts is at hand.

That inattentive citizens are likely to collect facts from the more politically attentive people with whom they have personal contact is an assertion neither novel nor shocking. It is something we have long known but keep forgetting. Probably owing to both the norms of popular democratic theory, which idealize the individual citizen as decision maker, and our intellectual dependence upon survey research as a method of observing the world, which constantly directs our focus to the individual as unit of analysis, our tendency is always to revert to thinking of the psychology of individual cognition as if in a social vacuum, the lonely contest of the individual citizen and his television set.

Consider the economy of fact gathering about policy choices. The citizen who would express his personal preferences in his choices between alternative candidates and parties must know the relevant choices (and the relevant set is always much smaller, more applied, more specific, and more technical than the more general preference questions to which they are related), who stands for what, how large is the relative difference between alternatives, and so forth. Two barriers stand in the way of individual fact gathering about policy choices: (1) the activity is extremely expensive, requiring an attentiveness to government and politics considerably beyond what most citizens seem willing to consider; and (2) having paid the high price of attentiveness to public affairs, the individual citizen gathering his or her own facts is very likely still to be wrong, to take a position contrary to what he or she would espouse with more expert knowledge on the matter.

The citizens who prefer to be inattentive to politics—and we tend to underestimate the reasonableness of that preference—could choose to bypass both costs and errors by simply looking to someone in their personal environments, someone whose views they know (often, probably without wishing to) for evidence of the relevant facts. The inference is simple and accurate enough on average to make it a reasonable guide: Joe Blow supports candidate X; therefore, X probably stands for the same things as Joe Blow. Fill in television's "Archie Bunker" for Joe Blow and Richard Nixon for X, and an inference that follows is that Nixon is not warmly disposed toward black Americans. We think it likely that this sort of reasoning is common. Indeed, the fictitious Mr. Bunker may even have been a source of considerable political "knowledge" during his prime-time run on American television.

Who would be those of known views in the individual's environment? The politically active, or others very like them, would seem prime candidates. They are the specialists who pay attention when others do not; their views are public, on display from lawn signs, campaign pins, and bumper stickers. Sometimes their views are known, in which case they give direct coloration to the parties and candidates they support. Sometimes their views on issues are unknown but advertised along with candidate support; a peace symbol and McGovern sticker on the same bumper told a story in 1972. Sometimes the association of political support with a subculture or lifestyle forms the basis of inferences about candidate views; if the McGovern sticker appeared on the bumper of an aging Volkswagen van of a certain distinctive type, the symbolic association of candidate and a cluster of left political views could be inferred.

The process of inferring candidate and party views from the views of the activist supporters would be most direct and powerful for members of primary groups including an activist cue-giver. There the constellation of issue positions associated with political support would generally be well known from direct conversation over a lengthy period. That may be supplemented, and in some cases replaced, by figures who are impersonally "known," such as politicians and movie stars, as well as by the altogether anonymous mechanisms, such as the bumper sticker.

What does it matter how citizens go about forming their beliefs of what parties and candidates stand for? We began this inquiry with a quandary: How can change be explained when the behaviors of two critical sets of actors, the mass electorate and elected politicians, are fundamentally inertial? Resolution of the quandary requires an important set of actors who are not inertial, and that set is the activists. The variability repeatedly visible in the year-to-year composition of the activist stratum now may be seen to be crucial. If the activists serve to define the issue positions of contending parties and candidates, then they are the missing dynamic element. The variability and responsiveness of their behavior is critical. For where others move slowly and predictably over time, gradually adjusting to a changing political environment but resisting sudden movements, the activists move at least relatively with lightning speed.

Change sometimes does happen quickly. How, for example, are we to understand the familiar phenomenon of almost unknown presidential candidates in March of election years who by June or July are surrounded by hordes of committed and enthusiastic supporters? Who are these people who come out of the woodwork, almost overnight, to form important political coalitions where none (of substance) before existed? Clearly the citizen activists are capable of such responsive behavior. They, too, are inertial in their commitments to parties and ideologies, but in their decisions to become active in a particular contest they are highly responsive to the political world. They create a large element of unpredictability, for the formula that produces responsiveness is not well understood. Like romance it seems to require a special chemistry that we can appreciate after the fact but find very hard to predict.

The posited role for citizen activists in the formation of party images resolves yet another quandary, this one specific to our own inquiry. We have repeatedly observed that the racial issue evolution proceeded at an impressive pace during periods such as the decade of the 1970s when racial concerns were not central to American party politics. The growth of party differentiation of image and polarization of the attitudes of party identifiers had their origins in the race-centered politics of the 1960s, but most of the growth in differentiation and polarization occurred after race was eclipsed as a central issue by Vietnam, Watergate, energy, and a series of economic miseries. If images became more distinctive at the same time that public debate contracted, then there must have been a source of those party images independent of what parties, candidates, and media chose to highlight. Citizen activists form that source.

It is possible in the racial case to establish time series of party images for the period during which national voting studies have been conducted. Based upon questions that ask respondents where the parties stand on an issue, as opposed to their own

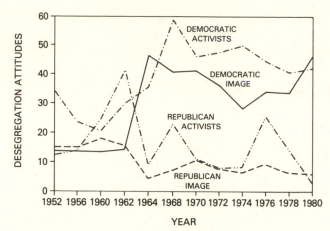

Figure 4.7 Desegregation Attitudes of Party Activists and Mass Party Images on Desegregation, 1952–1980. *Source*: SRC/CPS National Election Study Series, 1952–1980.

views of it, the party image series of Figure 4.7 represents the aggregated views of Americans on where the parties position themselves.[10] The largely familiar pattern of the figure shows no differentiation before 1964, followed by a sharp swing in perceptions that year, which sustains itself and even grows a bit by the end of the series. There is no difficulty understanding the sharp differentiation of 1964; Barry Goldwater's public opposition to civil rights legislation accounts for that. But understanding why images have remained distinctive after Goldwater and the racial politics of the 1960s is another matter. Figure 4.7 suggests that, if citizens formed their perceptions of what parties stood for by observing the attitudes of activists, the problem is neatly resolved. The activists of both parties became more distinctive and more differentiated after 1964. The 1964 contest appears to have set in motion a large and permanent reshuffling of the composition of campaign activists.

The same data are presented again as interparty difference scores (Democratic minus Republican) in Figure 4.8. The figure shows the exceptionally close fit between the views of campaign activists (we employ the activity weighting scheme here) and the racial images of the two parties over time. The visual pattern of Figure 4.8 suggests a close fit between the potential party images

[10] See Carmines and Stimson (1986) for details on the measurement of issue clarity.

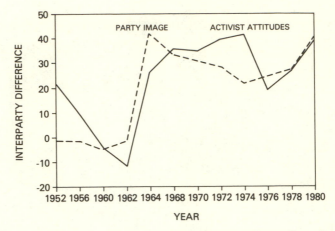

Figure 4.8 Desegregation Attitudes of Party Activists and Mass Party Images on Desegregation, Interparty Difference, 1952–1980. *Source*: SRC/CPS National Election Study Series, 1952–1980.

projected by activists and the actual party images perceived by voters. We may raise two sorts of statistical questions about the degree of fit: Do the two series tend to run together over time, a possibly true and nonetheless spurious association? And, more demanding, are the year-to-year changes in the two highly associated? The two regression analyses of Table 4.1 suggest a positive answer to each question. The degree of fit is so strong that it is highly significant even in a tiny sample and so robust that it remains significant even after the conservative measure of regressing first differences on first differences is taken. The policy images voters "see" are almost interchangeable with the policy images citizen activists project. That association is a crucial first step toward the causal linkage we wish to draw.

It could well be argued that our proposed direction of causation—that voters infer party positions from activist positions—is wrong, that the activists are merely a well-informed group who know their party's issue positions and adjust their behavior to fit. That too would produce a strong association. To deal with that contention we introduce as a control the group we have earlier referred to as informational activists, those who report following the campaign closely but through private and passive mechanisms—reading, listening, and viewing. The informational activists, whose number includes also some behavioral activists, may also be presumed to be unusually well informed about politics. Our operational criterion, a report of attending four out of four

TABLE 4.1
Party Image as a Function of Activist Attitudes:
Two Regressions

	Party Image Dependent	First Differenced Party Image Dependent
Weighted activist attitudes	1.73	———
Standard error	0.46	
t	3.76[a]	
Weighted activist attitudes (First differences)		1.49
Standard error		0.56
t		2.65[b]
Constant	5.14	2.73
Standard error	5.37	3.51
t	0.96	0.78
N	11	11
R^2	0.61	0.44

[a] $p < 0.001$.
[b] $p < 0.01$.

possible media (newspapers, magazines, television, and radio) is met by only about 9 percent of our national samples. There is every reason to suspect that the informational activists would be equally adept at knowing their party's position and adjusting to it, but they are not. The racial policy attitudes of the informational activists are associated neither with those of the behavioral activists ($B = -0.0019$, $R^2 = 0.000$) nor with the party images ($B = -0.1156$, $R^2 = 0.104$). Neither association is a statistical judgment call; both are of trivial magnitude and in the wrong direction. Although still less than fully decisive, that badly undermines the case for activists following party image rather than causing it.

One last, more suggestive, line of argument may be brought to bear on the thesis. The difficulty of testing our two-step, or mediated perception, thesis against a direct perception counter is that when perceptions are factually correct both models predict the same outcomes. They can be distinguished only when the im-

113

ages projected by activists are not fully in line with the words and deeds of candidates and parties. And this is where the mediated perception thesis shines. We have no difficulty understanding, for example, why themes such as "acid, amnesty, and abortion" stuck to McGovern, in spite of his real positions to the contrary; many people who visibly supported McGovern were associated with those themes. And if Jimmy Carter was not in fact weak on defense spending, his visible supporters in fact were. And if Ronald Reagan avows "not an ounce of prejudice" in his soul, it is still the case that traditional enemies of black rights are enthusiastically in the Reagan camp.

The mediating role of the citizen activists explains how policy cues too subtle to capture public attention can become translated into apparently policy conscious electoral behavior. The mediating activists do attend to minor distinctions and subtle cues and by their activity translate them into party image. This is particularly crucial in desegregation during the last two decades. Since the flash point of the civil rights movement, however popular it undoubtedly remains among millions of American voters, open advocacy of racial segregation is no longer a reputable political stance. The issue continues; it will remain with us for a long time. But the cues have gone underground. Racial conservatives no longer advocate the back of the bus or call for the dogs and fire hoses to deal with black demands. More likely they now support the goals of affirmative action and oppose effective means of implementation. Were it not for the activists, these cues would be lost in the noise of political communication. Because of the activists race is every bit as much alive in the politics of the 1980s as when the issues were squarely confronted.

We have written now of presidents, congresses, party leaders, and the elite element of citizens that is active in electoral politics. It is time to discuss ordinary citizens.

· 5 ·

THE IDEOLOGICAL AND PARTISAN
TRANSFORMATION OF RACIAL ISSUES

We have seen change in presidential stance, party platforms, congressional votes, and issue coloration of citizen party activists. In other words, we have seen partisan change, but we have yet to see issue evolution. All this change only suggests issue evolution because one key attribute of the process is yet to be examined. Issue evolutions necessarily involve ordinary citizens. Although true by definition, it is not merely definitional. Systematic policy changes at the level of political elites are not uncommon. All sorts of issues, particularly novel ones, can produce new party positions. But without response from the mass electorate, the new issue positions lack great consequence; there is no issue evolution.

We see the mass electorate as the environment of issue competition for attention in a very limited issue space. A mass public, necessarily inattentive by elite standards, is the source of those limits. When it grasps the new positions and responds to them, both rare phenomenons, then an issue evolution is underway. Most issue changes, like genetic changes in the biological world, are neutral or harmful. Their fate is to be selected against. Issue evolutions begin in the rare instances where something about an issue change is helpful in the usually losing contest to capture mass attention. When this happens the issue penetrates normal inattentiveness and attains the opportunity to affect the structure of mass beliefs about politics.

In this chapter and the next we examine mass response to elite changes in party positions on racial policy. We divide the topic into two parts: in Chapter 4 we consider the role of race in the evolution of belief structuring, and then we discuss the effect of race on citizen party identifications in Chapter 5. According to our thesis, the issue basis of an issue evolution should evolve into a position of centrality in mass conceptions of the meaning of the political world. Along the way we must deal with assertions that the level of belief structuring for all issues increased, at much the same time as the purported issue evolution.

Questions of belief structure are no less dynamic in theory

115

than our other foci. But investigation of this issue must be at the level of individuals, and that is limited by the availability of the requisite individual measures and their limited comparability. The Sullivan, Pierson, and Marcus (1978) results, discussed below, suggest that any over-time analysis of belief structure that crosses the boundaries of changing question design would be folly. Thus, our evidence for evolutionary processes, focusing on but a few discrete cross-sections, will be less direct on this matter than we would like, requiring inferences to stretch some distance beyond what analysis can safely support.

RACE AND THE GROWTH OF ISSUE CONSTRAINT

Throughout the 1950s and the early 1960s the dominant issues in American politics—primarily the social welfare issues of the New Deal—and the emerging issues of race were distinct and separate from each other. No mass ideology yet had encompassed both issue domains. Instead, race existed outside the New Deal's ideological framework (Kirby 1980). This separation was probably due to the fact that during this period racial issues were not defined in partisan terms. Both northern Democrats and Republicans took moderate stands on race. Antiblack forces were concentrated in the southern wing of the Democratic party. Thus, in sharp contrast to New Deal issues and their logical descendants (e.g., federal aid to education and national health care), issues of race were not partisan issues as recently as the early 1960s. And without partisanship to reinforce an underlying structure on responses to these issues, race moved along a separate ideological axis from other issues in American politics.

The mid-1960s witnessed a fundamental change in this situation. Racial concerns gained a prominent foothold on the national political agenda (Sundquist 1968), and in the process, they took on a clear partisan meaning (Pomper 1971, 1972). Breaking with a tradition of a hundred years, the Democratic party gradually became the home of racial liberalism. The New Deal ideology, having already justified the extension of its role for dealing with mass economic distress, provided the national government with responsibility for ending racial discrimination. And the Republican party, from political circumstances and deliberate choice, came to represent the opposing view: there were distinct limitations on the responsibility of the national government for dealing with not only social welfare but now also racial concerns.

This opposing view, racial conservatism, may be seen as a new issue species in the 1960s. Not derived from the strain of overt racism that characterized the Dixiecrats of the time, it was opposition to activist federal government involvement in programs to ameliorate the effects of racism. Because that involvement itself was new at the time, there had never before been a niche for the opposing view.

This partisan transformation in which the Democratic party came to represent racial liberalism and the Republican party racial conservatism was not lost on American voters. Gerald Pomper found this shift on racial issues clearly reflected in mass perceptions of the parties:

The most striking change has occurred on racial issues. In 1956, there was no consensus on the parties' stands on the issues of school integration and fair employment. Differences between the parties were less likely to be perceived on this issue than on others, and the Republicans were thought to favor civil rights as strongly as did the Democrats. By 1968, there was a startling reversal in this judgment. All partisan groups recognized the existence of different party positions on this issue, and all were convinced that the Democrats favor greater government action on civil rights than do Republicans. (Pomper 1971, 932)

Partisanship, the emerging issues of race, and the social welfare issues of the New Deal were now mutually reinforcing. As a consequence, responses to racial issues became associated with a set of liberal and conservative positions on a variety of policy issues. Reinforced by partisanship, racial issues gradually became aligned with other issues on the policy agenda, at last brought within the ideological orbit of the New Deal (Page 1978).

The key event in this transformation no doubt was the 1964 presidential election. For the first time in the twentieth century, voters were presented with a clear choice between major-party candidates holding sharply different positions on civil rights. Lyndon Johnson had become a strong advocate of civil rights, and his legendary political skills were instrumental in gaining passage of the 1964 Civil Rights Act. His opponent, Barry Goldwater, took the view that civil rights were the responsibility of the states, not the national government; he had voted against the 1964 Civil Rights Act. This election greatly clarified party images on race and citizens responded accordingly (Black and Rabinowitz 1980; Pomper 1972; Trilling 1978). In Ladd's (1978, 8–9) apt phrase, "the Goldwater Republicans seized the cloak of racial resistance that the Democrats, by themselves, had been unable to shed. Ever since, the Democrats have been the party of civil rights." Thus, the 1964 presidential election not only widened the gulf between the Republican party and the Democratic party on a number of policy issues, but it also drove a wedge between the parties on issues of race for the first time in this century. It sharply highlighted and permanently deepened the polarization between the parties on racial issues.

If this historical account is generally accurate, it provides a plausible explanation for the increased "constraint" (Converse 1964) of mass belief systems. Roughly the degree to which things thought to be alike go together and positions thought to be in conflict exclude one another, constraint is a measure of the degree of structure in systems of belief about politics. As the symbolic, emotionally charged issues of race took on a clear partisan complexion, they simultaneously moved to the center of political belief systems. The partisan evolution of race led to an increase in ideological constraint as mass responses to racial issues became aligned with attitudes toward other political issues.

A large and often contentious literature on belief structure seldom disputes that whatever structure is—and that is the core of disagreement—the more sophisticated portions of the electorate, however sophistication is measured, have more of it (Luskin 1987). But why are higher levels of constraint found among the politically sophisticated portion of the mass electorate? The issue evolution explanation suggests a possible answer to this question as well. The transformation in the political environment described above should have affected the belief systems of voters unequally. The ideological and partisan transformation of race was likely differentially to affect members of the mass public, depending upon levels of political awareness. Because of their lesser cognitive abilities and reduced attention to politics, the unsophisticated were likely to be largely unaffected by subtle shifts in the objective political situation. Indeed, they may not even have perceived less-than-obvious political developments. Their political beliefs, as a consequence, were likely to have been only very modestly influenced by alterations in the political environment. This does not mean, of course, that the politically unsophisticated do not hold strong opinions on race or that their racial views are inconsequential for their political behavior. It does mean, however, that they are less likely to recognize any "inconsistencies" between their racial attitudes and their positions on other issues and, hence, to take steps to bring them into greater conformity.

Stated somewhat differently, the unsophisticated, being less aware of subtle shifts in the political situation that tend to induce greater ideological consistency, are more likely to hold unconventional and idiosyncratic sets of beliefs. The structure underlying their political attitudes is less likely to be the broad liberal/conservative dimension found among political elites (Kritzer 1978) and valued in the "ideal" political culture (Sniderman 1975).

The situation differs sharply for the politically sophisticated. They have both the cognitive capability and the political awareness to recognize and respond to subtle changes in the political environment. The structure of their political beliefs should correspond more closely to the new political reality that brought racial issues within the partisan and ideological orbit of the New Deal. If this transformation led to a general increase in mass ideological constraint, then it should be most pronounced among the sophisticated segment of the electorate. It has both the cognitive ability and contextual knowledge to be able to understand and react to complex political stimuli. As a consequence, the underlying structure of its belief systems should reflect more fully the new ideological fusion of racial with other political beliefs.

Not only does this explanation suggest why there has been an increase in the constraint of mass belief systems, then, but it also points to the crucial role in this process played by the politically sophisticated portion of the electorate. In order to examine this thesis, we first present a partial reanalysis of the longitudinal data of Nie, Verba, and Petrocik (1976). We then turn to an analysis of data from the 1972 and 1976 National Election Studies, both well after the onset of the racial issue evolution and rich in racial policy materials; there we examine the structure of racial attitudes and the manner in which they have shaped mass belief systems.

INCREASED CONSTRAINT: A REANALYSIS

Nie with Andersen (1974) and later Nie, Verba, and Petrocik (1976) assert a striking increase in belief constraint between the 1956–1960 period, the basis of Converse's early work and pessimistic conclusions on belief structure, and the period of the 1960s and early 1970s. Most concur that much of that apparent increase is illusory, an artifact of the improved measures during the later period that produce greater evidence of constraint whatever the underlying phenomenon's true change.[1] We concur with this claim but note that it stops short of claiming that all measured change is illusion. The striking contrasts Nie and others produced overstate the case by a large margin. But even after the methodological argument some, albeit much more modest, real change remains to be explained. Dealing with that small real change in belief constraint over time is our task here.

The basic evidence in support of the change in belief constraint thesis is interitem correlations (gamma) across policy domains. Examining data for four issue areas—welfare, integration, welfare for blacks, and the Cold War—collected from a series of national election studies and from two National Opinion Research Center (NORC) surveys, Nie and coauthors discover two distinct periods in the evidence.[2] From 1956 through 1960 there were very low levels of issue constraint, while the upsurge of attitude consistency was dramatic in 1964 and continued through 1973.

The Nie correlational evidence is presented in Table 5.1, broken down into three dyadic types: nonracial issues, welfare and the Cold War; mixed issue dyads, one racial issue and one nonracial; and racial issues, integration and welfare for blacks.[3] One important aspect of the table is immediately discernible. The racial issues have been highly related to one another throughout

---

[1] Before 1964, issue questions were asked in a Likert format in which respondents were instructed to select an appropriate response along a five-point, agree-disagree scale. In contrast, the 1964 and subsequent surveys presented respondents with two alternative positions on an issue, and they were asked to choose between them. Sullivan, Pierson, and Marcus (1978) demonstrate that changes of a magnitude almost equal to those claimed by Nie et al. can be produced by using the alternative question formats at one point. For more detail about this controversy, see also Bishop, Tuchfarber, and Oldendick, (1978); Bishop, Tuchfarber, Oldendick, and Bennett (1979); Nie and Rabjohn (1979); and Sullivan, Pierson, Marcus, and Feldman (1979).

[2] We do not include the size of government in our analysis because its meaning has changed dramatically during this time period. See Nie and Rabjohn (1979).

[3] We report gamma correlations in this table because they were used in the original analysis conducted by Nie and his collaborators. However, the difference in average correlations between the mixed issue types and the nonrace issues is not an artifact of this particular statistic. We recomputed these relationships using tau-b correlations, where the same basic pattern emerges.

both periods. The 1956–1960 average correlation of 0.54 is especially noteworthy, for it suggests substantively that, even during the quiescent 1950s, there was substantial internal cohesion for the racial issue domain and methodologically that it is possible to observe substantial correlation even in the face of unreliable measurement.

Given the crudeness of measurement in survey data, particularly in the "old" SRC/CPS issue question formats, the 0.54 correlation within the racial issue domain is consistent with the view that racial attitudes are tightly bundled. That is precisely what we would expect from the knowledge that race is what we have elsewhere (Carmines and Stimson 1980a) called an "easy" issue, a matter that can be processed at the gut level, without interest or attention to politics or any sort of refined calculation. Near universal internal coherence of such issue domains is to be expected; there is no barrier to it.

The relative increase by issue type bears more directly on our thesis. The increase is only 0.07 for the nonracial issues, a change fully explainable by the method artifact. But where race is one of the two issues examined, the change (0.16) is more than twice as great. This differential increase suggests, simply, that during this transition period responses to racial issues became more highly associated with attitudes toward other political issues. Where other issue associations changed modestly—and, after correction for the artifact, perhaps not at all—the new association of racial positions with other positions probably accounts for all the observed real increase in issue constraint.

This increase we do *not* expect to be uniformly distributed across the electorate. Because comprehension and integration of the nonracial issues in Table 5.1 demand conceptual skill, we expect to see that integration of issue domains occurs disproportionately among the more sophisticated portion of the electorate. The barrier to integration is not race but the hard issues with which it must be associated.

One should not read too much into the data of Table 5.1. The evidence they provide is far from conclusive. Most important, the table is based on an analysis of only four issues. Whatever the limitations of these data, they suggest an important role for racial issues in the heightened internal consistency of mass belief systems.

TABLE 5.1
Levels of Issue Constraint by Time Period and Issue Type
(average gammas between issues)

	1956–1960 Average	1964–1973 Average	Change
Nonracial issues	0.15	0.22	+0.07
(Dyads with no racial content)			
Mixed issues	0.17	0.33	+0.16
(Dyads with both racial and other content)			
Racial issues	0.54	0.69	+0.15
(Dyads with only racial content)			

Source: These correlations were recomputed from those given in Nie, Verba, and Petrocik (1976).

RACIAL ISSUES AND ATTITUDE STRUCTURE IN THE 1972 PRESIDENTIAL ELECTION

The 1972 presidential campaign provides a demanding test of the thesis of increasing racial centrality. On the one hand, the campaign was, at least comparatively, preeminently an ideological and issue-oriented contest (Miller and Levitan 1976; Miller, Miller, Raine, and Brown 1976). Democrat George McGovern in particular seemed to represent the very personification of ideological choice in American presidential elections. Calling for major alterations in taxing and welfare policies, immediate peace in Vietnam, and massive spending to reduce unemployment among minorities and the poor, McGovern espoused policy positions of a consistently liberal persuasion. The objective issue differentiation between the candidates had a predictable effect on mass perceptions; across a variety of specific issues, McGovern was consistently seen as the more "liberal" candidate, at a considerable distance from Richard Nixon (Aldrich and McKelvey 1977).

Race—the issue we argue is central to the growth in issue constraint among the mass public—was largely absent from the rhetoric of the 1972 presidential campaign. Pursuing his southern strategy in political geography, Nixon nonetheless chose to focus his policy emphasis on foreign policy achievements while McGovern emphasized Vietnam and income redistribution schemes. The civil rights movement, unable to compete for public attention with the current Vietnam War and later Watergate, energy, and an ill-behaved economy, seemed to have become a thing of the past. It thus was not surprising that the major study of the election (Miller, Miller, Raine, and Brown 1976) found racial attitudes to be relatively unimportant in determining electoral behavior. Indeed, from our large variety of data collections it is clear that 1972 is the postcritical moment low point of various racial impacts.

Racial themes had been central to the 1964 and 1968 presidential contests, and Jimmy Carter's ambivalent appeal to both blacks and white southerners made 1976 confusing. But the inattention given to race, coupled with heightened concern for other issues, makes 1972 a good test of our thesis. If we find racial issues at the core of issue constraint in 1972, we have no reason to believe that it results from short-term stimulus factors associated with the presidential campaign. Instead, it would suggest that race has played a long-term and relatively powerful role in shaping mass belief systems. To argue that race is a long-term influence on American political beliefs presumes, among other things, that it is a durable attitude dimension. Its influence may come and go, but the attitude itself persists. The emotional intensity of the racial issue also leads us to expect a consistency between the various subdomains—housing, jobs, education, or whatever—forming the attitude dimension.

But the racial struggle in American politics has tended to be a series of skirmishes, some of which have resulted in cumulative victories—integrating the armed forces, outlawing de jure school segregation, and the like—while others—equal employment opportunities, for example—remain on the agenda year after year. We would consequently expect the centrality of the various subdomains to change over time as some issues leave the agenda to be replaced by others.

What then was the structure of response to racial issues in the 1970s? Only school busing achieved major public notice in the "benign neglect" Nixon years. Had it become the central racial issue? As the only specific racial issue assigned a seven-point proximity scale in recent NES national election studies[4] and the

---

[4] The NES studies also contain a seven-point item on governmental aid to minority groups; it is quite diffuse and captures some nonracial content as well (Miller, Miller, Raine, and Brown 1976, 764).

123

TABLE 5.2
The Dimensions of Racial Attitudes:
A Principal Factor Analysis (with varimax rotation)

Variable Activists	Factor 1: Segregation/ Integration	Factor 2: Affect Toward Blacks
Equal employment	0.480	−0.244
School integration	0.535	−0.268
Public accommodations	0.577	−0.137
Neighborhood integration	−0.594	0.037
School busing	0.385	−0.344
Aid minorities	0.459	−0.391
Civil rights too fast	−0.504	0.335
Blacks violent	−0.478	0.167
Blacks helped/hurt cause	0.461	−0.228
(De)segregation	0.615	−0.141
Prefer (de)segregated neighborhood	0.460	−0.211
Same intelligence	0.399	−0.098
Feeling thermometers		
Black militants	−0.151	0.791
Urban rioters	−0.120	0.776
Civil rights leaders	−0.490	0.528
Eigenvalue	5.16	1.42
(Percentage of explained variance)	(34.4)	(9.5)

Note: The sample consists of 2,191 respondents who were interviewed in both pre- and postelection waves.

only racial issue given more than fleeting attention in most analyses, busing seems a prime candidate for that role.

The 1972 NES study, particularly rich in racial items, allows mapping of patterns of association among a number of "old" racial issues, varied black images (through "feeling thermometers"), and, of course, busing. A principal components analysis of the correlations among these items (Table 5.2) indicates that they measure two fairly distinct dimensions of racial attitudes.[5] We will refer to the first factor as the "segregation/integration" dimension; the items that load most strongly on it are key ele-

[5] Two additional factors with eigenvalues of 1.2 and 1.08 were excluded.

ments of the traditional civil rights program (e.g., desegregation, school integration, and neighborhood integration). This factor indicates the extent to which respondents felt the federal government should promote racial desegregation. However, the items that load most strongly on the second factor tap feelings toward images of black leaders and activists. The difference between these factors suggests that respondents discriminate between the content of the civil rights program on the one hand and its public advocates on the other.[6] And where policies and advocates are most clearly linked, in the case of (traditional) civil rights leaders, so too are these factors.

The two NES seven-point scales—one on school busing, the other on government aid to minority groups—do not load cleanly on either factor. And this must question the assumption that these issues form the new exemplar of racial politics in America. These measures, the subjects of so much analysis, appear to have dubious validity as indicators of racial liberalism or conservatism. Response to busing particularly is not strongly correlated with the rest of the racial program, including school desegregation; this seems to reflect the simple fact that nobody likes busing. It is a sort of inverse apple pie, so uniformly disliked that it is a valence issue. However important it may be in its own right, the busing issue is not an important component of more general racial policy attitudes. To measure racial attitudes for our analysis we have abandoned the NES seven-point scales and instead use our two factor scales.

That brings us to the question of whether race, in any of its forms, is central to the political thinking of the American electorate. If an issue evolution were afoot, one manifestation should be an evolving centrality of the issue in question to mass mappings of political reality. Although we know race did not play that role before the onset of the evolution, we question here whether it later became central.

THE CENTRALITY OF RACE

The strategy we adopt to demonstrate empirically that racial attitudes became important to belief structuring is to compare 1970s levels of attitudinal consistency without controlling for ra-

---

[6] The apparent orthogonality of the two factors is not an artifact of the Varimax rotation. Oblique rotation also produces a near orthogonal solution.

cial attitudes to those found when controls are introduced. If race were central to belief structuring, we should find that controlling for racial issues greatly reduces levels of constraint. But if ideological constraint remains impressive when racial issues are controlled, then our thesis is called into question.

We have turned to principal component analysis to examine the unidimensional structure of mass political beliefs. This statistical technique is useful for assessing the extent to which a single basic continuum underlies responses to a set of items. The first principal component accounts for the largest proportion of variance among the items entered into the analysis. Thus, it indicates the strength of the unidimensional structure underlying the items. Three pieces of information are given in the first principal component solution. The first two relate to the presence and strength of the underlying continuum: the eigenvalue and its linear transformation, the proportion of variance in the items accounted for by the first principal component. The third piece of information, the loading, indicates the degree to which each item relates to the underlying linear dimension. These component loadings may be interpreted as the correlations between the individual items and the underlying dimension. The larger the loading, the stronger the relationship between the given item and the continuum.

We begin by documenting the fact of greater belief constraint among the more sophisticated, here indicated by a cognitive ability index combining levels of formal education with objective factual knowledge about politics. The index is employed to stratify the sample into quartiles of approximately equal size. Table 5.3 presents the results of a principal component analysis of the product-moment correlations among eight diverse political issues and two racial attitudes separately for each of four cognitive ability groups.[7] The political issues are measured by the familiar seven-point, self-placement scales on attitudes toward guaranteed jobs, tax reform, legalization of marijuana, national health insurance, women's rights, Vietnam withdrawal, controlling inflation, and protecting the rights of the accused. The two orthogonal racial scales are component scales derived from our earlier component analysis.[8]

[7] The cognitive ability index is a linear combination based on level of education and amount of political information. For further details about its construction, see Stimson (1975).

[8] For an extended discussion of these two racial attitude scales, see Carmines and Stimson (1980).

TABLE 5.3
Principal Component Analysis of Political Issues and
Racial Attitudes, by Cognitive Ability Group

Cognitive Ability Group	Eigenvalue of First Principal Component	Variance Explained by First Principal Component (in percentage)	Average Loading on First Principal Component
Group 1 (lowest) (N = 295)	2.07	20.7	0.35
Group 2 (N = 292)	2.19	21.9	0.37
Group 3 (N = 267)	2.88	28.8	0.45
Group 4 (highest) (N = 264)	3.34	33.4	0.51

Source: Computed from data collected in the Center for Political Studies, National Election Study, 1972.

The evidence in Table 5.3 is clear. The lowest ability groups show almost no evidence of unidimensional attitude constraint. The average loading on the first principal component for the lowest ability group is only 0.35. Similarly, for the lowest ability group only 20.7 percent of the variance among the variables is explained by the first component. Moving from those of low cognitive ability upward on the scale, there is monotonically increasing issue constraint. The average loading on the first principal component for the highest ability group is 0.51 and this component explains 33.4 percent of the total variance among the items. The evidence of Table 5.3 supports the basic conclusion that those of higher cognitive ability have more unidimensionally constrained belief systems.

To assess the postulated centrality of race we present in Table 5.4 the results of a principal component analysis of the intercorrelations among the eight political issues, but we now control for the two racial attitude scales. The analysis in this case is based on a product-moment partial correlation matrix. If racial attitudes were central to the higher levels of ideological constraint found among the upper ability groups, then this analysis should indicate evidence of sharply reduced levels of constraint in the

TABLE 5.4
Principal Component Analysis of Political Issues Controlling for Racial Attitudes, by Cognitive Ability Group

Cognitive Ability Group	Eigenvalue of First Principal Component	Variance Explained by First Principal Component (in percentage)	Average Loading on First Principal Component
Group 1 (lowest) (N = 295)	1.66	20.7	0.28
Group 2 (N = 292)	1.49	18.6	0.25
Group 3 (N = 267)	1.64	20.5	0.30
Group 4 (highest) (N = 264)	1.85	23.2	0.36

Source: Computed from data collected in the Center for Political Studies, National Election Study, 1972.

face of controls. Without the bonds of race, levels of attitudinal consistency should be substantially diminished. If racial attitudes were not central to the structure of belief systems, then no major effects should be observed; instead, the levels of issue constraint for the higher ability groups should parallel closely those found in Table 5.3.

Table 5.4 indicates that among the lower cognitive ability groups a lack of attitudinal consistency again emerges. Controlling for racial attitudes has little effect on the levels of constraint of those of lowest cognitive ability; with or without controls there is almost a complete absence of attitude integration. This is expected; given the already diminished level of issue constraint, controlling for racial attitudes could hardly be expected to reduce it further.

The differences between the two tables, however, are quite striking with respect to the higher ability groups. When controlling for racial attitudes, the two highest ability groups show almost a total lack of issue constraint. The first component, for example, accounts for only 23.2 percent of the total item variance among those of highest ability. Similarly, the average loading on the first principal component among the highest ability group is only 0.36. The differences in the two tables can be seen in a simple comparison: there is no more issue constraint among the highest ability group controlling for racial attitudes than there is among the lowest ability group not controlling for race.

But while the higher ability groups look very different from one another in the two tables, the differences between ability groups in Table 5.4 are minimal. Those of lowest and highest ability look quite similar to one another: both display little evidence of attitudinal consistency. In short, after controlling for racial attitudes, none of the ability groups shows evidence of attitude constraint. The conclusion seems inescapable: the higher levels of attitude integration found among the upper ability strata are almost completely nullified by controlling for racial attitudes. Race does seem to have been central to higher levels of issue constraint.

Before concluding that race alone is central to belief structuring, however, we must address an alternative hypothesis. Our procedure may be challenged as artifactual in one regard; if attitudes are tightly clustered—as they are for the upper ability groups—controlling *any* component of the cluster will eliminate common variance from the correlation matrix and thereby substantially reduce evidence of unidimensional structure. To argue that race is a principal source of issue constraint, it is necessary to demonstrate that other issues, when controlled, are not equally capable of eliminating evidence of structure.

We have replicated our partialling-out procedure for two additional issues. The "government responsibility to guarantee jobs" scale is the most likely candidate for a central role in issue constraint; it taps the domestic social welfare conflict fundamental to the New Deal party system. The Vietnam withdrawal controversy, while having no such theoretical claim, was unquestionably salient in the 1972 presidential contest and looms large in statistical analyses. Other issues are less central by both theoretical and statistical criteria.

Table 5.5 displays variance accounted for by the first principal component after controlling (separately) for the "job" scale and for Vietnam, again stratified by cognitive ability.[9] The contrast

[9] These principal component analyses are again based on a partial correlation matrix, but in this instance the appropriate issue, rather than the racial attitude scales, is controlled for. The results in Table 5.5, therefore, are not completely comparable to our earlier partialling of race because in that case we controlled for two orthogonal scales. On the one hand, controlling for two variables is likely to extract more systematic variance from the correlation matrix—and thereby bias the result in favor of racial attitudes (Sniderman and Tetlock 1986, 82). But

TABLE 5.5
Principal Component Analysis Controlling for Jobs
and Vietnam, by Cognitive Ability Group (in percentages)

	Cognitive Ability Group			
Controlling for:	1 (lowest)	2	3	4 (highest)
Government Responsibility to Provide Jobs and Decent Standard of Living	19.3	20.8	25.8	29.0
Vietnam Withdrawal	20.4	19.6	24.8	27.1

Source: Computed from data collected in the Center for Political Studies, National Election Study, 1972.

Note: Variance accounted for by first component.

with Table 5.4 is clear; although controlling for these issues reduces levels of ideological constraint, it does not eliminate the differentiation between those of high and low cognitive ability. Neither of these issues is as central to belief structuring among the upper ability groups as is race.

The evidence presented above indicates that racial attitudes are central to the higher levels of ideological constraint found among upper ability groups. The question naturally arises whether racial issues differentially affect the belief structure of subgroups in the population, especially racial groups and respondents living in different regions of the United States. Perhaps what we have observed is largely a regional or racial phenomenon.

As before we first establish a baseline. In Table 5.6 we report the results of a principal component analysis of the same eight political issues and two racial attitudes separately for four groups: southerners, nonsoutherners, whites, and blacks. Blacks display slightly more constrained belief systems than do whites, and this is also the case when we compare nonsoutherners to southerners. But overall the differences are small. The belief systems of these four groups are quite similar in terms of their overall levels of ideological constraint.

with both racial attitude scales left in the analyses of Table 5.5, we "force" two of the items to be orthogonal, limiting the possibilities of unidimensional constraint and creating a bias in the other direction.

TABLE 5.6
Principal Component Analysis of Political Issues
and Racial Attitudes, by Region and Race

Group	Eigenvalue of First Principal Component	Variance Explained by First Principal Component (in percentage)	Average Loading on First Principal Component
South (N = 260)	2.39	23.9	0.40
Nonsouth (N = 529)	2.71	27.1	0.47
Whites (N = 715)	2.41	24.1	0.41
Blacks (N = 71)	2.68	26.8	0.46

Source: Computed from data collected in the Center for Political Studies, National Election Study, 1972.

Table 5.7 reports an identical analysis, except controls are again introduced for racial attitudes. Again, blacks display more constrained belief systems than do whites, as do nonsoutherners when compared to southerners. Controlling for racial attitudes seems to have a similar impact on the issue constraint of each group. The unidimensional structure of their political beliefs is reduced, but the decrease is approximately the same for each of these racial and regional groups. The analysis provides no evidence for the conclusion that racial attitudes affect the political attitudes of only one segment of the population. It suggests just the opposite: racial issues shape the political beliefs of blacks and whites and southerners and nonsoutherners alike. These results suggest that by 1972 race had become "nationalized" as a central issue in American politics, giving shape and form to many voters' political belief systems.

IDEOLOGY AND RACE

Our analysis thus indicates that racial attitudes played a prominent role in the increased issue consistency of the 1972 electorate. Attitude structure historically has been associated with the

131

TABLE 5.7
Principal Component Analysis of Political Issues Controlling
for Racial Attitudes, by Region and Race

Group	Eigenvalue of First Principal Component	Variance Explained by First Principal Component (in percentages)	Average Loading on First Principal Component
South (N = 260)	1.51	18.9	0.28
Nonsouth (N = 529)	1.71	21.3	0.31
Whites (N = 715)	1.57	19.5	0.27
Blacks (N = 71)	1.96	24.5	0.38

Source: Computed from data collected in the Center for Political Studies, National Election Study, 1972.

liberal/conservative dimension. Through the use of this abstract ordering dimension, specific issue preferences were to be determined by underlying ideological beliefs of great generality concerning government's role in society. The question arises whether racial attitudes are related empirically to liberal/conservative beliefs, especially among that segment of the 1972 electorate that displayed relatively unidimensional belief systems. In fact, the multiple correlations between our two racial attitudes and the liberal/conservative, seven-point, self-placement scale for the four ability groups are 0.27, 0.29, 0.55, and 0.58 (from lowest to highest). Thus, not only do racial attitudes help to perform the structuring functions often associated with the liberal/conservative dimension, but much of the meaning of this ideological dimension is apparently racial in nature. This is especially true among the upper ability groups, which display the highest levels of attitudinal consistency.[10]

[10] Stimson (1975) provides additional support for this conclusion. Single racial issues—not factor scores, not multiple issues—show in that case that race is central to the liberal/conservative beliefs of all four cognitive ability groups, and most central in three of the four.

TABLE 5.8
Correlations Between Political Issues and
Liberal/Conservative Dimension: 1972

Product Moment Correlations of
The Liberal/Conservative Scale with:

Segregation/Integration	0.31 (n = 1547)
Affect toward black protest	0.37 (n = 1547)
Vietnam withdrawal	0.31 (n = 1494)
Jobs and living standards	0.32 (n = 1444)
Progressive tax rates	0.14 (n = 1422)
Control inflation	0.05 (n = 1437)
Legalize marijuana	0.32 (n = 1500)
Women's role	0.19 (n = 1497)
Protect rights of accused	0.32 (n = 1442)

This evidence does not indicate that liberal/conservative political beliefs are more highly related to racial than other political issues. It does suggest, however, that race should be among the more highly correlated issues with this ideological dimension. Table 5.8 indicates that this is indeed the case. Looking at the entire sample, the segregation/integration dimension is among the more highly correlated specific issues; the affect dimension is the very highest. In combination, the two dimensions produce a multiple correlation of 0.47, considerably greater than any other (single) issue.

Race is thus a prominent, if not dominant, connotation of the ideological labels, liberal and conservative. But we should not state the case too strongly. Other issues are manifestly associated with the liberal/conservative scale, and in combination those associations (R = 0.52) exceed that of race alone (R = 0.47). But if we ask simply, what do we know if we know someone avows a position on the liberal-conservative continuum? we answer that more than anything else we know that person's views on race.

Because the liberal/conservative scale was also included in the 1976 National Election Study, we can see whether racial attitudes continued to be correlated with this ideological dimension.[11] Table 5.9 shows some slippage in racial centrality. With a

[11] The 1976 scale is composed of four items—school integration, neighborhood

TABLE 5.9
Correlations Between Political Issues and
Liberal/Conservative Dimension: 1976

Product Moment Correlations of
The Liberal/Conservative Scale with:

Jobs and living standards	0.31 ($n = 1347$)
Rights of accused	0.25 ($n = 1387$)
Medical care	0.36 ($n = 1300$)
Urban unrest	0.31 ($n = 1118$)
Legalize marijuana	0.35 ($n = 1180$)
Progressive tax rates	0.13 ($n = 1196$)
Equal rights for women	0.24 ($n = 1256$)
Segregation/Integration	0.32 ($n = 1040$)

correlation of 0.32 the segregation/integration dimension is among the more highly correlated issues with the liberal/conservative scale, but not the very highest. Racial issues, in sum, seem not only to be at the core of the increase in mass issue consistency but also to provide a significant and stable element in the meaning of liberal/conservative political beliefs.

On the Time Bundling of Political Issues

Examining a large collection of attitudinal data from the 1950s, Converse was impressed with the lack of organization that existed among the issue preferences of the mass public. It was neither simply that members of the mass public were disinclined to mention ideological terms in their evaluations of parties and candidates nor merely that citizens could not cogently respond when asked about the meaning of such terms as liberalism or conservatism. These could be explained by voters' general unfamiliarity with the language of abstract political ideologies. But the lack of any discernible common structure underlying mass political attitudes could be neither explained nor rationalized so easily. For there was no question that the fragmentary, unorganized char-

---

integration, "civil rights too fast," and [de] segregation—central to the 1972 desegregation scale (see Table 5.2) and continued in the later study. No affect scale is available for 1976.

acter of public opinion was a major barrier to popular control of public policy. Thus, Converse's influential study had dire implications not only for the quality of citizen participation but also perhaps more important, for the possibilities of democratic governance.

More recent scholarship suggests that this was not a permanent condition of American politics. Recent studies have produced more substantial evidence of issue constraint. The unconstrained electorate of the 1950s has been replaced by an electorate that displays fairly coherent, well-integrated political belief systems. The liberal/conservative dimension, if not the terms themselves, seems to be in relatively widespread use.

This chapter has argued that the change in levels of attitudinal consistency was rooted in real-world political events. We have contended specifically that the increase in mass issue constraint was partly due to the ideological and partisan transformation of racial issues that occurred during the mid-1960s. As the symbolic, emotionally charged issues of race took on a clear partisan complexion, they simultaneously moved to the center of mass belief systems. No longer isolated from other political opinions and partisan orientations, the growing salience of racial issues had a significant impact on the structure of political beliefs.

We have found that: (1) nearly all the increase in the structure of political beliefs reported by Nie and his collaborators can be attributed to race, (2) controlling for race alone destroys the coherence of mass belief systems, and (3) racial matters are central to the apparent connotation of the terms of left/right discourse. These results all point to the centrality of racial issues in mass belief systems. But this centrality cannot be explained by conventional theories of issue constraint.

If one asks why some issues cluster together for mass publics, the invariable answer is Converse's three constraint-building forces: logical, psychological, and social. But neither individually nor collectively would they have predicted the results we observed. Race has no tight logical tie to other issues. If it is drawn into a cluster by psychological links to issues such as social welfare, it, not they, should be in a subsidiary role. And it cannot be explained by issue connections "learned" in the social background; this is a novel phenomenon, and the background is tied to the past. To account for the centrality of race, we extract from our earlier issue evolution account a fourth constraint-building force. What we call the "time bundling" of political issues shares elements of Converse's psychological and social explanations, but it is distinctively political.

Mass political involvement and issue discourse are episodic and discrete. Largely absent most of the time, they occur during political campaigns and particularly during presidential campaigns. Presidential campaigns are a time of relatively intense political learning. Candidates are the teachers. By becoming associated with positions on salient political issues, candidates define the contents of issue clusters.[12] And because in the norm there are only two major candidates, voters in this period of unusual political involvement face considerable persuasive pressure to constrain their own positions, but only on salient issues, to the same unidimensional and bipolar space occupied by the candidates.

The net effect to be expected from the candidate issue-bundling process is enhancement of mass issue consistency on the salient issues of a particular presidential campaign. This process is ordered in time in two regards. First, the salient issues of campaigns are always partly idiosyncratic. Candidates pick up standard issue positions of their party and blend them with newer and more personal positions in an attempt to enhance political leverage. The resulting combinations are not predictable before the campaign and dated after it. Second, because learning is episodic, we would expect a residue of issue "consistency" to remain after the campaign, even for issues altogether unrelated before it.[13] Thus, each election would be expected to contribute to the building of constraint for particular issues, unevenly so for particular individuals depending upon their involvement in the campaign, but the passage of time would normally lead to its decay. The crucial exception would be those issues that become permanently associated with the party system and the prevailing ideology. They have the capacity to sustain their influence by entering the regular bundles in subsequent contests.

[12] This tendency to become identified with stands on salient political issues is counterbalanced by the fact that presidential candidates typically do not emphasize their positions on divisive issues. For a discussion of this latter phenomenon see Page (1978) and Carmines and Gopoian (1981).

[13] For a recent illustration of the process recall that Ronald Reagan's program of simultaneous budget and tax cuts was characterized as "voodoo economics" by then opponent and later Vice President George Bush, a mainline Republican. Historically considered alternatives and advocated by opposite sides of the fence, by now, we suspect that most voters view budget cutting and tax cutting as consistent positions.

This is precisely what happened with regard to race. Racial issues were prominent in the issue bundles of the 1964 and 1968 presidential elections. Goldwater combined opposition to federal activity in civil rights with the self-description "conservative." George Wallace clearly linked racial advocacy with "liberalism" in both elections. Lyndon Johnson transformed "civil rights" into "poverty," which had a black face. Hubert Humphrey might have been the most important figure of them all had not Vietnam and protest so dominated the 1968 election that his famous racial liberalism was obscured.

The continuing prominence of racial issues in the presidential candidate issue bundles of 1964 and 1968 led to its ideological and partisan crystallization, which had a predictable effect by 1972. Even without race's salience in that campaign, it continued to be a powerful source of ideological constraint. Because racial issues had become a permanent feature of partisan divisions and ideological cleavages, they were embedded in the very fabric of American politics. By the 1980s, as we saw in Chapter 4, race no longer required candidate bundling because it was incorporated into elections by the views of activist supporters on both sides of the issue; by that time a Ronald Reagan could be known to be a full-fledged racial conservative without even addressing the issue.

Party and party identification are central to our understanding of American politics. If the purported issue evolution of race is also central, then we must find evidence of its impact on party ties. That is the subject of our next chapter.

· 6 ·

MODELING CHANGE
IN MASS IDENTIFICATION

Let us review the evidence. We saw in Chapter 3 a striking issue polarization in the pattern of roll-call votes on racial issues in the U.S. Senate and the House. In Chapter 4 we saw similar evidence of change in popular perceptions of where the parties stood, led by the changing attitude composition of party activists on both sides. And we saw in Chapter 5 that racial concerns have moved to a central position in the constellation of attitudes ordinary Americans hold toward political life, a position usually reserved for orientations of considerably greater abstraction. We have seen that much of the actual connotation of the popular concepts of liberalism and conservatism is racial in character.

Taken as a whole, this evidence suggests change of far-reaching character. It suggests redefinition of the normal grounds of political debate, a changing character of the experience of politics. At the beginning of our period racial issues were not aligned with the party system; they cut across it. Now they clearly are aligned. Racial issues have become an integral part of the normal struggle for political power.

The ultimate evidence of an issue evolution, however, is not to be found in the halls of Congress, the behavior of party activists, or even the ideological orientations of the electorate. It is to be found in the link between issues and citizens' partisan identifications. An issue evolution implies that the emergence of a new issue conflict has severed the connection between citizens and the ongoing party system—that, to be more precise, a mass partisan polarization has occurred along the new dimension of conflict. Have racial issues created a new partisan division in the electorate, overlaying the New Deal issue constellation? This is the question we will discuss in this chapter—the final piece of the issue evolution puzzle.

In Chapter 1 we posited three models of issue evolution: critical election, secular growth, and dynamic growth. All three lead to permanent changes in the issue basis of the party system, but they do so at different rates and involve different causal mechanisms. Here we focus on which model most accurately character-

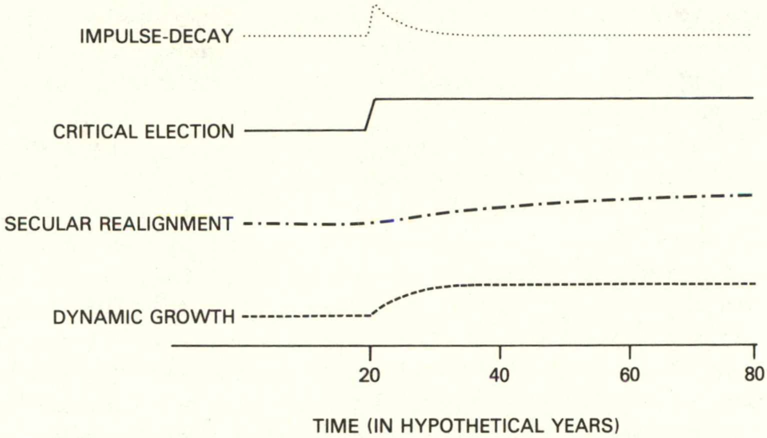

MASS IDENTIFICATION

IMPULSE-DECAY

CRITICAL ELECTION

SECULAR REALIGNMENT

DYNAMIC GROWTH

```
              20        40        60        80
```

TIME (IN HYPOTHETICAL YEARS)

Figure 6.1 Four Hypothetical Models of Partisan Change. *Source*: Compiled by the authors.

izes the evolution of racial issues. To address this question we construct hypothetical models of issue evolution, adding a fourth variation, temporary effects, to round out the hypothetical issue possibilities.

MODELS OF PARTISAN CHANGE

Imagine for the moment that we can measure polarization between parties over a particular issue, candidate, or event. A variety of techniques might be employed; the one we shall later use is the simple difference between the aggregate (mean) issue attitudes of the party groups (i.e., party identifiers) over time. Polarization might or might not exist before the process begins, but the increase[1] in polarization is important. Thus, we can presume without loss of generality a zero base-line. The models of Figure 6.1 track four hypothetical patterns of polarization of a party system to new issue conflict. The impulse-decay model of Figure 6.1 illustrates dramatic but transitory change. As soon as the temporary stimulus is removed, the system rapidly returns to its preexisting level of stability. The temporary nature of this change rather than its abruptness is its most distinctive characteristic.

[1] There are conditions under which one would want to model decreasing polarization as well. The decay of old alignments should produce decaying polarization, as we will show later.

139

Many different kinds of political phenomenons, especially presidential candidates, presumably have this type of dramatic but momentary effect on the party system. John Kennedy's nomination for the presidency by the Democrats in 1960, for example, led to a polarization of the electorate on the religious issue (Converse et al. 1961). Catholics became more heavily Democratic, just as Protestants became more Republican. But this increased partisan differentiation between religious groups was transient. It is convenient to digress to our underlying conception of causality in partisan change to explain why this must be the case.

We assume that the American party system exists in a state of equilibrium.[2] Because it has powerful implications, the equilibrium assumption is not to be taken lightly; equilibriums do not exist accidentally. Systems acquire that property when built-in causal forces tend to restore them after deviation (Stokes and Iversen 1966). We will not speculate here—in part, to be candid, because we do not know—about which particular mechanisms produce equilibrium, but one is hard pressed to account for the lengthy duration of any party system without recourse to the implicit causation of equilibrium.

It follows naturally that any temporary disturbance must have temporary effects. The disturbance can drive the system away from equilibrium, but it cannot keep it there after its causal force is no longer present. There is an important corollary. Two changes are required to alter the equilibrium level: one moves the system from equilibrium to a new level, and a second permanent redefinition of the grounds of party cleavage maintains its new level after the initial stimulus is no longer present.

To the extent that most political issues affect partisan change at all, they are likely to be of the impulse-decay type. Occasionally, the public may become aroused about specific political issues (e.g., Vietnam and Watergate), even to the point of decisive electoral impact. These issues are typically linked to political events that are a major source of disturbance in the existing political environment. Although these issues can be important in a particular election, their effects are short term. They may influence system outcomes, but they do not change the system. They move the system away from its equilibrium level, but they do not

[2] The equilibrium we presume is a short term interelection phenomenon. Riker (1982) argues persuasively that disequilibrium in the long run is to be expected from party systems.

keep it away. They have the important limitation of being unable to sustain themselves beyond the events that brought them into being. Thus, as the events fade in public memory, the issues lose their salience and with it their ability to influence citizen party identifications. The dramatic short-term electoral importance of these issues is thus more than counterbalanced by their inconsequential long-term effects on the party system. It is only a matter of time before the effects of these issues decay, leaving no permanent mark on the system.

The second panel of Figure 6.1 models the issue configuration of a classic critical election realignment, the earliest and most simplistic account of party system change. The party system is in equilibrium prior to the impact of some unspecified event after which it shifts dramatically and permanently to a new equilibrium. A long period of stability is followed by a sudden burst of dramatic change that shifts the party system to a new level of stability. The party system is stationary before the critical election—an intervention that leads to a radical and profound alteration of the system manifested in a sharp and sudden increase in issue polarization.

The scenario is familiar. A divisive political issue emerges that represents a major source of unresolved tension within the majority party's fragile electoral coalition. Despite its most strenuous efforts, the majority party is unable to keep the issue off the political agenda. Indeed, eventually it dominates the agenda. With the ascendence of the issue comes the inevitable and rapid collapse of the majority party fortunes; it can no longer command decisive support among the electorate. One party's misfortunes are another's opportunities as the minority party or a recently formed third party quickly assumes control of the major political institutions and forges a new direction in public policy.

Critical election realignments can result from either or both of two particular mechanisms of partisan change. The sharply discontinuous and episodic character of change specified in critical realignment models is consistent only with massive individual partisan conversions or equally rapid partisan mobilization of new voters previously uninvolved in politics.

Thus, from this perspective, abrupt and permanent transformations of the party system are caused by large numbers of voters discarding old party attachments in favor of new ones or massive numbers of newly active voters acquiring a distinctive partisan orientation. For example, the New Deal realignment, it is alternatively argued, occurred either because many Republicans came to identify with the Democratic party in response to the Great Depression (Sundquist 1983; Burnham 1970; Erikson and Tedin 1981) or because the ranks of the Democratic party were swelled by the massive mobilization of previously inactive voters, especially immigrants and women (Andersen 1976, 1979; see also Converse 1975; Salisbury and MacKuen 1981; Clubb, Flanigan, and Zingale 1980).

Population replacement, as we will argue, is capable of profound alteration of the party system, but this mechanism is sharply inconsistent with critical election realignment models. The more obvious inconsistency is that replacement effects by themselves are not large enough to produce dramatic change in a single election. The less obvious inconsistency is a theoretical Achilles' heel of critical election theories: unless conversion or mobilization is total at the time of the critical election, population replacement should cause steady increases in issue polarization in the years immediately after the critical election. Pre-realignment cohorts, those least polarized, will be successively replaced by newly eligible young voters who come of age when the alignment is at the peak of salience and should therefore be highly polarized (Beck 1974, 1979).

Replacement mechanisms entail a dynamic evolution to a new equilibrium level; they are inconsistent with a one-time shift. And if replacement is ruled out, only overnight conversion or implausibly rapid mobilization is left. We are left to postulate an event of such magnitude that it can alter the party system in one election and yet not be decisive enough to create distinctive party alignments of those coming of age in the years thereafter.

The third panel of Figure 6.1 is the political equivalent of Darwinian gradualism. The panel displays a gradual transformation of the party system that takes place over an extended period. The change effected through this transformation is permanent; it leaves an imprint on the political landscape. And the change can be quite substantial, fundamentally altering the complexion of the party system, but the process is slow, gradual, incremental. This is a noncritical, evolutionary model of partisan change, a model consistent with Key's notion of secular realignment. As Key observed:

A secular shift in party attachment may be regarded as a movement of the members of a population category from party to party that extends over several presidential elections and appears to be independent of the peculiar factors influencing the vote at individual elections. . . . A movement that extends over a half century is a more persuasive indication of the phenomenon in mind than is one that lasts less than a decade. (1959, 199)

Thus, Key viewed a secular realignment as a gradual shift in the partisan composition of the electorate. Though gradual, the shift is persistent, and herein lies its significance.

Although critical realignments look to individual conversion or rapid mobilization to explain the dynamics of partisan change, secular realignments can be accounted for by the far more common mechanism of normal population replacement. They can result from such essentially nonpolitical forces as differential birthrates between the party coalitions, interregional migration patterns, or economic-technological transformations that gradually produce new political generations exposed to different political forces than their parents. Secular realignments do not depend upon large-scale changes in individual partisan attachment, a characteristic noted for its substantial level of stability (Converse and Markus 1979), or upon massive partisan mobilizations of segments of the electorate. Instead, the gradual character of secular realignments means that they can be understood as a not atypical outcome of continuous population replacement.

The fourth panel portrays a dynamic evolutionary model of change in the party system. The model is dynamic because it presumes that at some point the system moves from a fairly stationary steady-state period to a fairly dramatic change; the change is manifested by a "critical moment" in the time series. Significantly, however, the change—the dynamic growth—does not end with the critical moment. Instead, it continues over an extended period, albeit at a much slower pace. This continued growth after the initial shock defines the evolutionary character of the model. The issue polarization, however, does not continue to grow indefinitely. Instead, after an extended period of increase, the polarization decays at a gradual pace. The pattern culminates in the establishment of a new equilibrium—one that shows a clear but lessened degree of polarization.

The dynamic growth and decay pattern of partisan change may be thought of as a synthesis of critical and secular realignment

143

models. The more pronounced the initial step compared to the eventual development of the issue polarization, the more closely the model follows a critical election realignment. Conversely, if the critical moment is modest compared to the continuous long-term component of change, then the model approximates a pure secular realignment. In either case, the main characteristic of the polarization is that it is not a one-shot, large-scale phenomenon but rather follows a discernible pattern over time. The polarization not only sustains itself but grows larger for a lengthy period until it begins a modest decay that eventually leads to a new equilibrium.[3] Thus, studied over a sufficiently long period, the evolutionary character of the change—the fact that the electorate is undergoing small, incremental change after the critical moment—is most impressive. The initial shock merely sets in motion a pattern of change that continues into the future.

Dynamic evolution is consistent with a variety of causal mechanisms of change. The initial step could be due partly to individual partisan conversions and partly to rapid partisan mobilization. The gradual change over an extended period of time is probably the result of population replacement.

The gradual growth and decay in polarization, a basic characteristic of dynamic issue evolutions, is well accounted for by normal population replacement. The growth in polarization comes about when older voters, relatively unaffected by the new issue cleavage due to their well-established partisan predispositions, inevitably leave the electorate and are replaced by newly eligible young voters whose weak partisan ties are easily influenced by the salience of the new issue. This dual impact of population replacement leads to a predictable increase in issue polarization. The later decay in polarization can be explained by the same mechanism. With the passage of time, the salience of the issue gradually declines as does its influence on mass partisanship. Its major influence is now concentrated among older voters—those whose partisanship was formed during the heat of political conflict. Young voters, having had no direct experience with the issue, are least likely to be polarized by it. Thus, both the gradual growth and partial decay in issue polarization are logical outcomes of normal population replacement.

Of the four models of partisan change we have presented, the

[3] The process is bounded by an asymptotic equilibrium. The new equilibrium occurs when the electorate becomes sufficiently polarized around an issue that replacement can no longer add to the process.

first (impulse-decay) is probably the most common issue impact, but it is not lengthy enough to be important in the evolution of party systems. Its fundamental limitation is that the partisan effects are wholly temporary. The second, critical election realignment, is too simplistic to accord with the complexities of partisan change. Resting on assumed massive partisan conversions or equally massive (and sudden) partisan mobilizations, it overestimates the degree of change occurring at a single point and underestimates the amount of change occurring over time. Pure secular realignment, which might be an adequate account of the impact of demographic shifts and the like, cannot explain issue evolution, for it fails to account for the reason why the process begins in the first place. It is a fire with no spark.

The dynamic growth and decay model is the most plausible account of partisan transformations. Where critical election accounts are conversion with no replacement and secular realignment posits replacement but no conversion or (rapid) mobilization, the dynamic evolution model posits all three mechanisms; conversion and mobilization start the process, and replacement sustains it. The "critical moment" of the dynamic growth model must be large enough to be visible—far less, however, than the convulsive change of the critical election. Long-term dynamic growth occurs when that "visible" shift is reinforced by recruitment (and derecruitment) that continues to emphasize the new cleavage in following years; and partial decay occurs when the issue loses its capacity to shape the partisan orientations of the newest members of the electorate.

Although we believe the dynamic evolution model provides a plausible account of issue evolution, it presents difficult problems of estimation. Most important, we lack the necessary information to track any single issue, including race, throughout its extended growth and partial decay. To compensate for this limitation, we will first turn to a limited analysis of an issue that represents the political conflict underlying the New Deal. Then we will conduct a more formal, statistical analysis of desegregation, which shows it still in its dynamic growth phase of partisan development.

THE NEW DEAL IN DECAY:
AN EMPIRICAL SKETCH

The New Deal, we all agree, is the basis of the current party alignment. Analysts have predicted its demise for at least three

145

decades, but it seems to persist. Few, however, would disagree that the alignment is in decay.

Decay has another face, the depolarization of attitudes that give policy content to the alignment. For the New Deal was not only a party coalition, an appeal to the common man; it was also a set of programs that reached out to the unemployed working man, saying "It is not your fault, you did not cause the Depression" and, most important, "It is the government's responsibility to do something about it." Thus, government responsibility was then and is still a controversial assertion. More than anything else, this cleavage issue separated partisans; it still does.

Contemporary survey data allow the study of this party cleavage issue. Recalled partisanship permits the reconstruction of parties of the past. Decay of polarization can be loosely estimated, which we will do, and modeled with some precision, which we will not do. The reconstruction methodology demands more than we can reasonably assume (Niemi, Katz, and Newman 1980). Recovering an event of the 1930s from respondents who lived on to be interviewed in the 1970s asks more than can be expected. Pushed further back in time, our sample becomes ever smaller and progressively age-biased. The technique requires memory of forty-year-old events, when Niemi and coauthors (1980) have found four years problematic. Thus, we shall paint no portrait of the New Deal, only a sketch.

No single issue portrays the New Deal realignment; it was a complex brew of issues, symbols, personalities, and coalitions. But most would concur that, if one issue had to be chosen, it would be the fundamental disagreement over the proper role of government intrusions into the marketplace to provide jobs for those who wanted to work. We, in turn, have chosen to look at its best empirical manifestation in the Center for Political Studies survey item on this question.[4]

Issue alignment is too subtle a phenomenon to tolerate the considerable noise introduced by variations in question wording over time. Thus, we must restrict our analysis to surveys where question wording is identical. We have chosen the CPS cross-sections of 1972, 1976, and 1978 for a reconstruction data base. They are current and present no question wording artifact, but they are long removed in time from many events of interest.

---

[4] The question is the familiar seven-point forced choice between "The Government should see to it that every person has a job and a good standard of living" and "Each person should get ahead on his own."

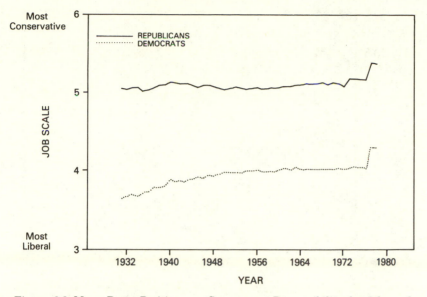

Figure 6.2 Mean Party Positions on Government Responsibility for Jobs and Standard of Living: A Reconstructed Time Series. *Source*: src/cps National Election Studies of 1972, 1976, 1978.

To model the New Deal realignment is a tempting prospect. A series can be reconstructed back to, perhaps even before, the event; however, the data are not good enough to sustain the modeling exercise.[5] Consequently, we settle for the more modest goal of sketching issue depolarization in progress.

The reconstructed attitudes graphed in Figure 6.2 show the issue dealignment we expected to see. Ignoring the sharp upward changes at the end of the series, attributable to sampling fluctuation, the sketch has some surprising features. For example, the decay of cleavage is asymmetric, accounted for entirely by changes among Democratic identifiers. Republican identifiers show no evidence of shift on New Deal issues from Hoover through Carter. Nothing happens.

Democrats are a more interesting lot. They, too, show no change over the last three decades, which also means that the New Deal cleavage has been stagnant for three decades. These

[5] We are in a much stronger position for the desegregation analysis because the events of interest are contemporary. We can measure alignment from a number of independent cross-sections before and after the beginning of the issue evolution.

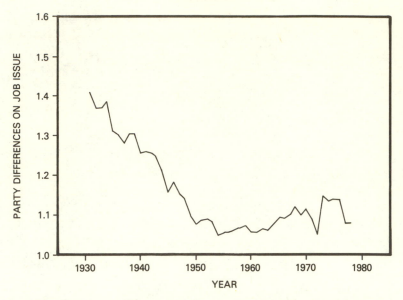

Figure 6.3 The Decay of Interparty Polarization of the Jobs and Standard of Living Issue. *Source*: Recomputed from Figure 6.2.

probably conservative estimates, however, show a decay of some 30 to 40 percent of the original party difference, all of which occurs in the 1930s and 1940s. This is unexpected in two regards. First, the method is far more sensitive to recent than ancient changes. Yet Figures 6.2 and 6.3, which shows the interparty difference computed from Figure 6.2, portray remarkable stability for recent decades and change in the past. Second, the pattern of decay could be produced only if the old in the 1970s samples were considerably more liberal than the young, which contradicts our normal expectation.

The pattern of the figures does make sense from another perspective. If one assumes that the generation that experiences realignment is peculiarly sensitive to the party-aligning issue but passes on its partisanship to its children (and they to theirs) more successfully than its issue position, then the gross patterns of Figures 6.2 and 6.3 are what would be expected. Party alignments decay to a new equilibrium as the generation of realignment loses its numbers and its intensity over the years. Our sketch of the New Deal in decay is an unintended confirmation of Beck's (1974) "socialization theory of partisan realignment." It is consistent with the view that the socialization mechanism can pass on partisanship as identification but not the vivid emotional context in which the identification was forged. Where the ties between generations are imperfect, as they surely are, any alignment formed from idiosyncratic events must of necessity decay (Carmines, McIver, and Stimson 1987).

The Polarization of Desegregation

If an issue persists relatively unchanged for a lengthy period, we can make several cross-sectional estimates of the polarization of issue and party and from these varying readings estimate what a continuous time series might have been if it had existed. That is our method here. We have used all the American national election studies for presidential and off-year elections (1956 through 1980) to construct an "even-year" time series of the desegregation attitudes of party identifiers.

Desegregation attitude scales are constructed for each cross-section by summing attitude items, each weighted equally, and transforming the scales obtained to a common metric (mean: 50, standard deviation: 25) for all years. The years 1945 to 1955 and odd-numbered years thereafter, except 1963, are then reconstructed from respondent reports of party identification change.[6] The intensity and continuity of racial attitudes make us comfortable with this procedure, but the need for intensity and continuity limits the method.

There are probably large numbers of issues of the impulse-decay type, for example, but we cannot study the decay of party alignments on them because questions cease to be asked when they are no longer topical. Other issues may have a lengthy history, but, because attitudes on them are not intense, cross-time measures are highly suspect from the intrusion of the varying cues of question wording.

Niemi, Katz, and Newman (1980) have demonstrated from panel data that recalled party identifications are frequently erroneous. Since the reconstruction methodology rests in part—thankfully not in large part—on the quality of recall, it, too, may be questioned. But we have shown elsewhere (Carmines and Stimson 1984, 154–58) that the reconstruction methodology is

[6] Party identifier attitudes for 1963 are estimated from a Harris survey of November 1963.

149

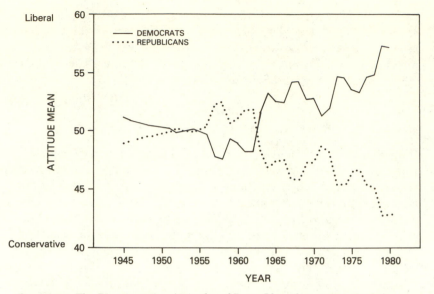

Figure 6.4 The Desegregation Attitudes of Party Identifiers, 1945–1980. *Source*: SRC/CPS National Election Study Series, 1956–1980, and Louis Harris and Associates, Study #1285.

fairly robust when applied to the reconstuction of racial attitudes.

Before proceeding to the business of modeling issue evolution on race, we pause to describe our expectations for the varying models of partisan change. Polarization is measured by the difference between the mean attitudes of the two party groups over time. Operationally, that entails simply computing party means for each year and subtracting one from the other. Arbitrarily, we subtract the Republican mean from the Democratic mean. That leaves us with three times series, one for each party and one for the difference between parties. The party mean series are graphed in Figure 6.4 for a first visual demonstration of the phenomenon.

Figure 6.4 shows a stable and very minor difference in the views of the two parties' identifiers through 1962, followed by the appearance of growing polarization in 1963–1964. A cautious spectator of the civil rights movement before that time, in 1963 the Kennedy administration, and implicitly the Democratic party, took up the cause of civil rights as its own. Whether that by itself would have been sufficient to create a partisan issue ev-

150

olution we shall never know, for it was quickly followed by Barry Goldwater's abandonment of the pro–civil rights Republican tradition the next year. Taken together, these events and these two years form our critical moment.

All four models of issue evolution may be expressed as variations of the first-order transfer function:

$$Y_t = [\omega_0/(1 - \delta_1 B)]I_t + N_t \qquad [6.1]$$

where:

Y_t is the interparty difference series to be explained
δ_1 is a first-order growth (or decay) rate parameter
B is the backshift operator such that $BX_t = X_{t-1}$
ω_0 is a zero-order initial impact parameter
I_t is an input series of zeros and ones
N_t is a noise model accounting for residual time dependence in the series.

Variation in three aspects of the intervention model of equation 6.1 can produce the outcomes of our four models of Figure 6.1. The input series I_t may be either a pulse ("1" for the critical moment and "0" at other times) or a step ("0" before, "1" after). The pulse input is used to model a temporary effect (e.g., impulse-decay), and the step is used to model any of our three permanent effects. The two parameters (ω_0, δ_1) model the size of initial impacts and dynamic effects, respectively.

Thus, for example, a critical election scenario would imply a very large ω_0 with no dynamic term. The pure secular formulation is the opposite combination; incremental change implies a small ω_0 coefficient while continuous growth over a long time span implies a δ_1 approaching the limit of 1.0. Evaluating the four models is an empirical question, given that each has a distinctive pattern of inputs and parameters, as shown in Table 6.1. Two can be ruled out by statistical inference, and the choice between the remaining two is a judgment call but not a difficult one. We consider them in order.

Model 1, the impulse-decay formulation, can be dismissed on visual evidence. It implies a sharp but temporary response of the issue/alignment series. The effect in Figure 6.4 is demonstrably not temporary. We have nonetheless modeled it and found what we expected to find; the decay rate parameter (δ_1) does not indicate decay. It takes on an unacceptable value, greater than 1.0, indicating the inappropriateness of a temporary effects model.

TABLE 6.1
Four Models of Issue Evolution

Model	Input	Dynamic (δ)	Impact (ω)
1. Impulse-Decay	Pulse		significant
2. Critical realignment	Step	zero	very large and significant
3. Pure secular	Step	large	small but significant
4. Dynamic growth "critical moment"	Step	large	"visible" and significant

Ruling out a temporary effects model, we can now distinguish between our three alternative permanent effects. We do so by fitting the first-order intervention of equation 6.1 with the input series (I_t) specified as "0" through 1962 and "1" in 1963 through 1980. The two parameters (ω_0, δ_1) from this fit and a third, θ_2 for a second-order moving average noise process, are displayed in Table 6.2. This same information is displayed graphically in Figure 6.5; it shows (1) the actual issue alignment series measured now as the net difference between the two parties; (2) a pure intervention model, the smooth curve, of the series; and (3) the best prediction of the series, including also the moving average noise component.

Reduction in mean square from 24.85 for the unmodeled series to 3.54 for the full model (analogous to an R^2 of about 0.86) indicates a good fit of the model to the issue alignment series.

Few would postulate a critical realignment around racial attitudes, and it comes as no surprise that the evidence at hand rules it out. This model fails both predictive criteria; the initial change ($\omega_0 = 5.42$) is not large enough to be "critical," and the continuing growth rate ($\delta_1 = 0.41$) is clearly significant.

The model of Table 6.2 clearly reflects the dynamic growth variety. The 1963–1964 change reverses the preintervention differentiation between parties, providing an easy distinction between the "visible" change of the dynamic growth formulation rather than the "small" change implied by the pure secular Model 3. The series approximates its asymptotic equilibrium level after approximately seven time points, far too quickly for the long, slow, gradual sort of change expected from pure secular realign-

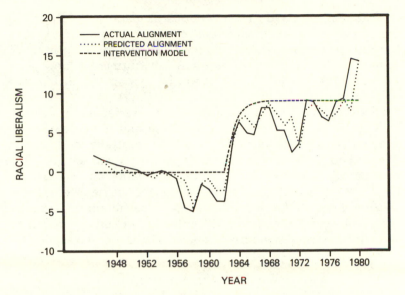

Figure 6.5 The Growth of Party Differentiation on Desegregation: Actual and Predicted. *Source*: Interparty differences recomputed from Figure 6.4.

TABLE 6.2
The Evolution of Interparty Differences on Desegregation:
A Dynamic Growth Model of Issue Evolution

	Parameter	Value	t	Description
Intervention: 1963	δ_1	0.41	2.9	Growth rate parameter
	ω_0	5.42	4.4	Initial impact
Noise Model: $(1 - B)Z_t = (1 - \theta B^2) a_t$	θ_2	0.94	40.8	Moving average (2)

Note: Residual Mean Square = 3.535; $X^2_{11} = 7.7$ (white noise).

ment. Issue evolution on desegregation, in short, seems to follow closely a dynamic growth pattern. The fact that it is dynamic growth is far less interesting than why it is.

Earlier we argued that population replacement should play a major role in the dynamic evolutionary model of partisan change because this mechanism can easily account for the steady, continuous, long-term increase in issue polarization following the critical moment. Partisan conversions, or massive mobilizations, associated with the critical moment may set into motion the initial differentiation between partisans on the evolving issue dimension, but the selective, successive recruitment of new partisan identifiers over time drives the system toward a new equilibrium.

This is precisely what we observe in the racial case (Carmines and Stimson 1981). Throughout the 1960s and 1970s new Republican and Democratic identifiers were substantially more distinctive in their racial attitudes than continuing identifiers. As these new partisans slowly but inevitably became an increasingly larger proportion of each party's base, the parties were driven steadily apart on the racial dimension. The cumulative result is the development of a significant polarization between partisans on racial desegregation largely due to population replacement.

WHY DYNAMIC GROWTH?
ISSUE EVOLUTION IN CONGRESS

Dynamic growth of issue polarization must consist of two components: the critical moment to account for departure from equilibrium and a permanent redefinition of the meaning of party alignment to account for continuing evolution. We have found evidence in support of both components in the racial evolution case. The critical moment is associated with events surrounding the 1963–1964 flashpoint in racial politics; the continuing evolution is due to the successive recruitment of new partisan identifiers with distinctive racial attitudes.

But we have not yet seen what accounts for the process itself. For mass issue evolutions do not occur within a political vacuum. They can only be understood as a delayed response, the most visible cumulative result of a more basic and profound issue redefinition of the parties occurring in the institutional structures of American politics.

There are many ways to examine the images of parties over time. Here we will look at only one, the aggregated voting records of the parties in Congress, which we have already discussed in Chapter 3. The racial voting series are a rich data base; much was happening during this period. They can be examined for many purposes, individual and aggregate, internal and external to Congress. Our purpose here is the development of a summary index of issue evolution in the most visible records of the national

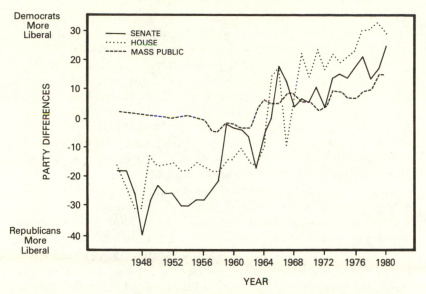

Figure 6.6 Growing Party Differentiation on Desegregation: Congress and the Mass Electorate. *Source*: Senate and House series compiled by the authors from analyses of annual roll-call votes of the U.S. Congress, 1945–1980. Mass electorate series compiled by the authors from SRC/CPS National Election Study Series, 1956–1980, and from Louis Harris and Associates, Study #1285.

parties in Washington. Except for the racially turbulent 1960s, we do not think citizens were paying much attention to congressional voting alignments, but the series do index a wide variety of more subtle displays of party image. They reflect the party images conveyed through the media, members' discussions about the relation of race and party with their constituents, and presidents' comments about Congress.

To examine the institutional series along with the mass series, we compute the interparty difference (Democratic minus Republican) of the series for each house. This information is graphed in Figure 6.6 for the 1945–1980 period, where data are available for both Congress and mass public. If citizens had paid attention to Congress, Figure 6.6 suggests they would have witnessed an issue evolution far more striking than what we have observed in the mass series. Both houses of Congress display an unmistakable issue evolution on race. Republicans were unquestionably the more racially liberal party through the 1950s, a pattern probably little changed since Reconstruction, and unquestionably the more conservative party after the transition of the 1960s. That

155

the congressional issue evolution occurs earlier than the mass response is less obvious but likewise important for causal analysis; the two congressional series lead the mass series.[7]

The result in Figure 6.6 easily confirms the image redefinition thesis. And it begins to suggest an answer to a troublesome anomaly—that evolution along racial lines is more striking in the 1970s after racial issues fell from the top of the public agenda than it had been during the peak salience period. If the congressional series are good indicators of party image—and we think they are—the answer is simple: the driving force of continuing mass evolution is continuing elite evolution.

And why should party elites, here congressmen and senators, continue to polarize after peak salience? The answer is both predictable and general for all issue evolutions. Most change among a party's visible officials occurs by replacement. Where officeholders can rely upon incumbency to retain office, (1) there will be inertial resistance to any new issue cleavage, and (2) the polarization process is likely to continue so long as a sizable proportion of "old" members retain office. For the American Congress, that time span is measured in decades.

Conclusion: Partisan Change without Critical Elections

Change is a stubborn fact of political life; it is especially pervasive in the electoral arena. Candidates change, issues change, and, on occasion, even the parties change. Not surprisingly there is a rich and varied literature on change in mass party systems. Although this literature abounds in rich historical detail and provides intriguing particularistic accounts, its theory is problematic at its core. It fails to provide a general account of political change.

The standard view of partisan change is that provided by critical election realignment theory. According to this theory, prolonged periods of partisan stability are interrupted by periodic realignments precipitated by critical elections. Thus, a stable party system undergoes a convulsive shock that leads to a sudden

[7] Our conceptual framework here is the Box-Jenkins transfer function model, where one dynamic series is postulated to be the causal result of another, after the removal of time dependence processes in both series. We turn to explicit transfer function modeling in the next chapter. See Box and Jenkins (1976, chaps. 10 and 11).

and permanent alteration in existing partisan alignment. A new majority party usually emerges in response to the changed political environment and rapidly becomes stabilized along the new issue dimension. The party system is thus characterized by a cyclical pattern of long periods of stability interposed by short but dramatic periods of change.

The problem with this prevailing account is not that it is necessarily wrong, but that it is clearly incomplete. Critical election realignment theory treats all partisan change as a single phenomenon that occurs through an abrupt, permanent transformation of the party system. As a consequence, it must ignore other types of partisan change—most important, change more gradual in character. Moreover, gradual transformations in the party system are probably more typical, occur more frequently, and account for the largest proportion of political change. Critical election realignment theory is thus not only a partial theory of partisan transformation, but it is also partial in a particularly perverse sense: it concentrates on the most unusual and infrequently occurring mode of change. A focus on the unusual and infrequent is unlikely to provide a satisfactory basis for a general theory of partisan change.

In this chapter we have examined a variety of models of partisan change and found the dynamic evolutionary model consistent with both the decay of the New Deal alignment and the growth in issue polarization on race. The model posits that the mass issue evolution begins with a "critical moment"—more visible than the creepingly slow change implied by pure secular realignment but much less pronounced than that presumed by critical election realignments. Equally significant, the initial increase in mass issue polarization does not complete the process but only begins it by setting in motion a change that grows over time.

Dynamic evolutions thus represent the political equivalent of biology's punctuated equilibrium. The critical moment corresponds to the punctuation point—a change of some magnitude but not a cataclysmic adaptation. The slower, continuous change following the critical moment is the drive toward a new equilibrium—the semipermanent redefinition of the link between issues and mass parties.

Dynamic issue evolutions can accommodate a variety of causal mechanisms. Unlike critical election models that imply either massive conversions or equally massive mobilizations, normal population replacement plays a central role in issue evolutions.

157

Conversion and mobilization account for the initial partisan differentiation on the issue, but population replacement accounts for its steady and continued growth.

This chapter, then, has provided a revised theoretical framework for understanding partisan change, one that looks to the dynamic evolution of new issues as the stimulus of change and to the continuous replacement of the electorate as its primary mechanism. In Chapter 7 we pursue our causal logic in a more integrated and systematic design for modeling and testing evolutionary assertions.

· 7 ·

ON THE STRUCTURE AND
SEQUENCE OF ISSUE EVOLUTION

Most issues most of the time lie dormant, stirring interest only in those especially informed and affected. They lend no weight to the color, tone, and meaning of partisan debate. They neither define party systems nor undergird party alignments. But issues occasionally rise from partisan obscurity and become so contentious, so partisan, and so long lasting that they actually define the party system in which they arise and transform the grounds of debate that were their origin. This joint transformation of issues and party systems, which we call "issue evolution," is a restructuring of mass and institutional politics, a dynamic process resulting in the change of issue alignments.

The evidence presented thus far sustains a portrait of issue evolution around racial desegregation. We have seen issue evolution in presidential acts and party platforms (in Chapter 2), in congressional roll calls (Chapter 3), in activist attitudes and party issue perceptions (Chapter 4), in the evolution of mass belief structures (Chapter 5), and, perhaps most important, in the alignment of issue with party loyalty (Chapter 6). The task of this chapter is to tie those diverse strands together into a single coherent model of the issue evolution process. We highlight two aspects of such a model: (1) the structure of issue evolution, what causes what, and (2) its sequence, how causal effects play upon one another over time.

The purpose of this chapter, then, is to examine the structure and sequence of issue evolution. We first outline a general causal model of the process, then look at specific evidence relating to its individual and separate elements, and finally conduct a more formal statistical analysis to uncover the dynamic causality inherent in the issue evolution process.

A MODEL OF ISSUE EVOLUTION

Most policy debate occurs among elected and appointed officials at the center of government. Most attracts no significant public notice. When occasionally an issue moves from the limited "pol-

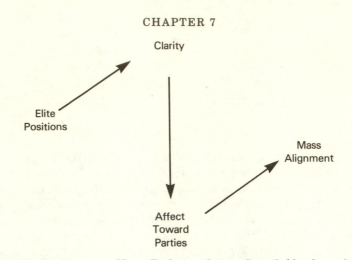

Figure 7.1 The Sequence of Issue Evolution. *Source*: Compiled by the authors.

icy" environment to the larger stage of partisan politics, we naturally look to those elite actors who framed the issue in partisan terms in the first instance for its partisan origin. Figure 7.1 outlines the ensuing sequence of the issue evolution process. A delayed, more inertial reaction in the mass electorate follows elite reorientations on contentious issues. When the elite polarization in progress is first squarely confronted by the mass electorate, the reaction often takes the general form of a "critical moment."[1] The critical moment is a mass polarization along the new line of issue cleavage large enough to be noticeable but considerably less dramatic than the critical election of traditional realignment theory. Partisan conversion and electoral mobilization are the causal mechanisms that produce such rapid change. Critical moments occur, we presume, with some frequency. Often the new issue/party links they establish lose electoral relevance as quickly as it was gained. But in some cases the critical moment becomes the signal event for a less dramatic but much more substantial secular redefinition of the issue bases of political life. This secular reorientation reflects the continuing recognition of

[1] The "critical moment" idea may appear to be, but is not, a reintroduction of a watered down version of the critical realignment baggage we shed earlier. The key distinction is that "critical elections" are thought to be either the whole of realigning change in some versions or a major part in others. The "critical moment," in contrast, is an important event for setting the stage for an evolutionary change that follows; it is not the change itself. It is the punctuation in a punctuated equilibrium approach to evolutionary sequences.

160

the changed positions of the parties after the critical moment, and it is driven by normal population replacement.

Changes in elite partisan behavior do not lead directly to mass partisan response. Rather, two intervening steps are necessary to link elite policy shift to mass issue realignment. First, the mass public must alter its perceptions of the parties with respect to the new issue dimension. Taking its cues from elite partisan actors and citizen party activists,[2] the mass electorate must recognize a difference in the positions of the parties on the new issue. But even changed perceptions, by themselves, are not likely to induce changes in mass issue alignment. For issues to move voters to change their partisan identifications (at the "critical moment") and bias the recruitment of new identifiers (thereafter), the issue must evoke a strong emotional response. Changing perceptions of the parties must carry with them a heavy dose of affection and disaffection for the parties if they are to weigh against the stubborn inertia of existing partisan identifications. The public must not only perceive a difference in party issue stands, but it must also care about this difference. Only when these two intervening conditions are met—clarified mass cognitive images of the parties and then polarized affection toward them—will issue redefinition among partisan elites lead to new policy alignments among the mass electorate.

Changes in the components of party image, moreover, should be temporally bounded between the elite policy reorientation that begins the process and mass issue alignment that ends it. Time ordering is critical. Redefinition of the link between issue and party, however tentative and perhaps even unintended it may be, is a process that must begin with elite actors. In an environment where many policy cues are given and most are ignored, the crucial role of the mass electorate is to choose to respond to some cues. Which set of actors—political leaders or mass public—is the more important element of the process is probably

---

[2] Recall from Chapter 4 that party images are an exceptionally close fit to the issue preferences of citizen party activists. We argued there that observation of the visible displays of activist attitudes is a likely means by which the more inert mass electorate comes to know where the parties stand. It would be natural to include the activists in a mediating role between elite behaviors and mass perceptions of them at this point. We do not do so because the data do not permit it. We can construct activist attitudes only when measures of activism itself are available in the election studies, and they often are not.

an unanswerable question; we shall not in any case attempt an answer. But priority in time we assign to political leaders.

We turn now to the evidence, which we present in two parts. First, we shall show the evidence for (the fact of) racial issue evolution. Because the case is made in earlier chapters, we shall be brief. In this first section we introduce individually the time series components of the model. Our point here is simple: something happened. Our analysis is accordingly simple; making minimal assumptions of our data, we shall for each interparty difference series present a simple before/after test for the hypothesis that 1964 represents a break point in all the series. The congressional series are annual; the others, with minor differences, biennial.

Second, we analyze the structure and sequence of issue evolution, the central focus of this chapter. When we turn to the evidence on structure and sequence, we shift tack to make stronger assumptions by treating all series as annual, to abandon the implicitly linear dynamics of the before/after test and its arbitrary focus on a single change point, and thus to explore the limits of refined analysis of causal dynamics.

The Evidence for Issue Evolution

We argue that visible changes in elite behavior serve to redefine party images, to affect emotional response to the parties, and ultimately to realign the constellation of voter issue attitudes and party identifications to reflect earlier changes among the elite. We require indicators of each concept: elite behavioral change, party image, citizen emotional response, and identification/issue alignment.

Party elite behavior is many things—acts of presidents, congresses, party officials, the parties in convention, and so forth. We have looked at all of these in this book, and each is arguably important in the issue case at hand, as would be the courts, except for their inability to lend partisan structure to issue conflicts. We choose to focus here on Congress, and specifically on roll-call votes, because these frequent and public acts present a clean summary measure of what the parties truly stand for. Although other elite actors, most particularly presidents, are undeniably important in reshaping party issue stances, none presents as regular a pattern of objectively (and cleanly) quantifiable behavior. Our focus on congressional behavior

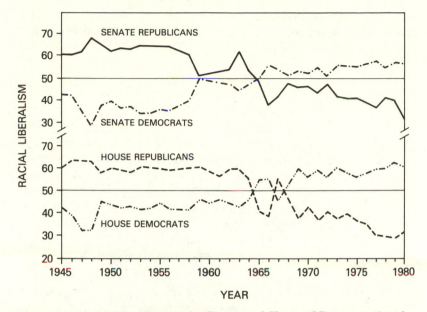

Figure 7.2 Racial Liberalism in the Senate and House of Representatives by Party, 1945–1980. *Source*: Compiled by the authors from analyses of annual roll-call votes of the U.S. Congress, 1945–1980.

should be seen not as an argument that Congress best defines what the parties support or oppose but rather that it presents the best leverage for developing operational indicators of the messier whole of elite party behavior.

For the purpose of charting elite policy stands, we use the roll-call vote scales developed in Chapter 3. These series represent the issue positions of the two parties on racial issues since the beginning of the postwar era.

Figure 7.2 presents the mean party positions on racial issues in the postwar era in the Senate and House. Examination of the figure reveals quite distinct and very strongly determined patterns of behavior. At the beginning of each series, as we saw in Chapter 3, the Republicans—then the "party of Lincoln"—were clearly the more moderate and liberal in relative terms of the two parties. Democrats were disproportionately southern in numbers, leadership, and image; the Democratic party had not yet developed its hard core of northern liberalism that would later counter southern influence and still later dominate it. By the end of the series the parties had reversed their positions; Democrats were

163

not only considerably more liberal in the aggregate, they were more liberal in all regions. Indeed, even southern Democrats are now less conservative on matters of race than the Republican party as a whole.

When we look at the *differences* between party positions over time, indicated by simply subtracting the Republican from Democratic mean positions for each year, striking patterns of racial issue evolution are in evidence. Beginning in the late 1950s the party behaviors track an unmistakable dynamic evolution toward a fundamental redefinition of the grounds of issue cleavage. Three significant movements in the Senate series (see Figure 7.2)—sharp movements in 1959 and 1965 and a gradual growth process beginning around 1970—contribute to the ultimate redefinition of party stands. The House series mirrors the 1959 Senate shifts on a smaller scale and then begins a continuing dynamic growth process in 1965. The 1959 through 1963 movements in both houses are not a new polarization over race; they are movements toward the erosion of the old pattern of greater Republican progressivism, a necessary precursor to new polarization. The politics of the time may be seen as the beginnings of assertion by northern Democrats of a new majority status in their party, a six-year struggle to control the direction of Democratic policy that culminated by 1964 in unquestioned liberal control. Earlier liberal attempts to pass civil rights legislation achieved only limited success at changing the law, but they appear highly successful in laying the groundwork for the new dominant Democratic liberalism of the later 1960s. All our indicators show significant issue evolution, but the congressional series are the most striking.

To establish an indicator of the public perception of the party stances we turn to the cps biennial national election series for a data source. Specifically, we examine questions tapping respondent perceptions of where the parties stand on racial issues. The data on perceived party issue positions are in three different question formats spanning three periods: (1) 1956–1958, (2) 1960–1968, and (3) 1970–1980. The most dramatic changes in issue perceptions occur, fortunately, *within* the common 1960 to 1968 format. To insure comparability of data collected under varying formats we reduced the level of measurement for all years to the categorical variable, "Democrats more liberal," "Republicans more liberal," or no perceived difference. With suitable

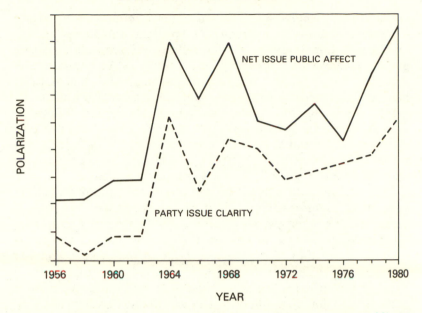

Figure 7.3 Polarizing Clarity of Party Racial Issue Stands and Issue Public Affect Toward the Two Parties. *Source*: SRC/CPS National Election Series, 1956–1980.

manipulation, all three question formats can be reformulated to yield the three categories.

The measure of mass perceptions of party issue positions—to be called "Clarity" following Pomper (1972)—is the aggregate percentage of each survey sample declaring the Democrats more liberal on desegregation minus the similar percentage of those perceiving the reverse ordering. Peak values are attained when respondents both see the parties as different and achieve consensus about which is more liberal. Lack of either consensus or perception of difference, both common before 1964, reduce the measure. We took considerable care to maintain the conceptual linkages between early and later series. The empirical evidence bears witness to our success; Figure 7.3 shows both consistent behavior in the series across format changes and impressive variation within common formats.

The voters of Figure 7.3 failed to distinguish between the two parties on racial grounds until just before 1964 (before/after $t = 5.5$; n = 12) as noted at the time by Converse, Clausen, and Miller (1965). As late as 1960 and, from other series, probably

165

through about mid-1963, voters saw no difference between the parties, responding 22.7 percent, 21.3 percent, and 55.9 percent—Democrats, Republicans, and "no difference," respectively—to a question asking which party "is more likely to see to it that Negroes get fair treatment in jobs and housing." That lags notably behind the congressional series that show clear signs of movement toward changing party positions following the 1958 elections, and it is equally, if less obviously, the case that mass perceptions lag behind the steady party polarization of later years as well, "catching up" at intermittent opportunities, such as 1980, years after the congressional parties changed.

We have seen quite direct evidence of the changing racial images of the Democratic and the Republican parties. Whether it *matters* we have not yet seen, for evolving mass party images by themselves are necessary but insufficient to account for issue evolution. More than clarity of perception is required if evolving party issue positions are to cause systematic issue sorting among the party identifiers. The issue must matter. It must strike home with enough force to influence the emotional ties between citizens and parties. As a first approximation of such emotional links we look to the simple affections and disaffections citizens display toward the parties over time.

To measure issue public affect we turn again to the CPS series and pursue a two-step indirect strategy. It is intentionally indirect to sidestep the "rationalization" and "projection" phenomenons (Brody and Page 1972) that are likely to plague any respondent commentary on the link among policy, affect, and party. Respondents who hold distinctive positions on the desegregation issue are isolated in the first step. Then the positive and negative feelings expressed for each of the parties, without regard to race, by these distinctive issue groups form a summary measure of net issue affect. Our indicators then tap whether racial liberals and conservatives have differential overall evaluations of the parties.

To isolate racial liberals and conservatives, we build a scale of desegregation liberalism for every study in the NES series where measures of both party affect and racial attitude are available (i.e., every presidential- and off-year study from 1956 onward, excluding 1958 and 1962). Racial liberals and conservatives are then defined arbitrarily to be the highest and lowest quartiles on the scale. The middle quartiles are excluded on the rationale that "indecisives" on an issue have no grounds for emotional response to party position taking. Our goal here is to develop an aggregate measure of party affection and disaffection among racial issue publics. These relatively extreme quartiles are taken as operational indicators of "issue publics."

Affection and disaffection for the parties are tapped by the best available valence measures in each study. That, in general, entails the use of open-ended "likes/dislikes" about the parties for presidential studies and feeling thermometer ratings in off-year studies when the open-ended materials are unavailable. Both measures are scored in the Democratic direction, that is, positive scores indicate greater warmth for the Democrats than for the Republicans, and both are adjusted to a standard (mean: 50, standard deviation: 25) metric for all years.

The net measure allows us to gauge whether citizens with distinctive issue positions reflect their issue biases in their emotional response to the two parties. Figure 7.3 shows a nonsignificant ordering of preferences before 1964. Racial issue publics, not excluding blacks, liked the two parties about equally well in 1956 and 1960. Affect toward the two parties became clearly related to issue positions after 1964 (before/after $t = 3.4$; n = 11). And although the data are altogether independent of the cognitive images of Figure 7.3, the two patterns in the figure are suggestively similar, a matter we discuss more formally below.

Systematic movements, something more than year-to-year fluctuation, would be expected to lead to something, and that is the final link in our analysis. The ultimate demonstration of the existence of an issue evolution is to show significant redistribution of public opinion on a policy issue among party identifiers. The new alignment of issues and party is the final result of the process of issue evolution and the one that justifies the importance of all the others. The semipermanent redefinition of the grounds of party issue conflict gives evolving issues an importance considerably beyond the normal grist of electoral politics.[3] Its measure here is the simple interparty difference on desegregation issues, the mean position of all Democratic identifiers for a given year less the Republican mean.

Figure 7.4 displays the causal effect to be explained, the grow-

---

[3] Such issue redefinition by similar logic could be expected to lead also to issue dealignment, a prospect explored in detail in Carmines, McIver, and Stimson (1987) but well beyond the scope of this chapter. The evidence of that analysis suggests quite clearly that racial and other policy attitudes do predict individual movements away from party identification.

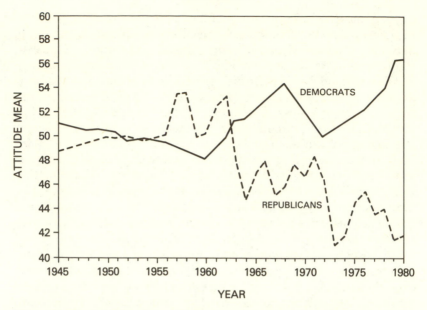

Figure 7.4 Racial Liberalism of Democratic and Republican Party Identifiers. *Source*: SRC/CPS National Election Series, 1956–1980, and Louis Harris and Associates, Study #1285.

ing racial attitude polarization of the identifiers of the two parties. Figure 7.4 plots the desegregation attitudes of party identifiers from the national election series for even-numbered years from 1956 to 1980 and from a Harris survey of November 1963. Racial attitudes, an equally weighted summation of the survey items available in each cross-section, are scaled with a common metric for all cross-sections and reconstructed backward in time to create a continuous annual series.[4]

[4] Each annual scale is composed of racial desegregation policy items that form the first principal component in analyses of all racial items. The items, in general, deal with respondent preferences for federal desegregation policy (not including school busing, where the evidence suggests powerful influence of extraneous issue dimensions). The now controversial reconstruction methodology and its specific application to reconstructing partisan racial attitudes are examined in detail in Carmines and Stimson (1984). That analysis confirms that the recall data are indeed problematic, as is reported "party identification" itself. We have limited the use of reconstruction methods to the period before 1956 and to odd-numbered years thereafter. One particularly crucial odd year, 1963, has been estimated from a Harris survey of November 1963, completed but not released before the Kennedy assassination. See Munger (1977) for more detail on this well-timed exploration of public attitudes. Each of our analyses to come will be

A sharp polarization along racial lines occurred in the turbulent 1960s (before/after 1964 $t = 5.3$; n $= 14$). Democrats became increasingly more liberal while Republicans became steadily more conservative, as some accounts suggest; see particularly Pomper (1972) and Converse, Clausen, and Miller (1965). Less expected—and hence more interesting—is the polarization's continued growth during the 1970s when racial issues were no longer prominent on the political agenda.

A pattern of growth *following* the decay of the stimuli that created the initial polarization suggests simply that something else was going on. Polarization with a self-sustaining dynamic must be more than a response to visible "events." By postulating intervening processes that lag behind and then dynamically adjust to the reality produced by initial events we account for that self-sustaining dynamic.

To this point we have asserted causal connections between the varied components of issue evolution and presented largely visual and intuitive evidence. We turn now to a more formal analysis of our causal assertions, using transfer function analysis to uncover the dynamic causality within and between the various series.

The Evidence for Structure and Sequence

To examine the sequence in issue evolution we will entertain dynamic formulations that allow the expression of causal effects between variables (series) in a manner that incorporates both empirical and a priori specification of delay, resistance, and dynamic adaptation. Our methodology is well developed in the time series literature but sufficiently distinct from normal political science approaches that some explanation is in order. We shall present our evidence fairly directly here, with little exposition of the statistical models and modeling techniques; we identify those matters in the appendix to this chapter.

Estimating dynamic relationships asks much of our data, and we have chosen to push them to their limit. In some cases that is easily done; our congressional series, based upon all the available roll-call data in both houses of Congress for thirty-six years each,

---

performed both on the annual time series, including those reconstructed, and independently on the shorter, mainly biennial, series that require no use of reconstructed partisanship. The latter results, presented in the Appendix to Chapter 7, in every case confirm our interpretation of the former.

present an exceptionally clean look at the aggregate party behaviors. The survey data, on the other hand, are limited by the biennial structure of American elections and the questions survey institutions choose to ask. We employ fifteen independent studies to construct our three series: *clarity*, what citizens think the parties stand for; *affect*, how issue publics feel about the parties; and *alignment*, the polarization of identifier issue attitudes. For alignment we reconstruct 1945 through 1951 and odd numbered years later, where independent surveys are not available, from recalled party identification of survey respondents. The perils of this technique are now well known (Niemi, Katz, and Newman 1980). They are manageable here because for the period of NES coverage, we rarely have to push recall beyond one year. The effect of errors of recall of party identification will be to introduce unwanted noise in the year-to-year changes of party identification/racial policy alignment (ΔAL).

Our intervening variables, clarity of issue perceptions and affect of issue publics toward the parties, are measured biennially at best. For these variables we postulate no change between elections (i.e., $\Delta X = 0$) or before the first available surveys. If independent evidence for these cases existed, we would expect to see only sampling variation in the year-to-year change measures between elections. This amounts to the assumption that only election years matter in the evolution of links between issues and parties. The style of our analysis with these variables is much akin to intervention analysis or regression with dummy variables, where 0 and 1 values are postulated to stand for absent and present. The difference here is that in place of the ones we have empirical estimates of the direction and magnitude of change; the zeros indicate the absence of expected change. Again, if the assumption is false, the expected effect is conservative; a constant zero will neither be predicted by, when dependent, nor aid in prediction of, when independent, another continuously measured series of first differences.

ESTIMATION

We begin estimation by examining the dependent variable itself, mass party identification issue alignment (AL). This examination serves a statistical, not theoretical, purpose; it erects a benchmark for later explanations by accounting for the variation in AL that can be explained by the history of the series itself. To establish an explanatory benchmark we first fit a univariate "noise" model to the dependent series. As is traditional in Box-Jenkins approaches, we treat this noise model for our dependent series as a matter of no theoretical consequence but a necessary prior step in order that later causal analyses will not be confounded by this source of extraneous variance. The AL raw series is nonstationary[5]—it does not fluctuate around a stable equilibrium—and thus we must model its first differences (ΔAL), the year-to-year changes that ultimately determine the level of the series.

The univariate AL noise series—that component of issue and identification alignment best accounted for by the history of the series itself—is well fit by a moving average process of order two, a sensible result given the two-year periodicity of American elections and of the election studies from which these data are constructed. The moving average process is marginally significant ($t = 1.8$) and produces a modest reduction in residual mean square (a measure of unexplained variance) from 5.40 for the series modeled with no parameters to 4.97 for the integrated moving average model. That latter value, the predictive error when the series is modeled entirely as a function of its own history, is a base-line against which the presumed causal explanations may be measured.[6] By treating the noise model as significant, the later causal explanations will not receive explanatory credit for this "noise" variance in the dependent series.

Elite to Mass Linkages

We introduce the Senate (S_t) net party difference time series in the transfer function[7] analysis of Model 1 (Table 7.1). Prewhit-

---

[5] Limitations of space prevent us from presenting either the method of fitting transfer functions, the best source for which remains Box and Jenkins (1976), or the step-by-step modeling process of our application of the technique. Each model presented and discussed is a final estimation, the result of a lengthy sequence of preliminary and intermediary identifications, estimations, and diagnoses.

[6] Our approach to causal analysis is the sometimes contentious notion of "Granger causality," that (in the simple recursive case) a series X_t may be said to (Granger) cause another series Y_t if the conditional expectation $E(Y_t|Y_t,X_t)$ produces superior predictions than an expectation based only upon the history of Y through $t - 1$. Thus, the univariate ARIMA model for alignment is the benchmark against which we judge predictive improvement. The residual mean square, unexplained sum of squares divided by degrees of freedom, is the criterion. See Freeman (1983) for a lucid, far more comprehensive treatment of Granger causality in the context of international political economy.

[7] On notation and terminology: Both "regular" transfer functions of the genre proposed by Box and Jenkins (1976), where one dynamic series exerts transfer

171

ened cross-correlations between the Senate and mass alignment series suggest an identification of the causal pattern between series that is in accord with what we expected to see. We know a priori (see Figure 7.5) that (1) the first significant party movement toward new issue alignments in the Senate series is in 1959, following the large-scale replacement of racially liberal northern Republicans by liberal Democrats in the 1958 Senate elections, and (2) the first notable sign of changing mass racial issue alignment appears in 1963, when the Kennedy administration first embraced the program of the civil rights movement as its own.[8] Thus, we have reason to suspect a four-year lag between the two series.

Because both the Senate and mass alignment series evolve toward greater issue polarization, we could not be certain a priori whether a static or dynamic causal connection would exist between the two series; the data indicate a static one. Using the Senate series to predict mass party alignment produces a significant parameter ($\omega_0 = 0.23$, $t = 5.9$) and reduces residual mean square on the order of 11 percent from the benchmark level. The form of the estimated model is linear because the postulated nonlinear dynamic adaptation process is already present in the independent Senate series, and since both track the same basic ("S" curve) dynamics, no additional interseries dynamic adaptation is present.

The House (H_t) issue alignment series is introduced as an additional explanatory variable in Model 2 of Table 7.1 (see also Figure 7.6). While the raw Senate and House time series show much the same evolutionary pattern, the first differences in the two series (ΔH_t and ΔS_t) are only partially collinear ($r = 0.28$). The House series is much more inertial. It resisted most of the racial polarization that appeared in the Senate for some six years

---

causality on another, and the more common Box-Tiao (1975) intervention models, where the independent series is a dummy variable, are properly referred to as "transfer functions." But there are important differences between the identification and diagnosis of the two. Henceforth, we shall use "transfer function" to mean "regular transfer function" and "intervention" to refer to the Box-Tiao or "interrupted time series" (Campbell and Stanley 1963) or "impact" (McCleary and Hay 1980) models.

[8] These are only the most visible discontinuities in the series, and such evidence can be only suggestive of the proper lag structure. The model specifies more generally that every change in S_t is followed by a response in AL_t four years later. When the changes take on a more continuous and subtle nature later in the series, connections become much more difficult to see but, the evidence suggests, no less present.

TABLE 7.1
Alignment of Racial Attitudes and Party Identification:
Two Transfer Function Models

	Explanatory Variables	
	Senate Alignment (zero order)	Senate and House Alignment (zero order)
Senate alignment[a] (lagged four periods)	0.23	0.12
	$(t = 5.9)$	$(t = 2.7)$
House alignment (lagged two periods)	—	0.13
		$(t = 3.3)$
Moving average (θ_2)	0.94	0.95
	$(t = 34.7)$	$(t = 25.9)$
Measures of fit		
Residual sum of squares	128.13	91.74
Degrees of freedom	29.0	28.0
Residual mean square	4.42	3.28
Improvement over benchmark		
Residual mean square (4.97)		
(in percentage)	11.1	34.0
Autocorrelation		
$Q^b \sim \chi^2$ (df)	5.9 (11)	13.0 (11)

Source: Annual time series computed by authors from SRC/CPS National Election Studies, 1952–1980, Harris Survey #1285, and from roll-call votes of the U.S. Senate and House of Representatives, 1945–1980.

Note: Mass issue alignment is dependent.

[a] All series, independent and dependent, are first differences.

[b] Q is the Box-Ljung (1976) Q statistic for small samples, distributed as χ^2:

$$Q = (N)(N+2) \sum_{i=1}^{k} \rho_i^2/(N-i)$$

from 1959 to 1965. But once the new alignment developed, it was more steadily maintained than in the Senate. Thus, the House offers a partially overlapping and partially different set of policy alignment cues that might have been publicly perceived.

Model 2 of Table 7.1 shows that the House and Senate series share about equally in explaining mass issue alignment. The combination of the two reduces residual mean square by about

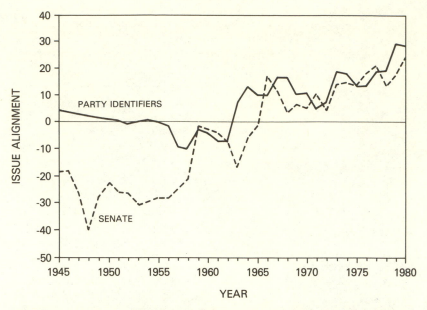

Figure 7.5 Senate and Party Identifier Alignments Together (Net, Democratic minus Republican Positions). *Source*: Senate series compiled by the authors from analyses of annual roll-call votes of the U.S. Congress, 1945–1980. Mass party identifier series compiled by the authors from the SRC/CPS National Election Study Series, 1956–1980, and from Louis Harris and Associates, Study #1285.

23 percent over that produced by the Senate alone and some 34 percent over the benchmark level. Taken together, the two models of Table 7.1 offer evidence that elite party behavior, as manifested in our congressional indicators, may cause later mass issue alignment.

Establishing simple causality next raises the question of whether the intervening causal connections we have postulated are correct. That is in part established by theory, for the intervening links are virtual logical requisites. The elite to mass issue alignment connection is fundamental. Empirical evidence of that linkage requires theoretical explication of plausible mechanisms that might translate change at one level into change at another, and perhaps in the process account for dampening and delay. Mass response to changing elite issue positions would seem to require reasonably accurate perceptions of those positions. And the polarization of affect in response to changes in party position requires clarity of issue perceptions. But we can and shall adduce empirical evidence for the linkages as well.

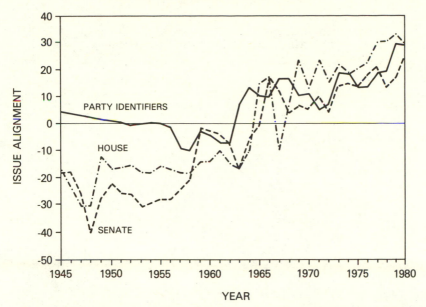

Figure 7.6 Senate, House and Party Identifier Alignments Together (Net, Democratic minus Republican Positions). *Source*: Senate and House series compiled by the authors from analyses of annual roll-call votes of the U.S. Congress, 1945–1980. Mass party identifier series compiled by the authors from SRC/CPS National Election Study Series, 1956–1980, and from Louis Harris and Associates, Study #1285.

Intervening Linkages

Working backward from mass alignment, we model the linkage between affect and alignment and then between clarity and alignment in the analyses of Table 7.2. In Model 1 we fit a first-order transfer function between affect and alignment. The resulting model produces the expected dynamic response—inertial resistance followed by adaptation—and a handsome improvement in our ability to account for alignment. The residual mean square (2.11) from this estimation of but two parameters represents a 57 percent reduction in unexplained variance from the univariate benchmark. An intervening link between elite party behavior (H_t and S_t) and mass alignment (AL_t), affect should be more strongly associated with the dependent series, and, by quite a margin, it is.

Following Pomper (1972) we postulate mass clarity of issue perception as a precondition of alignment. We further specify that the effect is indirect, through changing affect toward the

175

TABLE 7.2
Mass Issue Alignment as a Function of the Polarization of
Party Affect and the Clarity of Party Positions

	Explanatory Variables		
	Affect Only	Clarity Only	Affect and Clarity
Affect			
δ_1	0.27	—	0.27
	($t = 2.1$)		($t = 2.0$)
ω_0	0.58	—	0.59
	($t = 7.3$)		($t = 7.2$)
Clarity			
δ_0	—	0.35	—
		($t = 2.6$)	
ω_0	—	0.19	0.01
		($t = 6.3$)	($t = 0.4$)
Moving average (θ_2)	—	0.56	—
		($t = 3.0$)	
Measures of fit			
Residual sum of squares	69.77	71.67	69.38
Degrees of freedom	33	32	32
Residual mean square	2.11	2.24	2.17
Improvement over benchmark residual mean square (4.97) (in percentage)	57.5	54.9	56.4
Autocorrelation			
$Q \sim \chi^2$ (df)	11.5 (11)	15.1 (11)	11.3 (11)

Source: Annual time series computed by authors from SRC/CPS National Election Studies, 1952–1980, and Harris Survey #1285.

Note: Mass issue alignment is dependent.

parties among those who care deeply about an issue. That implies (1) a bivariate linkage between clarity and affect and (2) a mediated, not direct, link between clarity and alignment. We address the simple effect of clarity on alignment in Model 2 of Table 7.2.

The form of the causal impact of clarity on alignment, a first-order transfer function, is similar to the affect/alignment relationship. Clarity differs from affect by having (1) a considerably smaller initial impact, (2) joined with a larger dynamic adjustment, leaving (3) a smaller total effect. The clarity estimation leaves systematic variation in the model residuals, requiring an additional parameter to model an MA(2) process. The clarity/alignment linkage is clearly significant but slightly weaker than affect/alignment. It leaves more variance unaccounted for and requires an additional parameter in the process. The result is a marginally higher residual mean square.

The clarity to affect bivariate linkage is postulated to be instantaneous—both series are attitudes easily free to covary within our annual time interval—and thus can be estimated with a linear regression. The two series track one another quite closely even in their differenced form. The regression:

$$\Delta\text{Affect}_t = 0.57 + 0.40\ \Delta\text{Clarity}_t \qquad [7.1]$$

produces an R^2 of 0.89. Its slope is easily significant ($t = 16.8$), even in a small sample. Measured for aggregates (and therefore lacking the near automatic covariation from cognitive balance effects expected for individuals) and by very different techniques, the two components of party image retain nonetheless a striking empirical connection.

Whether clarity works directly on mass alignment or is indirect through affect is tested in Model 3 of Table 7.2. The result is unequivocal; the effect of clarity on alignment is entirely indirect, through affect. Model 3 with both series in the estimation equation looks virtually identical to Model 1 (affect only) with the addition of a substantively trivial and statistically nonsignificant parameter for the direct effect of clarity on alignment. That is reflected in a residual mean square higher than that produced by Model 1, a result of a lost degree of freedom without compensating gain in explanatory power. The appropriate diagnostic evidence, the cross-correlation function between prewhitened clarity and the Model 3 residuals, rules out misspecification as a possible explanation of this result; it shows no evidence of any connection between clarity and the residuals at any positive or negative lag.

The linkage between elite behaviors (here the Senate series)[9]

[9] Either Senate or House series alone is a significant predictor of clarity. But the small number of observations and the colinearity of the two series prevent statistically reliable estimation of their joint effect. A similar analysis, not reported, shows mediated but not direct linkages between the elite series and affect.

and clarity (of mass perception) can be modeled as a transfer function:

$$\Delta\text{Clarity}_t = 0.58\ \Delta\text{Senate}_{t-4} + (1 - 0.62B^2)a_t \quad [7.2]$$

which demonstrates significant association (t = 2.9) between movements in U.S. Senate voting patterns and perception of party positions, with the same four-year lag we have shown before.

The final causal question we consider is the linkage between party elite behavior and mass alignment, controlling for affect. Table 7.1, showing the simple effect of elite behavior on alignment, and Table 7.2, showing the much stronger effect of the proximate affect series, suggest that we are likely to observe no unmediated effect. Such is the message of the estimated model:

$$\Delta\text{AL}_t = [0.60/(1 - 0.24B)]\ \Delta\text{Affect}_t$$
$$- 0.02\ \Delta S_{t-4} + 0.04\ \Delta H_{t-2} + a_t \quad [7.3]$$

again virtually identical to the (affect only) Model 1 of Table 7.2, with the addition of two clearly nonsignificant parameters for the Senate (t = -0.5) and House (t = 0.3) series. As expected, the addition of nonsignificant parameters costs more than it gains, leaving the residual mean square (2.44) notably higher than the affect only model. This evidence demonstrates that the intervening causal mechanisms are necessary to connect elite to mass response.

We are left then with evidence strongly in support of the issue evolution model of Figure 7.1. All the hypothesized connections are significant: elite party behavior causes mass perception of party positions, which causes polarized affect toward the parties among issue publics, which in turn leads to alignment along issue lines. None of the longer linkages is significant when modeled with intervening terms in the equation.

We have now traveled the path from observed changes in elite party behavior, to accurate mass perception of party position, to polarized emotional response to the parties based upon issue positions, to mass party alignment, which is where we began. We have traced the issue evolution process through each of its empirically distinct but theoretically interdependent stages.

Concluding Reflections: On Organic Theory and Inadvertent Representation

Our purpose in this chapter has been to weave the separate and diverse strands of issue evolution into a coherent model of American political processes. The model is distinctive in two notable regards: first, it is an atypical conception of institutional/mass public interactions; second, it is a novel approach to political representation.

Conventional accounts of party realignment accord a fundamental role to mass electorates, treating institutional actors as responding to more central electoral forces. Such accounts provide a distorted picture of elite/mass dynamics. Tied to the normative democracy and the mechanistic metaphor of the Constitution, they require political professionals to have knowledge of issues—in both policy and political senses—that is less advanced than the amateur electorate. The origin of the policy dialogue between politicians and voters must lie, we believe, with the former, who provide definition to a multitude of issue conflicts.

The role of the electorate in issue evolution is to respond to some issues and not to others. The process is analogous to the natural selection of the biological world. Elites provide cues about issue definition. Numerous, complex, and contradictory, most are seeds on fallow ground, ignored by an inattentive electorate. The issue space, that tiny number of policy debates that can claim substantial attention in both center of government and among the passive electorate, is strikingly limited by mass inattention. Alternative issues, or alternative definitions of the same issue, may be seen as competing for a portion of that space, a highly selective and often unpredictable competition.

Although elites "lead"—in the sense of acting first in time sequence—they neither control nor manipulate. However strategic their behavior in developing issue positions as levers to influence, the number of policy cues is so large and their effect so unknowable that the process takes on an appearance of randomness. The competition for issue space produces very large numbers of possible issue definitions of party politics. One such definition is occasionally selected when it happens to be well suited to the political environment of the moment. Like organic behavior generally, issue evolutions come to seem sensible, perhaps even inevitable, after the fact; they are almost unknowable before it.

179

Issue evolution produces representation as a by-product. But unlike the demand-compliance notions that dominate thinking about representative processes, the by-product representation is inadvertent. It is systemic, not individual. It occurs without any single actor consciously attempting to produce it. Over the span of the desegregation issue, as should generally be the case, we can see evolution from a time when the party system was wholly unrepresentative—offering no coherent positions, no citizen choice—to the current pattern of issue-polarized parties, for better or for worse highly representative of their constituencies in the electorate. This representation is inadvertent because it was produced less by elite response to mass demands than by mass evolution toward existing elite positions.

We have now discussed the racial issue evolution in all its complexity, observing how the individual pieces fit together into a relatively complete process model. But what can this tell us about issue evolution more generally? We examine this question in the final chapter.

APPENDIX

Notes on First-Order Dynamic Specifications

For many of the links in the model of Figure 7.1 we postulate first-order dynamics. That entails a change in some variable X followed, after a possible lag of k years, by a series of changes in the effect variable Y. In the model we entertain we expect a change in X (ΔX) at t to be followed after k lags by a perceptible change in ΔY (estimated by the parameter ω_0) and a continuing sequence of ever smaller changes in ΔY until it achieves an equilibrium adaptation to ΔX. But before the equilibrium response to ΔX is achieved, Y is also responding to later innovations, both positive and negative, in X, ΔX_t, ΔX_{t+1}, ΔX_{t+2}, ... The decay in the sequence of changes is estimated by the parameter δ_1 (where $0 < \delta_1 < 1.0$) that distributes the causal effect of ΔX to a sequence of ΔY, which, though mathematically infinite, in practice decays to a trivial level after a few periods:

$$\Delta Y_t = [(\omega_0)/(1 - \delta_1 B)]\Delta X_{t-k} + N_t \qquad [7.4]$$

If we assume the lack of a systematic "noise" process in the model residuals—which we do here to simplify illustration but do not do in the analysis—the model can be written in this more intuitively satisfying form:

$$\Delta Y_t = \delta_1 \Delta Y_{t-1} + \omega_0 \Delta X_t + a_t \qquad [7.5]$$

which expresses the current change in Y as a function of ΔX lagged k periods, and the previous ΔY, and a random disturbance a_t. Since the previous ΔY is also a function of its previous value and δ_1 must be less than one, then the causal effect of changes in X must decay over time:

$$\Delta Y_t = \omega_0 \Delta X_{t-k} + \delta_1 \omega_0 \Delta X_{t-k-1} + \delta_1^2 \omega_0 \Delta X_{t-k-2} \\ + \delta_1^3 \omega_0 \Delta X_{t-k-3} \ldots + a_t. \qquad [7.6]$$

Equation 7.6 accurately expresses change in Y only as a function of previous changes in X—this is not a lagged endogenous formulation—and of random error. The sequence of exponentially decaying change in ΔY becomes growth when ΔY is cumulated back into Y, because the *rate of change* is decaying.

The first-order model is an attractive conception of dynamic causality. It is likely to find application wherever inertia limits the responsiveness with which effect variables can adjust to changes in their causal environment, a very large class of problems. In the present instance, for example, party identification, if it is to deserve the special status it holds in theories of electoral behavior, cannot be understood as a labile response to the constellation of factors that cause it. The party identification of our theories is, at least in degree, a lifelong commitment, a standing decision, an ego identification, an ingrained loyalty, a habit, and an expression of solidarity with racial, religious, ethnic, and linguistic peers. The "identification" in party identification gives it a rootedness that makes it not impermeable to changes in the political world but certainly highly resistant to them. Policy conflict between the individual and his or her party (or attraction to the opposition) over matters of great material or symbolic importance may be understood to produce change in party identification. But the contest between ingrained loyalty and a short-term party attraction or revulsion is unequal; we expect loyalty nearly always to win. But even as rock erodes under the force of a trickle of running water, sustained for a very long time, so party identification is likely to change in response to long-sustained policy cues on matters of personal importance.

Two static approaches to the estimation of such dynamic causal

TABLE 7.A
Regression Respecification of Table 7.1

	Mass Alignment (ΔAL) Dependent	
	Senate Only	Senate and House
S_{t-4}: Senate (lagged 4 years)	0.15	0.23[a]
(standard error)	(0.12)	(0.13)
H_{t-2}: House (lagged 2 years)		0.21[b]
(standard error)		(0.14)
Constant	0.64	-0.36
(standard error)	(1.20)	(1.31)
N	13.00	13.00
R^2	0.12	0.28
R^2	0.04	0.14

Source: Annual time series computed by authors from SRC/CPS National Election Studies, 1952–1980, Harris Survey #1285, and from roll-call votes of the U.S. Senate and House of Representatives, 1945–1980.
[a] $p < 0.05$ one tailed test.
[b] $p < 0.10$ one tailed test.

relationships are common but problematic. If we conceive of cause as an event in X at t, the effect of which is distributed over several later values of Y, we can approach the problem statistically (1) by relating cumulative cause with cumulative effect or (2) by relating change in X with change in Y, perhaps with some lag k. The cumulative approach—for example, relating the congressional racial time series to the party identification/issue alignment series—will produce stunning levels of apparent covariation, much of which invariably is spurious. If causal connection is present, the cumulative approach will find it but with very little likelihood of identifying the correct functional form or direction. It is also likely to find it if it is not present. Cumulation, even of purely random variations, induces systematic behavior in time series, any two of which will have high levels of incidental covariation.

The problem of cumulation is Type I error; it leads to the inference of cause when it is not in fact present. The examination of static relationships between change in X and change in Y has the opposite problem. If the effect of ΔX is distributed over several

TABLE 7.B
Regression Respecification of Table 7.2

	Mass Alignment (ΔAL) Dependent		
	Affect Only	Clarity Only	Affect and Clarity
Affect	1.72[a]		1.20[a]
(standard error)	(0.33)		(0.58)
Clarity		0.20[a]	0.08
(standard error)		(0.05)	(0.07)
Constant	0.12	0.47	0.17
(standard error)	(0.67)	(0.75)	(0.67)
N	13.00	13.00	13.00
R^2	0.72	0.64	0.75
R^2	0.69	0.60	0.69

Source: Annual time series computed by authors from SRC/CPS National Election Studies, 1952–1980, and Harris Survey #1285.

[a] $p < 0.05$ one tailed test.

lags of ΔY, then even choosing the empirically optimal lag between X and Y, even with perfect measurement, always understates the true relationship. If inertial drag limits responsiveness, then response time becomes stochastic, and we expect to see a distribution around some optimal value of k. No more than a fraction, and perhaps a very small one, of the effect of ΔX_t will appear in ΔY_{t+k}. If cause is not present, the method will not find it; it is also fairly unlikely to find it when it is present.

The first-order dynamic model is a middle course. It deals with variations in X and Y, not their cumulations, and hence avoids the spuriousness problem. It is, in fact, exceptionally rigorous against spurious covariation, an attractive property. But within the constraint of a parsimonious formulation, it also allows for a distributed effect of ΔX on ΔY, both more realistic than a static formulation and much less vulnerable to Type II errors. It errs on balance on the conservative side because true causal effects that do not conform to the constraint of the first-order model do not count for the hypothesis.

· 8 ·

RACIAL ISSUE EVOLUTION:
STRATEGY, CHANCE, AND OPPORTUNITY

> Nothing at first can appear more difficult to believe than
> that the more complex organs and instincts should have
> been perfected, not by means superior to, though analo-
> gous with, human reason, but by the accumulation of in-
> numerable slight variations, each good for the individual
> possessor. Nevertheless, this difficulty, though appearing
> to our imagination insuperably great, cannot be consid-
> ered real if we admit the following propositions, namely,
> —that gradations in the perfection of any organ or in-
> stinct, which we may consider, either do now exist or
> could have existed, each good of its kind,—that all organs
> and instincts are, in ever so slight a degree, variable,—
> and lastly, that there is a struggle for existence leading to
> the preservation of each profitable deviation of structure
> or instinct. The truth of these propositions cannot, I think,
> be disputed.
> —Charles Darwin, *On The Origin of Species by Means of*
>   *Natural Selection, or the Preservation of*
>   *Favoured Races in the Struggle for Life*

The preceding chapters have presented the issue evolution of race.
We have woven a portrait of presidents, party leaders, congressmen and senators, citizen activists, and the electorate, moved by
ordinary political motivations but part of a larger and longer picture of issues in evolution. We have postulated patterns, fit models, and looked at evidence. But a fifty-year longitudinal analysis
is history, even if it does not have much of that appearance. We
turn in this final chapter to a more conventional narrative history of the issues and the times. Necessarily incomplete and over-
simple, our goal is to abstract some familiar political elements of
that history and recast them in our evolutionary conception.

THE EVOLUTION OF RACE:
SOURCES OF ISSUE COMPETITION

As recently as 1960 it is arguably the case that issues of race
were not partisan issues. Advocates of racial liberalism were to

be found about equally among northern Democrats and Republicans. Hostility to the aspirations of black Americans was almost exclusively the province of the southern wing of the Democratic party. For the mass electorate, race was a regional concern; on this question the union halls and country clubs were in easy agreement. Neither party found it advantageous to stake out distinctive activist positions on this potentially volatile issue, and citizens responded accordingly. Except for the Dixiecrats, race was an irrelevant cue for the development of party attachments.

Nor was race a reference point in American political ideology. To be liberal was to advocate activist positive government, but this advocacy need not cross the color line. Democrats from Roosevelt to Kennedy found it advantageous to cast the role of the common man with a white face. Indeed, ideological liberalism and race baiting sometimes marched hand in hand among southern advocates of the early New Deal. And opponents of the New Deal—those contemporary conservatives—were often sincere advocates of racial equality.

All of this, of course, has now changed. The Democratic party has become the home of racial liberalism. The strident Dixiecrats of old have all but vanished from the American political scene. Gone also, and not replaced, are the racially liberal Republicans who played a key role in the early legislative victories for civil rights. Racial attitudes are now tightly linked to prevailing political ideology. Once separable, it is now all but inconceivable to be a liberal and not a racial liberal or to be a conservative and not oppose activist racial policies.

Over the last half-century racial issues have transformed American politics. We have seen the issue develop from a regional concern into a national issue, from partisan obscurity to a fundamental division between the parties, from being unconnected to mass political beliefs to being at the core of mass ideology. As we view the full history of this issue, the question naturally arises: Could this history have been different? Why does the racial issue evolution follow the pattern it does rather than some plausible alternative route?

It was after all obvious well before the 1960s that the increased salience of race was incompatible with continued Democratic domination. The New Deal Democratic coalition—largely composed of southern conservatives, northern liberals, and blacks—

would surely rupture beyond repair if race came to prominence in national discussion and debate. What was it about the mid-1960s that fundamentally changed the direction of the evolution? Why did the critical moment occur then, not sooner, not later? If the outcome was so inevitable, why then was the process so delayed, so halting? The answer of course is that it only appears inevitable in hindsight. It depended upon a number of discrete and separate forces, some notably absent before the time, coming together to mark the dynamic break in the evolution of race. Ultimately, then, it happened when it happened because all the sources of issue competition were favorably disposed toward race then but not earlier.

Internal Contradiction: The Unstable Democratic Coalition

The logical outgrowth of the New Deal issue agenda led, as we have demonstrated, to an internal contradiction in the New Deal coalition. If the New Deal was premised on help for the needy, on power for the dispossessed, and on respect for all, how long could it avoid the plight of black Americans? But both granting and protecting black rights were bound to offend and alienate southern whites. The potential for conflict was always present, but it took several decades for the logic underlying the New Deal to unravel upon itself.

Part of the internal unraveling was the electoral success of racially liberal Democrats in the 1958–1962 period, most particularly in 1958. The effect of large numbers of new liberals on the Democratic party was to deprive its southern wing of its traditional congressional dominance and its moderate leadership of its ability to paper over racial conflict within the party and keep race off the party agenda. Lyndon Johnson's role as Senate majority leader in preventing divisive conflict over race in the late 1950s was legislative skill at its zenith. But given the liberals' greater numbers and greater influence, probably not even Johnson could long have held back the urge of powerful liberal forces to assert a new defiantly pro–civil rights position for the party. It would remain for the opposition Republicans to exploit the schism, but the Democratic party could not long contain defiant liberals and unreconstructed racists—at least if race could not be kept underground.

Strategic Behavior: The Goldwater Gamble

The strategic behavior of politicians represents a second source of issue competition. Losing but rationally calculating politicians, as Riker (1982) argues and as we pointed out in Chapter 1, have an ever-present motive to introduce new issues so as to defeat the governing status quo and institute a new one of their own. The current majority, in contrast, should act to keep coalition-splitting issues off the agenda.

With regard to race, Franklin Roosevelt's presidency is an obvious example of strategic issue suppression, and the Goldwater presidential campaign exemplifies strategic issue introduction. FDR clearly recognized that race represented a serious threat to the continued success of his New Deal. The "Solid South" had long been the cornerstone of Democratic electoral strategy. With the new addition of millions of northern voters the Democratic majority looked secure and long-lasting. But like all coalitions, this one was internally unstable, written in sand more than stone. Disequilibrium was only one issue away, and it was manifestly clear which issue that would be. The Democratic coalition now included the racial extremes, blacks and liberal whites at one end and racial bigots at the other. If race became a central national concern, the Democratic coalition would split at the seams. If it remained submerged, then Democratic hegemony was possible.

Roosevelt was a master at distancing himself from the racial struggle. The economic relief provided during his presidency benefited blacks along with other Americans, but blacks were not singled out for special attention. His administration, particularly in the person of Eleanor Roosevelt, made numerous symbolic gestures affirming the importance of blacks. But, at the same time, FDR resolutely refused to endorse federal antilynching legislation and failed to desegregate the armed forces. And only when he was threatened with a massive march on Washington did he issue an executive order preventing racial discrimination in defense industries. His public position, in sum, was decidedly ambiguous, designed to assuage blacks without alienating southern whites.

Barry Goldwater's 1964 presidential campaign is a clear instance of the calculated use of a new issue cleavage to upset an established majority. But it did not work; at least it did not work for Goldwater at the time. But it is the clearest instance of stra-

187

tegically using new issues that can be found. Goldwater's campaign theme, "A Choice not an Echo," was predicated on the strategic assertion of a very large supply of "hidden" conservative, and potentially Republican, voters. Any elementary electoral arithmetic would show that the preponderance of those "hidden" conservatives were white southerners. The means to move them from their established loyalty was, and could only be, racial conservatism.

The evidence is overwhelming that Goldwater's racial conservatism worked. It did not save Goldwater from disastrous defeat, but it did break the tie of southern whites to the Democratic party. It was a break that would later be helpful to Richard Nixon in 1968 and 1972 and decisive for Ronald Reagan in the 1980s. But 1964 was the critical moment, the time of unambiguous issue signal. That was the time when voters on both sides of the new issue divide clearly perceived the issue transformation. That was the time when votes moved on both sides of the cleavage, leading to Goldwater victories in five deep southern states but losses in traditionally Republican but racially progressive areas.

Faced with a permanent Democratic majority based on New Deal domestic issues, Goldwater sought to introduce a new, unpredictable issue cleavage into American politics. We cannot fault his logic. It was a gamble by a politician who could readily anticipate defeat in a contest based upon the old alignment. The new cleavage may have been volatile and unpredictable—and, in retrospect, probably did the 1964 Republicans more harm than good—but the old cleavage all too predictably led to Democratic victory at the polls. It was the sort of move the Republican party had to make on some new issue eventually. In the long run it may well have accomplished what it so clearly failed to do for Goldwater.

Why then if the strategy of the new issue cleavage was so beneficial to the GOP did no candidate before Goldwater attempt to exploit it? Why not Herbert Hoover, at the origin of the illogical Democratic coalition? Why not Thomas Dewey, when internal dissension over race produced a massive walkout from the 1948 Democratic National Convention? Why not Richard Nixon after the violence at Little Rock foretold the power of racial emotions? Why were Republicans not ready to step into the breach when race so obviously troubled the Democratic party? To answer these questions we need to look at external disruptions and local variations, two more sources of issue competition.

External Disruption:
The Civil Rights Movement

A first answer to our strategic queries is this: never before 1964 were racial concerns so obviously on the minds of American voters. That may be understood as a simple response to the civil rights movement of the early 1960s. External, because the forces originated outside the party system and at least initially had no eye on electoral politics, the sit-ins and freedom rides of 1962–1963 moved racial consciousness to a national level of concern it had never before attained. Always lurking near the surface of southern politics, racial consciousness existed in the North as well at times of strife and riot. But race was never a partisan political issue because the parties offered voters no choices, and it was always a local affair. The civil rights movement, fired by the imaginations of young blacks, with traditional black leaders scrambling to catch up, brought racial conflict to all American television sets and to the center of political consciousness. The great March on Washington, the Kennedy endorsement of the civil rights program, and the Civil Rights Act of 1964—the dramatic legislative struggle of our times—kept it there. It was ripe for exploitation.

Local Variation:
Racial Conservatism as Issue Adaptation

Plausible as is the account of the ripeness of race for party politics, it is far from the whole story. The Republicans were severely constrained in moving rightward on race because the party had a racially progressive image, in contrast to the large segregationist streak of the opposition. Inertia lays a strong hand on the issue maneuverings of political parties. Parties can and do alter their positions to take advantage of strategic opportunities, but the process is neither open-ended nor conducive to rapid reversal. Historically, the Republicans were the "party of Lincoln." Born from abolitionist fervor and without a southern constituency, the GOP could never become a party of racism. The Loyal Opposition's challenge to the Democratic majority took many forms during the 1930s, 1940s, and 1950s; a racist appeal was not one of them.

189

Thus, if we ask why Herbert Hoover, Thomas Dewey, Dwight Eisenhower, or the Richard Nixon of 1960 did not exploit Democratic disharmony on race, much of the answer is that they were not racists. They did not wish to take a racist position, nor would they have been believable if they had done so. Their public records, like their party's, were of moderation and sometimes progressivism. It took a new racial issue for the GOP to drive a wedge between Democratic factions.

That occurred in 1964. Racial conservatism was a new issue. It consisted of opposition to strong federal intervention in civil rights, itself new in the 1960s. Before 1964 the two sides of the racial debate were progressivism and racism. Racial conservatism was a new species, originating as a minor adaptation—what we have called a local variation—from generalized conservatism.

Evolutionary theory makes a useful distinction between two kinds of similar adaptations. Homologous adaptations are similarities that arise by inheritance from the ancestral species. Related species are similar because they share genes from a common ancestral pool. Analogous adaptations, on the other hand, are similarities that arise independently because two genetically separate species undergo similar adaptations in response to similar environmental conditions. The distinction is crucial because, depending upon which it is, the same evidence, similarity, has very different theoretical standing. Homologous similarities are explained by genetic argument, analogous ones by ecology. Racism and racial conservatism are clearly of the latter, analogous, variety. They are strains of pragmatic thought with similar appeals but entirely different ancestors. Although racial conservatism had considerable appeal to outright racists, its origin in western Republican conservative doctrine was altogether different in situation, culture, and ideology from southern white racism. It was a new species.

The racial transformation of the GOP awaited the adaptation of Goldwater's generalized policy conservatism. Barry Goldwater was not a racist, nor was his band of ideological followers. The followers were conservative ideologues consistently opposed in principle to modern liberalism, symbolized in Roosevelt's New Deal. They opposed the New Deal welfare state because they felt it undermined free-market capitalism, constrained individual freedoms, and led to inefficient overpowerful government. They had to offer ideological opposition to the new civil rights initiatives because the new measures suffered from these same "defects." But this was racial policy conservatism, not racism. Although it would and did appeal to bigots, the new conservative position was advocated without open bigotry and espousal of segregationist goals. The Goldwater conservatives held that civil rights advocacy was inappropriate activism for the national government. That was also the basis of their opposition to the emerging American welfare state.

Normative arguments that racial conservatism is only racism dressed up, made respectable, may or may not accurately account for the impact of the position. We will pass on that complex issue. But they are surely wrong on the important matter of accounting for its origin. Racial conservatism evolved from Goldwater's conservatism, not from traditional racism, and it depended for its expression upon the new conservative dominance of the Republican party. We can even date its origin with some confidence, for it arises from Goldwater's coherent statement of the issue in *Conscience of a Conservative* (1960), very widely read and undoubtedly influential in the months before the 1964 election. The origins of the process were thus both intended and accidental, but once started the new adaptation took on a life of its own. The infusion of Goldwater activists into the party moved it to the right; the strategy of appealing to increasingly disaffected southern whites kept it there.[1]

THE LOGIC OF ISSUE EVOLUTION:
REFLECTIONS ON THE RACIAL CASE

Hazard lies in generalization from a case, even one well studied. It is instructive nonetheless to abstract some elements from the five decades or so of the racial issue evolution and the one decade of our study of it. Some of these elements are inherent in issue evolution and so would likely also be found in the issue evolutions of the past and those, more numerous, yet to occur.

Four attributes of the racial evolution seem particularly wor-

---

[1] One other event played a crucial role in reinforcing the GOP move to the racial right. As noted in Chapter 2, the coming of the Voting Rights Act of 1965 banished blatant racism from southern Democratic politics. With large numbers of new black voters a significant force in the Democratic primaries of every southern state, this appeal to the lowest element of white segregationists did not gain enough votes to justify writing off black voters. Whatever the personal views of southern Democratic politicians, they projected racial moderation after the Voting Rights Act as a strategic imperative. That, for the first time, left an opening to Republican candidates to successfully pick up the banner of the racial right.

191

thy of note; each is tied more to the inherent logic of issue evolution than to the racial case per se, and all seem likely to generalize to other cases. Thus, issue evolutions are dynamic, complex, effectively subtle, and long lasting. We will consider each attribute in turn.

A Dynamic Trace

Issue evolution is inherently dynamic, a process not to be understood except in the context of growth and decay through time. We have looked to "critical moments" for punctuation points, for an understanding of one-time changes that might set dynamic processes in motion, but virtually all change wrought by this issue evolution occurred in the gradual dynamic phase, not in the originating events. Dynamic adaptations are highly consistent with inertial notions of political change, holding that systems are to some degree driven by internal momentum; in political systems its major source is party loyalty. Thus, dynamic adaptations by their very nature tend to resist sudden change of any kind but gradually adjust themselves to it over time.

Complexity

Neither the nature of the racial change nor its causes is amenable to any sort of straightforward account. They are much more complex stories than the realignments of American history, much more complex than the story we started out to tell. This account is at war most particularly with simple cause and effect notions of partisan change, such as the "depression causes realignment" scenario that is so familiar from textbook accounts of the New Deal.

Allied with complexity, this account is completely at odds also with notions of historical inevitability, whether explicit as in the Marxist dialectic or the less well-articulated but no less common notion in western social theory that some events inevitably follow from others. We do not deny cause and effect, as indeed it is not denied in the genetic theory on which we so heavily draw. Instead we are led to point out again and again that the critical causal events had a very low probability of occurring as they did, as do all others. That is less an assertion of inherent randomness in the world than a recognition that chance is an essential actor in evolution. What it implies, of course, is that if we could restart the whole process from where it was, say in the 1930s, that it is exceedingly unlikely that we would witness the same result. That does not imply that the particular observed outcome was improbable so much as that all possible outcomes are improbable, even the one most probable.

Subtlety

We came at our topic in the conventional manner of social science, looking for notable effects that would justify the research. And there are indeed some notable effects to be found in the mid-1960s. But the lesson of this work is that most changes to be observed are subtle. They are so small in any given year that, unless one is looking very specifically with finely honed statistical instruments, they will not be seen at all. But subtle movements cumulated over a lengthy span have notably unsubtle effects, as we have observed so clearly in the racial case. This situation has implications for the design and analysis of political research, some of which we draw out below.

Extended Time Horizons

Conventional election studies have no time horizon at all; their great limitation is now widely recognized. The more popular accounts of electoral realignment also often write of party system change, under the influence of an earthquake metaphor, as if partisan change occurred in a single wrenching movement—and then concede to the evidence that it probably takes more than one critical election to effect a realignment.[2] The fifty years we allot to racial issue evolution is, of course, an analytic convenience; we can date neither the origin nor the termination of the phenomenon, and probably neither exists in any meaningful sense. But a necessary corollary of emphases on complex, subtle, dynamic movements is quite clear: they must take a very long time to complete themselves.

WHAT THEN OF HISTORICAL PARTISAN CHANGE?

Our account of the racial issue evolution is unprecedented in some respects. After a decade of analysis we have approached it

[2] Sundquist (1983) is an always notable exception to our treatments of realignment research; his long-time horizon and relatively complex scenarios of events and dynamic "aftershocks" are much more consistent with and in some ways anticipate our account of issue evolutions.

from many angles. Because the phenomenon is in part contemporary, we have the luxury of contemporary data collections. We are the beneficiaries of rich survey research on racial attitudes and opinions conducted early in the evolutionary sequence and before the critical moment. Thus, we can know quite directly not only what government did but also what citizens saw of what government did and how year by year it affected their attitudes, loyalties, and attachments to the parties while the events were afoot.

The episodes of party system change of the American past are not similarly well documented. They are studied by historiography and by the skillful, often imaginative spinning of stories from fragmentary evidence. The process is a sort of political paleontology, whereby a few bones and teeth of evidence are the necessary base for constructing a portrait of change in a complex political system. The limitation of this effort lies not in the analysts but in the limited raw material from which they necessarily construct and test theory. Theories are necessarily quite simple because fragmentary evidence and the requisites of parsimony can support nothing else.

By studying multiple actors with varied and contemporary data, we have found it necessary to construct a complex and subtle evolutionary scheme to fit evidence to explanation. With simple data, principally election outcomes, and often painfully irrelevant demographic information, students of past party system change have produced simple, direct, brief, cause-and-effect accounts of the movement from one to another party system, called realignment. Given the partial and fragmentary evidence, this theoretical outcome was to have been expected.

We are sorely tempted to apply issue evolution notions to the "realignments" of the American past. But because we are also captives of the same limited historical record, such an account is bound to lack a full measure of richness, complexity, and depth. We shall not attempt it here. About issue evolutions of the past we can only say that it is unlikely that they much resemble the simple creatures of traditional realignment theory.

Process, Dynamics, and Organic Theory: Reflections on Studying Political Change

We have learned much about American politics in the course of this research; that was our intent. We have also learned much about American political science, its culture and doctrines of everyday procedure; that was not our intent. And it was far more difficult knowledge because we are not anthropologists standing off at a distance observing a tribe; we are members of the tribe, subscribers to its culture. This knowledge is altogether inadvertent. It is the spin-off of research decisions, some with a fluky character, of ideas impressed on data that sometimes would not yield and of arguments about how to do things and how to see things.

Our perspectives on how to study American politics were quite typical of behavioral political scientists at the outset. They are less typical now, as a result of this process. Thus, there may be some value in reflecting on the perspective of behavioral political science derived from the lessons of this research.

We step back from our subject and our more narrow gauge findings here to speculate on the process that produced them. At the outset we decided that our focus would be the process by which issues develop. Thus, our understanding of partisan change could only be dynamic; time would be inherent in any suitable model of issue change.[3] Before we were even entirely sure quite what we were studying, we were convinced that a crucial part of how it would be done was over time. It is much clearer in retrospect that we had such a commitment than why we had it.

That in turn led us to search for a theory that would account for dynamic processes. There are a limited number of explanatory possibilities for dynamic phenomenons. We considered and rejected most of them as inadequate to deal with a phenomenon not only of change but a phenomenon that was itself changing while the study proceeded. We grasped at natural selection as a possibility, at the outset more in fun than as serious social science.

Having grasped at natural selection as an explanatory hook, we began to take it seriously. It suggested topics for exploration and a means of doing it. Most crucially it had a powerful effect in conditioning our expectation of what evidence would be appropriate. And as the evidence began to come in, it was consistent with

[3] That is quite different from the electoral realignment tradition, which has largely taken cross-sectional notions of change, as best evidenced in the dichotomous notion of an election being or not being a realignment, and grafted them onto a longitudinal problem. Although few scholars now think that electoral realignments could be accomplished in a single election, that the question is even considered meaningful indicates a cross-sectional approach.

195

our organic framework, while being quite unimpressive in terms of the cross-sectional perspective we had so recently entertained. For an evolving process one expects gradual but cumulative changes, so slight at any one time as to appear trivial but capable over the long haul of producing profound transformations. That is what we saw. And as we saw this same pattern of evidence over and over again, the organic framework—issue change as natural selection and evolution of issues—came to dominate our thinking.

Of what consequence is all this for our assertions? Critical is that the dynamic traces readers will have seen in this book on topic after topic carry an interesting methodological point. Most demonstrate change over time that can be called substantial, or even profound, with little danger of overstatement. Consider this evidence in another light, not as a pattern of systematic movement over almost fifty years but as one slice in time (or even fifty separate slices). If this same evidence were decomposed in this fashion—if the question, that is, were subtly changed from how much change does this process produce? to how much of the observed change in a particular variable in a given year is attributable to the process in question?—then inferences drawn by a reasonable analyst would have a strikingly different character. In few cases would the effects in any given year be notable. Only a few would be statistically significant.

If similar judgments were to be made relatively—this issue or process weighed against other alternatives—in most annual slices the issue would be found wanting, not as important as some more immediately relevant concern of the time. In some such analyses it would be judged trivial, for race has not always been a potent influence on immediate behaviors. We would have concluded from such a perspective, indeed the literature on American mass behavior has concluded, that the racial changes were crucially important for a few years in the mid-1960s, not very much before or since, and that the issue mattered then, not before and not after. That conclusion would be an appropriate reading of the cross-sectional evidence and, we believe, a profoundly mistaken reading of reality. Without the organic perspective, it is very unlikely then that this book would have been written.

The problem with evaluating the import of a particular issue from its immediate effects is only partly methodological. Also wanting in this quite typical approach to explaining political reality is a theory of issue effects. For if the argument of this book is even close to being true, if, that is, the way in which issues shape the niches in which they find expression is half as elaborate and inherently dynamic as we make it, then most times we would be led to expect evidence of little or no issue effect of a particular kind at a particular moment. But we must question if the particular moment matters. Political science owes much of its origin to political journalism. And like political journalism we have an excessive tendency to concentrate on the here and now, a blindness toward movements on a grander time scale. Processes are not so easily captured, but the postulate on which this work must stand is that they matter more.

Concern with process led us to dynamic formulations. They required explanation, for which we turned to organic theorizing. Having adopted natural selection as an explanatory framework, for whatever reason, we have acquired and interpreted evidence of processes quite different from the norm of our discipline. Organic thinking leads away from our normal emphases on immediate outcomes and their explanation and toward process itself as a centrally interesting fact of political life.

American constitutional democracy is an exercise in eighteenth-century political mechanics. But the clockworks and balance wheels of its conception seem ill suited to explain its subsequent survival, development, and metamorphoses. For that, we suggest there is much to be gained from the organic thinking of a later century.

197

BIBLIOGRAPHY

Aldrich, John H., and Richard D. McKelvey. 1977. "A Method of Scaling with Applications to the 1968 and 1972 Presidential Elections." *American Political Science Review* 71: 111–30.

Andersen, Kristi. 1976. "Generation, Partisan Shift and Realignment: A Glance Back to the New Deal." In *The Changing American Voter*, eds. Norman H. Nie, Sidney Verba, and John R. Petrocik. Cambridge: Harvard University Press.

Andersen, Kristi. 1979. *The Creation of a Democratic Majority, 1928–1936*. Chicago: University of Chicago Press.

Anderson, J. W. 1964. *Eisenhower, Brownell, and the Congress*. University: University of Alabama Press.

Axelrod, Robert. 1984. *The Evolution of Cooperation*. New York: Basic Books.

Bartley, Numan V., and Hugh D. Graham. 1978. *Southern Elections: County and Precinct Data, 1950–1972*. Baton Rouge: Louisiana State University Press.

Beck, Paul Allen. 1974. "A Socialization Theory of Partisan Realignment." In *The Politics of Future Citizens*, ed. Richard G. Niemi. San Francisco: Jossey-Bass.

———. 1979. "The Electoral Cycle and Patterns of American Politics." *British Journal of Political Science* 9: 129–56.

———. 1982. "Realignment Begins?: The Republican Surge in Florida." *American Politics Quarterly* 10: 421–37.

Beck, Paul Allen, and M. Kent Jennings. 1979. "Political Periods and Political Participation." *American Political Science Review* 73: 737–50.

———. 1984. "Updating Political Periods and Political Participation." *American Political Science Review* 78: 198–201.

Bensel, Richard Franklin. 1984. *Sectionalism and American Political Development, 1880–1980*. Madison: University of Wisconsin Press.

Berelson, Bernard R., Paul R. Lazarsfeld, and William N. McPhee. 1954. *Voting: A Study of Opinion Formation in a Presidential Campaign*. Chicago: University of Chicago Press.

Berman, William C. 1970. *The Politics of Civil Rights in the Truman Administration*. Columbus: Ohio State University Press.

Bishop, George F., Alfred J. Tuchfarber, and Robert W. Oldendick. 1978. "Change in the Structure of American Political Attitudes: The Nagging Question of Question Wording." *American Journal of Political Science* 22: 250–69.

Bishop, George F., Alfred J. Tuchfarber, Robert W. Oldendick, and Stephen E. Bennett. 1979. "Questions About Question Wording: A Rejoinder to Revisiting Mass Belief Systems Revisited." *American Journal of Political Science* 23: 187–92.

Black, Merle, and George B. Rabinowitz. 1980. "American Electoral Change: 1952–1972 (with a note on 1976)." In *The Party Symbol*, ed. William Crotty. San Francisco: W. H. Freeman.

Box, George E. P., and Gwilym M. Jenkins. 1976. *Times Series Analysis: Forecasting and Control*. San Francisco: Holden Day.

Box, George E. P., and George C. Tiao. 1975. "Intervention Analysis with Applications to Economic and Environmental Problems." *Journal of the American Statistical Association* 70: 70–79.

Boyd, Robert, and Peter J. Richerson. 1985. *Culture and the Evolutionary Process*. Chicago: University of Chicago Press.

Brady, David. 1978. "Critical Elections, Congressional Parties and Clusters of Policy Changes." *British Journal of Political Science* 8: 79–99.

Brauer, Carl M. 1977. *John F. Kennedy and the Second Reconstruction*. New York: Columbia University Press.

Brody, Richard A., and Benjamin I. Page. 1972. "Comment: The Assessment of Policy Voting." *American Political Science Review* 66: 450–58.

Burnham, Walter Dean. 1970. *Critical Elections and the Mainsprings of American Politics*. New York: Norton.

———. 1981. "The 1980 Earthquake: Realignment, Reaction, or What?" In *The Hidden Election*, eds. Thomas Ferguson and Joel Rogers. New York: Pantheon.

Campbell, Angus, Philip E. Converse, Warren E. Miller, and Donald E. Stokes. 1960. *The American Voter*. New York: John Wiley & Sons.

Campbell, Donald T., and Julian C. Stanley. 1963. *Experimental and Quasi-Experimental Designs for Research*. Chicago: Rand McNally.

Carmines, Edward G., and Lawrence C. Dodd. 1985. "Bicameralism in Congress: The Changing Partnership." In *Congress

Reconsidered, 3rd ed. eds. Lawrence C. Dodd and Bruce I. Oppenheimer. Washington, D.C.: Congressional Quarterly.

Carmines, Edward G., and J. David Gopoian. 1981. "Issue Coalitions, Issueless Campaigns: The Paradox of Rationality in American Presidential Elections." *Journal of Politics* 43: 1170–89.

Carmines, Edward G., and James H. Kuklinski. 1989. "Incentives, Opportunities, and the Logic of Public Opinion in American Political Representation." In *Information and Democratic Processes*, eds. John Ferejohn and James H. Kuklinski. Champaign: University of Illinois Press.

Carmines, Edward G., John P. McIver, and James A. Stimson. 1987. "Unrealized Partisanship: A Theory of Dealignment." *Journal of Politics* 49: 376–400.

Carmines, Edward G., and James A. Stimson. 1980a. "The Two Faces of Issue Voting." *American Political Science Review* 74: 78–91.

———. 1980b. "The Racial Reorientation of American Politics." In *The Electorate Reconsidered*, eds. John C. Pierce and John L. Sullivan. Beverly Hills, Calif.: Sage Publications.

———. 1981. "Issue Evolution, Population Replacement, and Normal Partisan Change." *American Political Science Review* 75: 107–18.

———. 1982. "Racial Issues and the Structure of Mass Belief Systems." *Journal of Politics* 44: 2–20.

———. 1984. "The Dynamics of Issue Evolution The United States." In *Electoral Change in Industrial Democracies*, eds. Russell J. Dalton, Paul Allen Beck, and Scott C. Flanagan. Princeton: Princeton University Press.

———. 1986a. "On the Structure and Sequence of Issue Evolution." *American Political Science Review* 80: 902–21.

———. 1986b. "The Politics and Policy of Race in Congress." In *Congress and Policy Change*, eds. Gerald Wright, Leroy Rieselbach, and Lawrence Dodd. New York: Agathon Press.

Carmines, Edward G., Steven H. Renten, and James A. Stimson. 1984. "Events and Alignments: The Party Image Link." In *Controversies in Voting Behavior*, eds. Richard E. Niemi and Herbert F. Weisberg. Washington, D.C.: Congressional Quarterly.

Cavanagh, Thomas E., and James L. Sundquist. 1985. "The New Two-Party System." In *The New Direction in American Pol-*

itics, eds. John E. Chubb and Paul E. Peterson. Washington, D.C.: The Brookings Institution.

Clausen, Aage. 1973. *How Congressmen Decide: A Policy Focus*. New York: St. Martins Press.

Clubb, Jerome M., William H. Flanigan, and Nancy H. Zingale. 1980. *Partisan Realignment*. Beverly Hills, Calif.: Sage Publications.

Congressional Quarterly. 1967. *Revolution and Civil Rights*, 3rd ed. Washington, D.C.: Congressional Quarterly.

————. 1971. *Civil Rights: Progress Report 1970*. Washington, D.C.: Congressional Quarterly.

————. 1983. *National Party Conventions, 1831–1980*. Washington, D.C.: Congressional Quarterly.

Converse, Philip E. 1964. "The Nature of Belief Systems in Mass Publics." In *Ideology and Discontent*, ed. David E. Apter. New York: Free Press.

————. 1975. "Public Opinion and Voting Behavior." In *Handbook of Political Science*, eds. Fred I. Greenstein and Nelson W. Polsby. Reading, Mass.: Addison-Wesley.

Converse, Philip E., Angus Campbell, Warren E. Miller, and Donald E. Stokes. 1961. "Stability and Change in 1960: A Reinstating Election." *American Political Science Review* 55: 269–80.

Converse, Philip E., Aage R. Clausen, and Warren E. Miller. 1965. "Electoral Myth and Reality: The 1964 Election." *American Political Science Review* 59: 321–34.

Converse, Philip E., and Gregory B. Markus. 1979. "Plus ca Change . . . : The New CPS Election Study Panel." *American Political Science Review* 73: 32–49.

Cosman, Bernard. 1966. *Five States for Goldwater*. University: University of Alabama Press.

Darwin, Charles. 1859. *On The Origin of Species by Means of Natural Selection, or the Preservation of Favoured Races in the Struggle for Life*. London: John Murray; reprint, New York: Penguin, 1968.

Dawkins, Richard. 1976. *The Selfish Gene*. New York: Oxford University Press.

————. 1986. *The Blind Watchmaker*. New York: W. W. Norton.

Dugger, Ronnie. 1983. *On Reagan*. New York: McGraw-Hill.

Duram, James C. 1981. *A Moderate Among Extremists*. Chicago: Nelson-Hall.

Erikson, Robert S., and Kent L. Tedin. 1981. "The 1928–1932

Partisan Realignment: The Case for the Conversion Hypothesis." *American Political Science Review* 75: 951–62.

Flanagan, Scott C., and Russel J. Dalton. 1984. "Parties Under Stress: Realignment and Dealignment in Advanced Industrial Societies." *West European Politics* 7: 7–23.

Freeman, John R. 1983. "Granger Causality and the Time Series Analysis of Political Relationships." *American Journal of Political Science* 27: 327–58.

Freidel, Frank. 1965. *F.D.R. and the South*. Baton Rouge: Louisiana State University Press.

Goldwater, Barry. 1960. *The Conscience of a Conservative*. New York: Hillman Books.

Gould, Stephen Jay. 1980. *The Panda's Thumb*. New York: W. W. Norton.

———. 1981. *The Mismeasure of Man*. New York: W. W. Norton.

———. 1983. *Hen's Teeth and Horse's Toes: Further Reflections in Natural History*. New York: W. W. Norton.

———. 1985. *The Flamingo's Smile: Reflections in Natural History*. New York: W. W. Norton.

Huckfeldt, Robert, and C. W. Kohfeld. 1989. *Race and the Decline of Class in American Politics*. Champaign: University of Illinois Press.

Johnson, Donald Bruce. 1978. *National Party Platforms Volume II, 1960–1976*. Champaign: University of Illinois Press.

———. 1982. *National Party Platforms of 1980*. Champaign: University of Illinois Press.

Johnson, Donald Bruce, and Kirk H. Porter. 1973. *National Party Platforms 1840–1972*. Champaign: University of Illinois Press.

Key, V. O., Jr. 1955. "A Theory of Critical Elections." *Journal of Politics* 17: 3–18.

———. 1959. "Secular Realignment and the Party System." *Journal of Politics* 21: 198–210.

Kingdon, John W. 1973. *Congressmen's Voting Decisions*. New York: Harper and Row.

———. 1984. *Agendas, Alternatives, and Public Policies*. Boston: Little, Brown & Company.

Kirby, John B. 1980. *Black Americans in the Roosevelt Era*. Knoxville: University of Tennessee Press.

Kritzer, Herbert M. 1978. "Ideology and American Political Elites." *Public Opinion Quarterly* 42: 484–502.

Ladd, Everett Carl. 1978. *Where Have All the Voters Gone?* New York: W. W. Norton.

Lipset, Seymour Martin, and Stein Rokkan. 1967. "Cleavage Structures, Party Systems, and Voter Alignments: An Introduction." In *Party Systems and Voter Alignments*, eds. Lipset and Rokkan. New York: Free Press.

Ljung, G. M., and George E. P. Box. 1976. "A Modification of Overall v^2 Test for Lack of Fit in Time Series Models." University of Wisconsin, Department of Statistics, Technical Report 477.

Luskin, Robert. 1987. "Measuring Political Sophistication." *American Journal of Political Science* 31: 856–99.

MacDonald, Stuart Elaine, and George Rabinowitz. 1987. "The Dynamics of Structural Realignment." *American Political Science Review* 81: 775–96.

MacRae, Duncan, Jr. 1970. *Issues and Parties in Legislative Voting*. New York: Harper and Row.

Martin, John Frederick. 1979. *Civil Rights and the Crisis of Liberalism*. New York: St. Martin's Press.

Mayhew, David R. 1974. "Congressional Elections: The Case of the Vanishing Marginals." *Polity* 6: 295–317.

McCleary, Richard, and Richard A. Hay, Jr. 1980. *Applied Time Series Analysis*. Beverly Hills, Calif.: Sage.

McCoy, Donald R., and Richard T. Ruetten. 1973. *Quest and Response*. Lawrence: University Press of Kansas.

Miller, Arthur H., Warren E. Miller, Alden S. Raine, and Theodore A. Brown. 1976. "A Majority Party in Disarray: Policy Polarization the 1972 Election." *American Political Science Review* 70: 753–78.

Miller, Merle. 1980. *Lyndon*. New York: C. P. Putnam's Sons.

Miller, Warren E., and Teresa Levitin. 1976. *Leadership and Change*. Cambridge, Mass.: Winthrop.

Miller, Warren E., and Donald E. Stokes. 1963. "Constituency Influence in Congress." *American Political Science Review* 57: 45–56.

Morgan, Ruth P. 1970. *The President and Civil Rights*. New York: St. Martin's Press.

Munger, Frank. 1977. "Kennedy vs. Goldwater: Issues in an Election That Never Was." Presented at the meetings of the Southern Political Science Association, New Orleans, November 1977.

Murphy, Reg, and Hal Gulliver. 1971. *Southern Strategy*. New York: Charles Scribner's Sons.

Nelson, Richard R., and Sidney G. Winter. 1982. *An Evolutionary Theory of Economic Change*. Cambridge: Harvard University Press.

Nexon, David. 1971. "Asymmetry in the Political System: Occasional Activists in the Republican and Democratic Parties." *American Political Science Review* 65: 716–30.

Neuman, W. Russel. 1986. *The Paradox of Mass Politics*. Cambridge: Harvard University Press.

Nie, Norman H., with Kristi Andersen. 1974. "Mass Belief Systems Revisited: Political Change and Attitude Structure." *Journal of Politics* 36: 540–90.

Nie, Norman H., and James N. Rabjohn. 1979. "Revisiting Mass Belief Systems Revisited: Or Doing Research is Like Watching a Tennis Match." *American Journal of Political Science* 23: 139–75.

Nie, Norman H., Sidney Verba, and John R. Petrocik. 1976. *The Changing American Voter*. Cambridge: Harvard University Press.

Niemi, Richard, Richard Katz, and David Newman. 1980. "Reconstructing Past Partisanship: The Failure of the Party Identification Recall Questions." *American Journal of Political Science* 24: 633–51.

Norpoth, Helmut, and Jerrold G. Rusk. 1982. "Partisan Dealignment in the American Electorate: Itemizing the Deductions Since 1964." *American Political Science Review* 76: 522–37.

Oakes, Stephen B. 1982. *Let the Trumpet Sound*. New York: Harper and Row.

Page, Benjamin I. 1978. *Choices and Echoes in Presidential Elections*. Chicago: University of Chicago Press.

Petrocik, John R. 1981. *Party Coalitions*. Chicago: University of Chicago Press.

Pomper, Gerald M. 1968. *Elections in America: Control and Influence in Democratic Politics*. New York: Dodd, Mead.

———. 1971. "Toward A More Responsible Two-Party System: What, Again?" *Journal of Politics* 33: 916–40.

———. 1972. "From Confusion to Clarity: Issues and American Voters, 1956–1968." *American Political Science Review* 66: 28–45.

Pritchett, C. Herman. 1984. *Constitutional Civil Liberties*. Englewood Cliffs, N.J.: Prentice-Hall.

Public Papers of the United States. 1932–1980. Washington, D.C.: Government Printing Office.

Radnitzky, Gerard, and W. W. Bartley, III. 1987. *Evolutionary Epistemology, Theory of Rationality, and the Sociology of Knowledge.* LaSalle, Ill.: Open Court.

Raup, David M. 1986. *The Nemesis Affair.* New York: W. W. Norton.

Riker, William H. 1982. *Liberalism Against Populism.* San Francisco: W. H. Freeman.

Rubin, Richard L. 1976. *Party Dynamics.* New York: Oxford University Press.

Salisbury, Robert H., and Michael MacKuen. 1981. "On the Study of Party Realignment." *Journal of Politics* 43: 523–30.

Schattschneider, E. E. 1960. *The Semi-Sovereign People: A Realist's View of Democracy in America.* New York: Holt, Rinehart, and Winston.

Simon, Herbert A. 1985. "Human Nature in Politics: The Dialogue of Psychology with Political Science." *American Political Science Review* 79: 293–304.

Sitkoff, Harvard. 1971. "Harry Truman and the Election of 1948: The Coming of Age of Civil Rights in American Politics." *Journal of Southern History* 37: 597–616.

———. 1978. *A New Deal for Blacks.* New York: Oxford University Press.

Smith, Tom W. 1985. "The Polls: America's Most Important Problems." *Public Opinion Quarterly* 49: 268–74.

Sniderman, Paul M. 1975. *Personality and Democratic Politics.* Berkeley: University of California Press.

Sniderman, Paul M., and Philip E. Tetlock. 1986. "Interrelationships of Political Ideology and Public Opinion." In *Political Psychology*, ed. Margaret G. Herman. San Francisco: Jossey-Bass.

Stampp, Kenneth M. 1965. *The Era of Reconstruction.* New York: Random House.

Stevenson, Adlai E. 1953. *Major Campaign Speeches of Adlai E. Stevenson, 1952.* New York: Random House.

Stimson, James A. 1975. "Belief Systems: Constraint, Complexity, and the 1972 Election." *American Journal of Political Science* 19: 383–418.

———. 1985. "Regression Models in Space and Time: A Statistical Essay." *American Journal of Political Science* 29: 914–47.

Stokes, Donald E., and Gudmund Iversen. 1966. "On the Existence of Forces Restoring Party Competition." In *Elections and the Political Order*, eds. Angus Campbell, Philip E. Converse, Warren E. Miller, and Donald E. Stokes. New York: Wiley.

Sullivan, John L., James E. Pierson, and George E. Marcus. 1978. "Ideological Constraint in the Mass Public: A Methodological Critique and Some New Findings." *American Journal of Political Science* 22: 233–49.

Sullivan, John L., James E. Pierson, George E. Marcus, and Stanley Feldman. 1979. "The More Things Change, the More They Stay the Same: The Stability of Mass Belief Systems." *American Journal of Political Science* 23: 176–86.

Sundquist, James L. 1968. *Politics and Policy*. Washington, D.C.: Brookings Institution.

———. 1983. *Dynamics of the Party System*. Rev. ed. Washington, D.C.: Brookings Institution.

Trilling, Richard J. 1978. *Party Image and Electoral Behavior*. New York: John Wiley.

Verba, Sidney, and Norman H. Nie. 1972. *Participation in America*. New York: Harper and Row.

Weiss, Nancy J. 1983. *Farewell to the Party of Lincoln*. Princeton, N.J.: Princeton University Press.

Woodward, C. Vann. 1974. *The Strange Career of Jim Crow*. New York: Oxford University Press.

INDEX

Achen, Chris, xvii
"acid, amnesty, and abortion," 107
activism: asymmetry thesis, 100; atypicality of, 89; attitudes and party
images, 111n; benefits of, 95; com-
pensations of, 91; measures of, 92–
94
activists: age of, 92, 96–99; compared
to mass electorate and political
elite, 90; explanations of variability,
95; and ideological campaigns, 100;
ideology of, 101; informational, 94;
occasional, 89; as opinion leaders,
93; party loyalties of, 99, 101; personal attributes, 94–106; potential
v. actual numbers, 91; recruitment
of, 90–92; Republican advantage,
99; role in issue evolution, 16, 89–
114; as vanguard of issue evolution,
109
affect dimension of civil rights issues,
125
affect toward parties, 160, 166–67,
170, 174–80
aid to education, 10
aid to minority groups, 125
Aldrich, John, 122
alignment of race and party identification, 170, 173–80
all deliberate speed, 37
analogous adaptation, 190
Andersen, Kristi, 22, 119–22, 142
Anderson, J. W., 37, 104n
Andre, Carolyn, 33
anomaly of continuing polarization,
156
antilynching legislation, 187
Archie Bunker, tie to Nixon racial attitudes, 109
asymmetry in New Deal decay, 147
asymptotic equilibrium, 152
Axelrod, Robert, 17n

baby boom, as explanation of youthful
activism, 98–99n

Bartley, Numan, 17n
Bartley, W. W., 17n
Beall, J. Glenn, 69, 71
Beck, Paul, xvii, 91n, 93n, 142, 148
belief structure, and issue evolution,
115–16; racial transformation of,
115–37
benign neglect, 123
Bennett, Stephen, 120n
Bensel, Richard, 24
Berelson, Bernard, 93, 108
Berman, William, 34, 37
bigots, 187, 191; in southern Demo-
cratic primaries, 74
biological theory, uses and abuses, 4
biology, 3
biopolitics, 18
Bishop, George, 120n
Black, Merle, 117
black political power during Recon-
struction, 29
black power, 87
black pride, 87
black registration, 49
black vote, growth of in cities, 33
Bookheimer, Samuel, xvii
border Democrats, 73
Box, G.E.P., 66, 156n, 171n
Box-Jenkins approach, 171
Box-Ljung Q statistic, 173
Box-Tiao intervention analysis, 66,
172n
Boyd, Robert, 17n
Brady, David, 22
Brauer, Carl, 39
Brody, Richard, 166
Brown v. Board of Education of To-
peka, 35, 37, 61
Brown, Theodore, 122–23
Buckley, James, 73
Bumpers, Dale, 73
Burnham, Walter Dean, 16, 17n, 21n,
23, 142
Bush, George, 136n

209